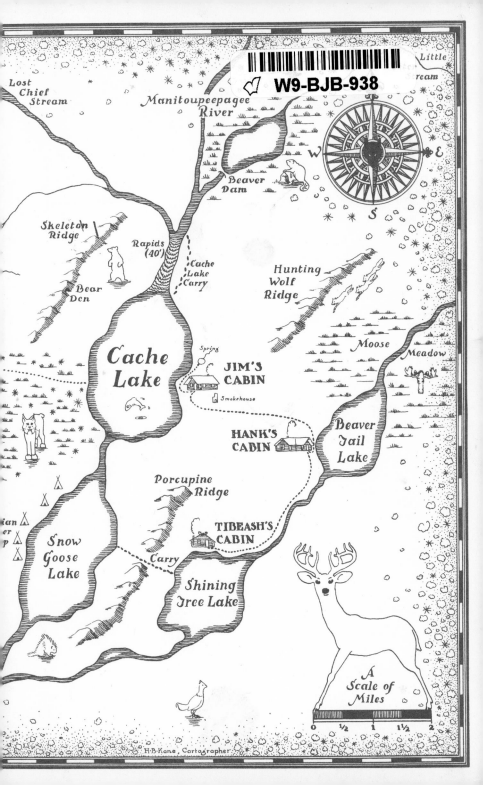

Cache Lake Country

Cache Lake

Cache Lake Country

LIFE IN THE NORTH WOODS

BY JOHN J. ROWLANDS

Illustrated by HENRY B. KANE

Wilderness Edition

W · W · NORTON & COMPANY · INC · *New York*

TO
Chief Tibeash

Library of Congress Catalog Card No. 59-13370

Book Design by John Woodlock

PRINTED IN THE UNITED STATES OF AMERICA

Contents

CACHE LAKE   Portage to Contentment   9

JANUARY   Long Nights and Deep Snows   28

FEBRUARY   The Stars and the Silence   48

MARCH   Strong Winds in the Sugar Bush   67

APRIL   Thundering Ice and Black Water   88

MAY   The Green Tide Flows North   109

JUNE   Soft Twilights and Fireflies   128

JULY   The Moose Are in the Lakes   148

AUGUST   Harvest of the Wilderness   170

SEPTEMBER   The Moon When the Birds Fly
Away   191

OCTOBER   Frost on Scarlet Leaves   210

NOVEMBER   Gray Skies and Cold Rains   230

DECEMBER   Blizzards and Wailing Winds   249

Woodcraft Index   271

Foreword

IT IS NOW better than a dozen years since *Cache Lake Country* was first published and in that. fragment of time the world has seen great changes. We have watched the dawning of the Atomic Age, bringing new triumphs for man, new hopes and also new and haunting fears.

But Cache Lake has not changed. Serene, remote, untouched, it lives on as always, a symbol of the beauty, simplicity and natural honesty of the Northern wilderness in which it lies, the abiding place of peace and contentment.

In *Cache Lake Country* I have recounted not only the happy and rewarding experiences of life in the North, but the deep satisfaction and excitement of discovering how inventive and resourceful man can be when his living depends upon making the most effective use of whatever comes to hand. He must learn—often with only an axe for a tool— to build himself a home. He must know where to look for and how to procure food if he is to survive, and he must learn to find his way through a world of trackless forest.

There is more that he must learn, for now and then he must walk alone, trying to conquer fears he has never known before—fear of illness, fear of death and, now and then, fear of the motives of men. If the man of the wilderness thinks of security at all, it is as something that lies in the future and has to be earned. He would never dream of demanding security in advance. He has no fear of failure, for he thinks of failure as one of many steps in the business of getting ahead.

Many readers of *Cache Lake Country* have told me that its simple philosophy—our way of thinking to get the best out of life—has been helpful in easing the tensions of the hard fast pace of modern civilization. Many, too, have discovered for themselves the satisfaction and pleasure of developing skills of the hand by working out various ideas and projects in the book. And no less pleasing has been their delight in joining us in spirit on the trails and on the waterways and in sharing the warmth of life at Cache.

"Cache" is the woodsman's term for a safe and secure place in which to store valuable possessions, food and equipment, against the day of need. In *Cache Lake Country* are stored the best and most treasured memories of my life, a keeping place of conviction and contentment from which I may draw when I feel the need.

There is a Cache Lake for everyone, but it won't be found beside a four-lane highway nor will there be a clear trail to lead to it. If it is worth finding, it will be far from the sights and sounds of civilization, quiet and clear, and without pretension. Unless you know what to look for you may pass it by.

To my great satisfaction *Cache Lake Country* has lived on through the years and appears to have found its special place in the affections of readers old and young. I greet this new Wilderness Edition with pleasure, and hope that it may find new readers in years to come who will share the ageless rewards and riches that I found at Cache Lake in·time gone by.

John J. Rowlands

CACHE LAKE

Portage to Contentment

On most maps Cache Lake is only a speck hidden among other blue patches big enough to have names, and unless you know where to look you will never find it. But a place like Cache Lake is seldom discovered on a map. You just come on it—that is if you are lucky. Most men who travel the north woods sooner or later happen on a lake or stream that somehow they cannot forget and always want to go back to. Generally they never do go back.

Cache Lake lies deep in a wilderness of spruce and pine which, except for a timber cruiser like myself and maybe a trapper now and then, few white men know. But the Indians find it good game country, and so do the big gray timber wolves that run its hills. So like many other worth-while things, there's no easy trail to Cache Lake, for it is protected by distance, mile after forgotten mile of woods and water, and it is still clean and clear and safe from civilization.

Strange it is how things work out sometimes. A man starts out for a place in mind, but before he gets there he comes on something more to his liking than he thought a spot ever could be. That's how it was with Cache Lake. I was working north through a chain of lakes and streams to look over some timber for the lumber company. I had never been in the region before, but knew in a general way where I was heading. It was in the Snow Goose Lake country and I figured I would go up the Manitoupeepagee River and make myself a camp handy to the district I had to look over. A trapper told me I would find Wabun Lake a likely place for living. Just by way of remarking, Wabun is Indian for "east" or "dawn."

The time was early September, which is one of the best months for traveling in the north when the days are clear and sunny and the nights sharp with frost to make a fire feel good and remind you that fall is coming on. I stopped one night at the south end of Snow Goose Lake, where the Indians camp in the summer, and at dawn I started on. At that time of day the water is apt to be quiet and since my canoe with outfit and supplies was riding almost to the gunwales, the smoother the water the easier it was for me.

You leave the north end of Snow Goose Lake by a narrow creek or thoroughfare, a dark and deep neck of still water with muskeg and tamarack on the west side and heavy spruce on the east where the ground rises. It was so quiet I could hear the drops from the paddle hitting the water. The map showed that the waterway linked Snow Goose Lake with a small lake which had no name, so I didn't think much about it. Lake Wabun was a day's paddling ahead with some tracking up the river to boot, and my mind was set on getting there as soon as I could make it.

After I cleared the thoroughfare and came out on the small lake, I stopped paddling like a fellow will when he sees new water for the first time. The sun had come up and mist hung motionless like a big cobweb just above the surface. "Ghosts' breath" we called it when we were young. Over to my right, to the eastward, the shore was lined with jack pines and in one place close down by the water I could see a natural clearing. On the west was part of the great swamp I had passed coming up from Snow Goose Lake, but going north on that side the land lifted and the white boles of big canoe birches showed on the slopes of a low ridge.

I have seen maybe a thousand northern lakes, and they all look alike in many ways, but there was something different about that little lake that held me hard. I sat there perhaps half an hour, like a man under a spell, just looking it over.

On rigid wings with feet outstretched for a landing

This lake gave me the queer feeling that I had been there before. The tall pine tops were moving in the first soft breeze of morning and as the mist drifted away dark shadows began to edge across the water into the woods just as they had somewhere, sometime long ago. Then, as the sun cleared the hills and turned the still black water into shining gold, I remembered. This was the lake of my boyhood dreams! This was the lake I used to picture when I camped with my chum by a little millpond near a meadow on a farm. We made believe it was a lake in the far northern wilderness. The cows that came down to drink were deer and moose; the dogs that barked were wolves, and the perch we caught were fighting trout. Our flat-bottomed boat was a birch bark canoe.

Then I remembered the little brook that hustled into one end of the pond and now as I looked toward the north I saw the froth of white water at the far end where the Manitoupeepagee comes down over a rock-spiked forty-foot pitch. This was my lake at last, even to the black duck that came out of the shadows of a cove to fly clear against the sky and drop down on rigid wings with feet outstretched for a landing. In our millpond it was a kingfisher.

Then, for no reason that I understood, I paddled ashore, built a fire and made myself a pail of tea. And there was the big tree, not the elm that stood by the old millpond, but a tall white pine just where it ought to be. I knew then I had found the place I had always wanted to be.

After a while I headed on my way, but, when I pulled out for the carry at the head of the lake and looked back, I knew I would one day return. The fact is, I was back in a week and I pitched my tent in the clearing and worked out of Cache Lake on my job of cruising the timber country. The longer I stayed the better I liked the lake and after a while I began thinking about giving it a name, for by then I had a feeling that it belonged to me. It could be called a lot of pleasant names and all of them would fit, but I liked "Cache" because here was stored the best the north had to give: fine timber to build a cabin and keep a man warm, fish and game and berries for food, and the kind of peace and contentment that is found only in the woods. Where you store your belongings in the north, the things you can't live without, that's a cache. I could think of no better name.

Cache Lake brought me luck, for I hadn't been there long when I learned that Chief Tibeash, a Cree Indian I had known years before when my father and I came north to fish, was living on Shining Tree Lake about two miles from my camp. It was a meeting, I can tell you, for I had lost track of the Chief when we moved to another part of the country and many a time after I came back to the north again I had tried to get trace of him. But Indians don't leave forwarding addresses.

I was young and green when I first met the Chief and in those days I thought I knew the ways of the woods, but it didn't take me long to realize that I couldn't see much more than a puppy when his eyes open. Not until I traveled the woods with the Chief for several summers did I know the real meaning of a newly bent blade of grass, a broken twig, or water slowly oozing into a hoof-print in the mud. I hadn't learned to see an animal standing motionless in the woods, much less catch the quick movement at the moment of its escape. But the Chief saw it all. With him I learned to use my eyes and my nose and my ears in ways only the woods people know. Here in the clean air of the forest the sense of smell becomes keen and in time you learn to detect many things, lynx and bear, moose and other animals, by their scents. Gradually the eyes learn to see and the ears to hear, for every sound in the wilderness has a meaning, be it the faint rustle of a deer mouse in dry grass or the quavering howl of a timber wolf.

Chief Tibeash is not the kind of Indian you might picture. He is small and lean and his muscles are as tough and strong as a rawhide thong. The warm brown of dry pine spills is the color of his skin, and the many fine lines about his eyes come from years of squinting across glaring snow and ice

Deer Tracks

and shining water. You might expect his eyes to be dark, but they are gray and keen. If you could summon his ancestors back it wouldn't surprise me if you would find among the darker skins a fine looking *voyageur* with gray eyes. The Chief figures he is about seventy now. His mother told him that he was born in "the winter of the deep snows," which could be any one of many winters up here, so he can't be sure. But his age doesn't matter, for he is faster on the trail and can last longer in a canoe than many a younger man. He still takes a hundred-pound pack over a five-mile portage without stopping to rest.

It was the Chief who showed me how to handle a canoe like an Indian with the short stroke that begins at the waist and ends with a thrust from the shoulders and never tires. The proudest moment of my early years in the woods was when I was taken for an Indian because of the way I worked my paddle. I learned to live in shelters made from what came to hand in the woods and to know and use the natural foods of the wilderness. It was the Chief who helped me to make my first hunting sled and taught me to drive a dog team. I helped him tan deer and moose hides and make them into moccasins. Now I was back with him again as though there had been no space of years since I had seen Chief Tibeash.

When I finished cruising the timber and started out to make my report to the company, I promised the Chief I would come back someday, but right then I didn't know just when it would be. Well, when the company people got my report they asked me how I would like to make a permanent camp on Cache Lake and keep watch over the timber country. It didn't take me more than two breaths to say I would take the job and be glad to have it. All I asked was that they send in tools, spikes, and tar paper roofing to build a log cabin, and supplies to keep me fit through the winter. That they did with a large hand, including good windows for the cabin, two stoves and plenty of pipe.

The stuff came in three freight canoes and the six young

fellows that brought it stayed on to help me build the cabin, for by then it was late October and we had no time to lose before the snow came. The way those men went to work getting out logs, singing and yelling as they cut, was a caution. We used white pine for the walls and tamarack for the roof timbers. Green logs mean you must watch the chinking, for they open up as they dry, but winter was coming and we couldn't wait for them to season, a process which takes at least six months.

While the boys cut and placed the logs the Chief and I brought in plenty of sphagnum moss and gray clay for chinking, and in two weeks the cabin was closed in with the roof on. I found enough down timber that was dry to make the floor of hand-squared logs. A pretty sight it is to watch a man, who knows how to use an adz, square a timber almost as straight as if it was sawed. They did a fine job of fitting.

The boys stayed on to cut twenty cords of firewood, for no man in his right mind faces a north woods winter without having his wood cut and stacked. Mostly wood is cut in the winter and yarded to season until the fall. In that way you can take your time and choose the weather. But cutting wood day by day to keep warm when the temperature drops to the bottom of the thermometer is something I don't like to think about. When the crew left, all the Chief and I had to do was to finish the inside of my home and make it snug with bunks, tables, and chairs.

The site I chose for my cabin is on a knoll and from my window I can look out across the lake and over the ridge to hills far beyond. Tall jack pines lift high above my roof, and down in the marshy ground along the lake's edge to the south fish-net willows grow side by side with alder and high bush cranberries.

One of the things that means a lot to me at Cache Lake is my spring which lies back a little way in the woods just north of the cabin. I have always had a soft spot in my heart for springs. In a great valley I have run across a spring forty feet wide with water bubbling up under pressure. I have

ADZES

The Indians had an adz made out of stone......

.... and the steel adz we use is not too much different.

even cooked eggs in a pool so hot the water would scald you, and on one occasion I saw a spring of cold, sweet water in a hollow in the rocks on a tiny island far out in the ocean. But above all I love the little springs that are hidden in the moist and shadowed places in the north woods.

Paths to springs are not laid out by men. They choose their own way, twisting between trees, side-stepping rocks, and skirting marshy places. So it is with the path to my spring, for roots, lightly covered by moss, lie in wait to catch your toe, and when bruised on hot summer days give off the pleasant scent of spruce or balsam sap. You walk on through a patch of sphagnum moss, soft and heavy with water, and if you look you find the little star-shaped tufts that grow between the rocks, green on top and brown below. Everywhere balsam and spruce seedlings, some of them only a few inches high, are fighting their way toward the sky that shows in little patches through the tops of the trees high above, but in this struggle for survival only a few will grow up to feel the warmth of the sun. And overhead from the dead branches long whisps of gray moss hang like the beards of old, old men.

Suddenly from under your feet a bird startles up into the air and is gone before you hardly have a chance to see it, although there is no mistaking the sound of a partridge, and maybe a little further on a fool hen will lumber into the air and light on a low spruce limb where you could knock it over if you wanted to. I have flushed hundreds of partridges in my day but my heart always jumps when they whirr off the ground.

A great dead pine blown over by winter winds years ago lies part way into the spring, and in the dark cavern under its roots where the soil still clings, a hole shows where a chipmunk makes its home. All about it are ferns—thin, pale fronds that reach up only a few inches—and a little way beyond, where there is too much shade for their good, are a few thin raspberry bushes.

Going to my spring you walk from open pine woods into

a quiet world of green shadows and broken sunbeams where life begins with little seedlings and ends in sodden boles resting under blankets of moss, slowly sinking into the dark soil from which they once lifted their heads to the sun. There is beauty even in decay.

The first sign that you are close to the spring is a granite boulder which shoulders its way out of the moss. Here, close to one side of the big stone, you come upon a pool, clear, cool, and sweet. When your eyes get used to looking down you see grains of white sand jumping up like little fountains where the water comes in. The stream that carries the run-off is only a few inches wide, but further along it nourishes skunk cabbage and marsh plants as it makes its way toward the lake below.

Then if you glance up and away to the east where the ground begins to rise again you think you are looking into a smoky haze, but it is only the gray trunks of the spruce standing close in the dim light. And when you turn back, if it happens to be early June, lady's-slippers will be growing in a cool, shady place that gets just a little sun. And in mid-summer on the higher ground where the pine needles are deep, Indian pipes stand like little groups of ivory statues.

Indian Pipes

I had been living on Cache Lake for several years when one June day the plane that the company kept to patrol the timber limits dropped down on the lake and brought in a young fellow who was making his living by drawing and photographing wild animals and birds. And a first rate artist he was. His name was Henry—we called him Hank—and the letter he brought from the company asked me to be neighborly and make him at home for as long as he wanted to stay. I was glad to have this new friend who came loaded with drawing paper, pencils and ink, several cameras, and gear enough to keep him going for a long time.

The Chief took a strong liking to Hank and the three of us had a good summer. It was so good Hank decided he would stay on, so the Chief and I turned to and helped him

HBK

From my cabin on the knoll I look down on the lake

build a cabin over on Beaver Tail Lake, which is about two miles to the east of me, and a mighty sightly place.

The Cache Lake country is a land of rolling hills, none of them very high, with more lakes and streams than can easily be counted. It is a country of heavy forest, broken by muskegs and swamps where the black spruce grows. There is fine timber, white pine the best of all, and big hemlocks with the twigs on top that usually point to the east. Hundreds of square miles are covered with banksian pine, which we call jack pine, and others know as Labrador or Hudson Bay pine. It is one of the trees that comes back after a forest fire, for they say its seeds sprout faster if the cones have been scorched. And everywhere you go there is plenty of spruce and balsam, that good tree which provides man with a bed to sleep on and gum to heal wounds or to cover the seams of birch bark canoes.

Aspen

Up on the sandy ridge the quaking aspen grows, and when the soft breeze blows on the leaves they make a whispering sound. The Chief calls them "the trees that talk to themselves." And on the slopes of these whispering hills you find poplar and white birch, "the ladies of the woods." The Indians call it canoe birch, for it provides them with bark for canoes and from it they also make good paddles, snowshoe frames, and sleds. In the swamps, some of them many miles across and lonely, the feathery tamarack stand in close ranks, and there is no finer cover for deer and moose than the cedar that grows in the lowland.

Canoe Birch

Up in the northwest is Faraway See Hill, the highest point of land anywhere around here. It was used by the Indians as a lookout for generations, for Cache Lake lies on one of the ancient highways of the north, and from my cabin on the knoll I like to look down on the lake and imagine the scenes of the old days when big canoes and dog trains passed this way and became part of the rich history of the great fur trade of the north country.

Cedar

After I had been living at Cache Lake about two years, a geologist came by and stopped in for the night as men do up

Black Spruce

here. They always know they are welcome. He was making a study of the minerals of the country and knew a lot about how these northern lakes and rivers were formed. I took him up on Faraway See Hill and, looking down on Cache Lake, he told me he was sure that my lake had been formed by beaver works hundreds, maybe thousands, of years ago, and that the narrows between Cache Lake and Snow Goose Lake was where the great beaver dams had been built centuries before.

When the ice went out a year ago and scarred the banks in the narrows I found an old, yellowed beaver tooth sticking out of the soil. Likely as not, he told me, if I dug deep I would find the sticks of the beaver dam preserved in the mud and water.

Long before men ever thought of flood control, which you hear so much about today, beavers were at work. Behind their dams the soil brought down by the water settled in the low places and began to build up rich land. The fact is, my friend said, some of the finest farming land on this continent was made by beavers. Until I began studying their history I had never heard that beavers were plentiful ages ago in Europe and Asia. The kind we have in this country is a close relative of the European species and they tell me our beaver is even kin to the squirrel family.

From that welcome day in spring when the rivers break the icy thongs of winter, and flow free and wild, until the last leaf skitters down in late October, Cache Lake country is a land of ever-changing color and activity. The sifting rains of April release again the scents of rich earth, brown wood, and sodden leaves, and soon fresh grass shows in the clearings and the buds on the trees burst their winter sheaths. The Canada geese and the ducks, heading north, drop down to feed in the lakes that steal their color from the sharp blue sky. Then the singing birds come back from the south. May brings the peepers singing in the swamps and birds getting ready to nest in June, when the young animals will be out exploring their new world for the first time.

Summer comes with a rush, bringing long, hot days to help plant life blossom and ripen its seeds. The mosquitoes and black flies are at their worst when July comes along, and you know August is here when the drowsy warmth of dog days raises the acid odor of rotting pine spills while heat waves dance in the hazy woods. It is not a pleasant smell to some to be sure, for it's the odor of rotting vegetation turning back to the earth from which it first came.

Almost before you know it the blueberries are ripening in the clearings and in other places, especially where the land has been cut over, raspberries hang like rubies in the sunlight. About that time, if you know where to look, juicy blackberries can be found too.

Late in August when the leaves of the poplars stir with the sound of a host of fluttering wings, you may feel the first cool breath of early autumn in the night air. Now the summer foliage slowly turns to crimson and gold, a violet haze dims the far hills and the blue lakes turn to silver.

To me there is something almost comical about the first flurry of snow that comes usually in September. It's the way the clumsy big flakes float down, dipping and rising as if afraid to hit the ground. But they are not timid very long. In another month the snow has gained experience and the flakes, small and solid, drive down in close slanting lines, sure of where they are going and the job they have to do in the winter months ahead.

I like the feeling of danger in the cold autumn air that carries a quiet warning that winter is on the way and that time is running short. You would best be prepared for Pawatchicananum, the Whirlwind Moon of December, and Kushapawasticanum, January's Moon of the Great Cold, and Kichi, the Big Moon that rides the February sky.

There's no mistaking the signs of the first heavy storm of December. An old friend of mine used to say: "Snow like meal, snow a great deal." And that is pretty nearly always true, for when I hear the peculiar whispering of fine snow sifting down through the still air when the temperature is up around the freezing mark, I stack more wood on the porch and get ready to hole up for a few days. As the storm tucks the woods under its heavy white blanket the temperature is apt to fall, and when the weather clears it may be far below zero.

Some folks say the north is savage and a heartless country. In a way that is true, for winter shows little feeling for the man who takes no steps to prepare for its heavy snow and ice and the fury of its bitter winds. Here in the big winds the strong win and the weak lose, which, to be fair to the north, is the way folks everywhere work out life among themselves.

The white silence that closes down on the woods in winter like some kind of fog is strangely different from the hush of summer, when there are soft sounds that cannot be denied even though it may seem quiet. But when deep snow blankets the land and ice holds it in its rigid grip, there are few things left from which sound can escape except the wild creatures and the cracking of frost in the trees. So when the brittle silence of winter is broken by a noise it seems louder and is the more startling.

The Old Lady in the Clouds is generous when she starts plucking her geese and in normal years we are likely to have five feet of snow in the woods where the wind can't blow it away or pack it hard. And in low and sheltered places I have seen it actually twenty feet deep. On the waterways where the strong winds keep it moving the snow is seldom very deep and its surface, beaten hard by the winds, is fine for traveling.

After a heavy storm with little wind, snow burdens the trees and great snow bosses form between the branches of the spruce and balsam, while the slender cedar saplings in the swamps give up the fight and bow their heads to the ground. Many of them never quite straighten out again. Every stump becomes a gigantic white toadstool and in some open places the wind makes beautiful ripples on the snow like the marks of waves on a sandy beach. Along the streams where rabbits girdle the willows, the marks of their sharp teeth may be ten feet above the ground when spring carries the snow away.

Chief Tibeash is the head man of the Indians who come from their hunting grounds to camp during the summer on the west shore of Snow Goose Lake. A Chief doesn't inherit his position, but is chosen by general agreement on his qualities as a wise and intelligent leader. So it is to my old friend, the Chief, that the Indians of the Cache Lake Country turn with their problems, or to settle their disputes. They respect his natural dignity and his word is law, although they would resent it if he made his decisions in that spirit. No matter how thorny the problem, the Chief's way of working it out is based on the rules of common sense, the greatest gift that a man can have.

Our Indians are not what they might be pictured, for there have been many changes in their ways of living in the thirty years since I have known them. They buy many things that once they made for themselves from what they found in the forest. Some use tents and cabins instead of bark and hide tepees, and in the summer the footgear that most of them wear is made in some clanging factory hundreds of miles away. You don't see the Indian at his best in the summer camp near civilization, for it is in winter as a trapper and hunter that he turns again to the ways of his forefathers. Moccasins take the place of his summer shoes and although most of the canoes that carry the Indian families across the lakes and up the rivers to their winter homes are made by white men, some still cling to the fine birch bark craft, which has served them so well for centuries. To be sure it is not as fast as a manufactured canoe, it is hard to keep watertight, and is cranky in a wind, but a good birch canoe will carry far more freight than one the white man can make. But I've come to believe that the canoes made of light thin metal that can be molded into sweet and easy lines come closer to the birch bark craft than any other in weight and carrying capacity.

I admire the Indians in their respect for all things in na-

The Indians have a great respect for the spirit that dwells in the bear

ture. To them everything—water, land, trees, and animals—has a spirit and feelings. They hunt and kill game not
for the sport, but to live; and they believe that when they
shoot a deer or a moose or a bear the animal will understand
that it must be so. The Indian believes that the spirit of an
Indian chief dwells in the bull moose. He believes, too, that
birds can bring him good luck or evil fortune, and that they
can understand his language. The Indian mother is confident
that if her baby dies very young its spirit will become part of
a bird and that in its sweet song she is hearing the voice of
her little one. Every Indian boy from the time he turns toward manhood has a guardian spirit or "po-argen." which
is in the form of an animal or bird of which he has dreamed.
The Indians have a great respect for the spirit that dwells in
the bear which they believe to be very powerful and may
harm or help you according to your attitude in approaching
the animal if it is to be killed.

Indians are a warmhearted and generous people and when
the Chief and I visit them at their summer camp or go to their
winter lodges in the hunting country, the best food they
have is cooked for us and the most comfortable sleeping
place in the lodge or cabin is offered to us. By the standards
of our womenfolk their lodges are not always as clean as
they might be, yet their skill in using all the resources of the
wilderness in making their homes and in providing food
would astonish a white woman from the city. An Indian
mother, having established herself in a lodge one day, may
be called upon to tear it apart and move a few miles the next
for no better reason than to be near the carcass of a bear
killed by her menfolk who consider it more convenient to
move the home to the bear than carry the bear to camp.

In his hunting country far from the influences of civilization, the Indian is a shrewd, hard-working and skillful
hunter, using his simple and often meager resources to great
purpose. For whatever he does, whether it be the hitch on his
snowshoes or his method of tracking game, the form of his
shelter or the kind of clothes he wears, he has a practical

reason which has been tested by time, sometimes by centuries of experience.

Patience is one of the qualities you must learn if you live with the Indians, who think of time only in terms of useless effort for which there is nothing to show. A successful hunt has meaning only in time. Life in the woods has taught the Indian that he can't hurry trees and rivers, the rain and the sunshine, or most important of all, the game he hunts and traps. He never rushes in the way we do, though that doesn't mean he cannot and does not act with astonishing speed when he needs to. But he knows that the longest way round a swamp is often the shortest, for many reasons. He may spend days stalking a moose on which his family depends for life, but he makes sure that when the moment to shoot comes his chances of taking meat home are practically certain. So time to an Indian may be a moose.

Time is a strange standard of measure, for its value changes so much, depending on what you're doing and where you are. In the city most folks are slaves of minutes and hours. Time tells them what to do and when to do it. Here in the north woods it is different. It is not the hours or the days, but what happens at various seasons of the year that counts. Time is a snow storm, a downpour of rain, a day in spring, mosquitoes, and black flies. Time may be a dry spell or a forest fire, the freeze-up or the day when the ice goes out. In nature time doesn't trot right along. Often it stops for a while and sometimes backtracks on its own trail. It loafs along in winter and hustles in the spring and summer.

Anybody who lives in the woods knows how easy it is to lose all trace of time in terms of days and weeks. When I first came here I nailed a calendar on the wall and thought I was all set, but within a month I didn't know what day it was. When someone came my way I would get straightened out again and begin checking off the days until going on a cruising trip I would once more get out of step with time.

I remember one Thanksgiving Day when the Chief, Hank, and I celebrated the day with a fine dinner. The only thing

wrong was that we were two weeks ahead of the correct date. But what did that matter? The spirit was there. Maybe some day I will build myself a contraption to keep track of the days, but somehow I don't believe I would use it very much. Sunrise and sunset are close enough to mark off time for me.

Time has a way of doing strange things to a man who lives in the woods all alone, which is not a healthy thing for anybody. When you live by yourself for a long spell time begins to seem like a pail with a hole in the bottom. You can dip up water with it, but it leaks out before you can make use of it. Going over a portage one summer I met a fine old man who lives up here and helps the Indians. He was going in to see a young fellow who had been trapping for a year all alone, for the Indians had told him the young man was under the influence of a Weendigo, an evil spirit, and that they feared him. When we got to the man's cabin he was sitting in the doorway talking to himself. He had been there a mite too long and the old man persuaded him to go outside where he'd see his friends. That's all he needed. No, living alone, be it in the woods or the big city, where you can be as lonely as in any wilderness, is bad business. Men were not meant to live alone.

Long Nights and Deep Snows

STARTING a new year is like heading into strange country with no map to show you what's round the next turn in the trail or what lies behind the hills. It is what happens along the way to the meeting place of next year that makes going on worth all the work. You never know when a storm may break; never can be sure you won't hit white water round a bend in the river, and the big lakes you thought would be rough and dangerous as often as not turn out to be easy traveling. Best it is that a man not try to look too far along the trail. Have you ever watched a good Indian packer going over a portage with a heavy load? He keeps his eyes on the trail at his feet, looking for the roots and the rocks that might trip him. Generally he gets where he's going without falling.

This month was named after Janus, an old-time character, a sort of god. It seems that this fellow had two faces so he could look behind and ahead at the same time. Taking to mind what had happened in the past, it was his job to map out what would go on in the new year. Good enough as long as you keep in mind that things don't always work out to a plan.

This is the month the Indians up here call Kushapawasticanum o Pesim—the Moon of Great Cold. It is midwinter the way our cold season runs and the snow is light and dry with about four feet on the level and deep drifts in the hollows.

28

January is a season of rest, for this month almost everything in nature is asleep and storing up strength for the job that must be started when spring comes. Many of the animals are dozing away the winter deep in their burrows under rocks, in logs or maybe nests in the trees where the squirrels and deer mice go. A strange and wonderful thing this winter sleep they call hibernation.

The plants that grew last summer and scattered their seeds to carry on their kind have died, and now January is shredding the fallen leaves and dead grass with icy knives to make new soil to blend with the earth in the spring and nourish the plants and the living trees. That is the way nature works up her own fertilizer and if she didn't there wouldn't be any forests.

This is a month when, as the Chief says, "the earth is far below the snow"; and it is a good thing, for the snow holds some of the warmth of the earth and protects it from freezing too deep. Without its white blanket the land would lose a lot of moisture by evaporation. In January we generally have a thaw that reminds us of a spell of April weather, which is to make sure that the water is spread around fairly.

Every so often at this time of the year I go over to see Chief Tibeash at his cabin on Shining Tree Lake. On my last trip I hitched old Wolf to the light sled to bring back my small canoe which had been cached by the lake since the fall. I will want to make some repairs on it one of these days when I'm held home by the storms. I never saw a sled dog that loved his work more than Wolf, the best dog I have ever owned, and a fine leader in a team. He is a big black and white husky, strong and knowing, and as gentle as a doe with those he knows. Just to see him on the trail with his muzzle down and his bushy tail curled over his back is a sight to make any dog driver envy me.

It was one of those very quiet and cold mornings and the moon was still high and white when I started out, using bear-paw snowshoes to break trail for Wolf. The snow was deep and dry and he needed all the help I could give him. We don't often use one dog on a sled, consequently I plan to have another dog later on.

By the time I got to the Chief's place the sun was just hoisting itself stiffly over the ridge to the eastward of Shining Tree Lake and the tops of the trees, sharp against the pale sky, were as jagged as the teeth on Paul Bunyan's saw.

There is never a time, day or night, in the north when you are not welcome to walk in on a man for a meal or a bunk, for a human being and a voice mean a lot, especially in the winter months. So by the time I had slipped off my snowshoes and stuck them in the snow, the Chief was at the door telling me he had breakfast just about ready, which he didn't have to mention, for the smell of frying bacon and boiling coffee was notice enough. You can always count on having a good breakfast with the Chief, and that morning he had fried oatmeal with plenty of bacon. That is a good way to use up any left-over oatmeal because when it is cold you can cut it in half-inch slices, dust it with flour and fry it brown in bacon fat. As nourishing a thing as you can eat and it stays by you.

The sun was lost behind gray clouds when the Chief came out with me to get the canoe down from its staging on the shore and he took a couple of sniffs and said, "Kona!" And when the Chief smells snow you pay attention. Wolf and I hadn't more than got the canoe back to Cache Lake and laid in an extra tier of firewood when the Old Lady of the Clouds got down to business and that night a whining blizzard rode out of the north on the wings of a gale. Winter shows for certain who is master of life in the woods this time of year. On the south side of the cabin one big drift piled up clear to the roof. It keeps out the wind and cold like the insulation that folks in the city have to pay for to keep their houses warm. I got mine delivered by the wind free of charge.

Did you ever sit and listen to the sounds of a great night storm? From the darkness high overhead comes a deep rumbling. It is not the soughing of the wind in the thrashing

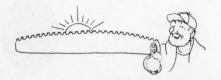

pine tops and it is not the sound of the gale beating down on the cabin. I have heard the very same rumble over a great city; I have listened to it on a ship in a storm at sea; and it is the same noise I once heard in a blizzard in flat country where there wasn't a tree or a rock in sight. It must be the roar of the mighty waves of the wind, tumbling across the cold black sea of night. Chief Tibeash says his people used to call it the war drums of the Manitoupeepagee Din-ens, "the Wind Devil."

Every now and then in such a storm there's a lull. Suddenly the wind stops as if someone had shut a door, and the snow that was streaking across the window, drifts straight down in dead silence for a little time. During a quiet spell in the blizzard that night I heard the scream of the big Canada lynx that lives and hunts in the Great Tamarack Swamp at the lower end of the lake. Once you hear that sound you never forget it. I have been in these woods close to twenty years, but I never hear that wild cry without shivering. Even old Wolf gets uneasy. The hackles on his shoulders rise and he growls and swings his muzzle for the scent.

After a lull in the storm the wind comes back with a rush as if it had gathered new strength in the few seconds of calm. At the height of our big storms we sometimes have winds of more than fifty miles an hour. You might ask how I know. The answer is a wind gauge which I made last summer, for I am always interested in the weather, especially how hard the wind is blowing.

Putting the wind gauge together was not much of a job once the idea was worked out, as you will see by Hank's sketches. The body of the contraption is about the shape and size of a ping-pong bat, which, as a matter of fact, would have served the purpose very well. The vertical lever has a slot in the lower end so that the counterweight can be raised or lowered and then set by a small bolt. The wind vane, which fits on a slot in the top, should be made of a very thin piece of light wood. Thin sheet aluminum would be even better. Once the parts are assembled you have to experiment

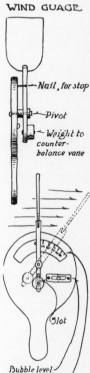

WIND GUAGE

Nail, for stop

Pivot

Weight to counter-balonce vane

Slot

Bubble level
Graduated scale

Wind vane displaced
by a 22 mile wind.

on adjustment by moving the counterweight up and down and trying various sizes of wind vanes. It is not practical to try to register wind speeds below ten miles an hour and sixty miles was set as the top speed, which is about as high as will ever be needed, and that not very often. The small bubble level must be set carefully so that when the bubble is centered the vertical lever is just balanced against the nail stop. In high winds the velocity often changes quickly, so it is best to take several readings to get a close check on the average speed.

When the gauge was finished we had to find some way of setting the various speeds on the dial. The only method we could figure out was to tramp out to the settlement where a friend of mine had a car. While he drove up and down the road at various speeds I held the gauge out the window and as he called the speeds I marked them on the dial. We picked a calm day when there was no breeze stirring so the speed of the car would represent actual wind velocity. I don't claim my gauge is accurate to the mile, but it's not far off and plenty close enough for my purpose.

I can't tell you how much pleasure that wind gauge has given me, for all I have to do when I want to know how fast the wind is blowing is to step outdoors where I get a clean sweep and hold it at arm's length and the dial swings over to give the answer.

Mal de raquette, or snowshoe lameness, is something you have to watch out for at this time of year. I had a touch of it a while back after a hard trip out to the settlement, and the only thing to do is to take it easy and keep off your feet as much as you can for a few days. *Mal de raquette* starts in the tendon that moves the big toe, and creeps up the ankle, making it mighty painful to walk. It is caused by the constant bending of your toes on the snowshoes where the foot dips through the slot.

I have lots to do these stormbound days and the number

MAL DE RACQUET!

one job is making myself two pairs of moccasins from a fine piece of moose hide the Chief brought over. It was the Chief who taught me many years ago how to make moccasins and his are the finest I've ever seen. Once you get on to the trick it's not much of a job. The best way is to make your first pair out of a piece of old blanket or heavy cloth to get the knack of cutting and stitching, and to make sure the size is right. A friend of mine who was just learning got himself one of those pieces of chamois for polishing things that you can buy in the stores. It feels like fine buckskin, but it's not as strong. Just the thing to practice on though, and chamois moccasins are good over socks in shoepacks or overshoes. Matter of fact we make a special kind of doeskin sock for just that purpose.

The way to start is to make a drawing of your foot on a large piece of cardboard. Then draw the cutting lines outside your footprint, leaving enough space so that the toe piece will fold back to about the base of your big toe. The sides should be wide enough to turn in over your foot leaving maybe two inches to fit the vamp in, and just under the ankle bone further back. In drawing the cutting lines on your pattern do not follow the exact shape of your foot. That is the natural thing to do, but it is not the best way, take my word for it. What you want is a well-rounded toe and straight sides to your moccasins. They don't have to be shaped to the foot like shoes, but can and should be changed from one foot to the other to get even wear. The kind I make is the Cree or Ojibwa moccasin, which to my mind is the best. The high tops wrap around the ankle snugly and keep the snow out. Once you get the hang of puckering the toe and sewing in the vamp, the rest is easy. Take your time, and don't rush the stitching. Just remember to sew the pieces together with the edges on the outside so that there won't be any ridges inside to chafe. That is important. With Hank's sketches you ought to be able to do a fine job.

I guess maybe you will think the three of us are queer, but not long ago we went on a midwinter picnic. It was Hank's

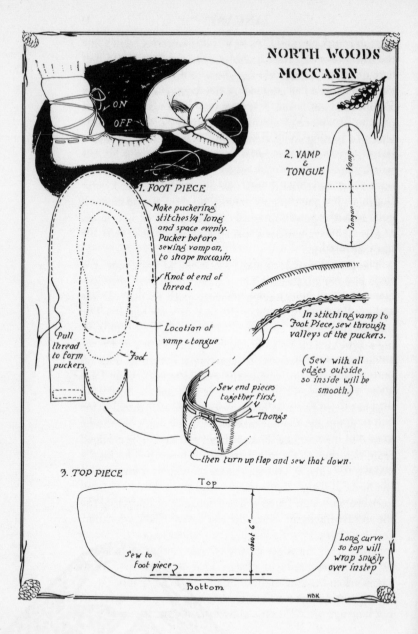

NORTH WOODS MOCCASIN

ON
OFF

1. FOOT PIECE

Make puckering stitches ¼" long and space evenly. Pucker before sewing vamp on, to shape moccasin.

Knot at end of thread.

Location of vamp & tongue

Pull thread to form puckers

Foot

2. VAMP & TONGUE

Vamp

Tongue

In stitching vamp to Foot Piece, sew through valleys of the puckers.

(Sew with all edges outside, so inside will be smooth.)

Sew end pieces together first,

Thongs

then turn up flap and sew that down.

3. TOP PIECE

Top

Sew to foot piece

Bottom

about 6"

Long curve so top will wrap snugly over instep

HBK

idea, and the Chief and I fell in with it. It was a cold day and the thermometer showed twenty-three below zero, but here in the north the cold is dry and with the right clothes you don't feel it half as much as the damp air farther south. We loaded a pack of extra special food on the sled and Wolf did the hauling. We snowshoed northeast, passing to the west of Hunting Wolf Ridge, and then went on up to the beaver works on Little Otter Stream. Beaver dams are the worst places in the world to get around in summer; what with water and down timber and dry-ki the going is hard. But in winter you can just walk right over it all and get a good idea of what they've been doing.

The rounded white mounds rising above the level of the snow-covered pond mark the location of the beaver houses where, surrounded by water and locked fast in heavy ice, they live happily, safe from the cold and their enemies. Some of those houses, built of small logs, saplings, twigs, and mud, are ten feet across. Down in the mud on the bottom they have stored for the winter a fine food supply of juicy green poplar logs and other choice wood. The beaver enters his house through a sloping tunnel that starts near the bottom well below the ice and leads up to his living quarters above the water level. They are clean animals and have a drying-off shelf, so to speak, where they drain off water before going up to the sleeping room lined with nice dry grass and leaves of water plants. In the winter they try to keep an air hole open somewhere in the pond, but if the hole freezes over they can breathe all right with the small amount of air that leaks into their houses.

A beaver is a critter that uses his head in more ways than one. Some folks say they know how to drop a tree where

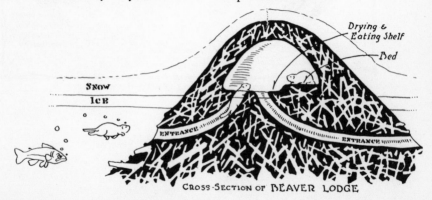

CROSS-SECTION OF BEAVER LODGE

Snow Buntings . . . fly up and strike the weed-tops

they want it to fall, but I don't believe that is so. They just keep on gnawing right around the trunk until it comes down. I have always wanted to see what a beaver does at the moment a good-sized tree falls.

On the way up we came into a clearing which is full of flowers and weeds in the summer and saw what we expected, snow buntings feeding on the seeds of dead weeds. They fly up and strike the tops of the weeds to knock the seeds out, then settle down in the snow to eat them. They are pretty little birds, white feathers below and brown mixed with white on top. The wings and tail are tipped with black. When they fly they circle and dip in a pattern as perfect as a lot of airplanes following a leader in formation. You see them flying in the worst blizzards, and they seem to enjoy it. Sometimes we see horned larks, too. They have little feathers that stand up on their heads and look like horns. If there are weeds to feed on, they don't mind snow or cold either.

Once the sun cleared the hills the glare on the snow was so bright that we had to put on our snow goggles. Snow blindness is something you have to watch for, especially late in winter when the glare is hard on a man's eyes. That's why we use snow goggles. Something like spectacles, they are, but instead of glass you look through very thin slits.

We make our blinders of wood or bone, but all you really need to see how they work is some good stiff cardboard. If you have a pair of old spectacles handy, lay them on the cardboard and trace the shape. Then cut along the line, leaving the eyepieces solid and the nosepiece wide. Next with the point of a sharp knife cut thin slits across the middle of the eyepieces, but not right to the edges. If you have done a good job the slits should be exactly opposite your eyes, and you can then smooth them by running a strip of very fine sandpaper gently back and forth so the edges won't be fuzzy. Now tie the snow glasses on with string to reach around your head. Don't use wire earpieces; they freeze to your skin in cold weather. Try those glasses on bright snow, ice, or shining water, or even dazzling sand on a beach or desert, and see if you don't think they're fine to beat the glare. Fitting a little visor over the slits and painting the outside flat black helps to keep out reflected glare.

If you like the idea carve yourself a pair of goggles out of soft pine wood. Make the slit as thin as paper and curve the goggles to fit your forehead, hollowing out the eyepieces so your eyelashes won't rub. Snow blindness doesn't always come from the glare of the sun on ice or snow, but from the steady whiteness of everything, even when the sun is hidden by thin clouds. Men have been known to go snow blind while stormbound in a tent. You can suffer from this misery any time of the year, but to my mind the glare of the sun on crusted snow from February on into the spring break-up is the worst.

If you get snow blindness when you are alone on the trail you're in a fix and no mistake, so the wise thing is to put on snow goggles or dark glasses, which serve the same purpose. And speaking of dark glasses, some of them can do your eyes a lot of damage, so you want to get the best, which are made of good optical glass.

Snow blindness, I can tell you from experience, is painful, and about all you can do is try to shield your eyes from the light as much as possible. If you are at home it is a good thing to keep your cabin or tent dark. A solution of granular boracic acid in water helps to ease the pain, and I always have some with me in my first-aid kit. It is also good for small cuts and insect bites. One thing to make sure of is that you don't try to use your eyes for reading or close work while you are suffering from snow blindness. That only makes it worse.

Once when he had left his goggles at home I saw the Chief cut a slit in a piece of birch bark and tie it across his eyes, which did a pretty good job in the emergency. He made a

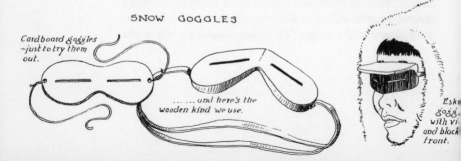

SNOW   GOGGLES

Cardboard goggles ~just to try them out.

......and here's the wooden kind we use.

Esk
gogg
with vi
and block
front.

little notch for the bridge of his nose and that's all there was
to it. He's a wonderful old man and there's never a day I
don't learn from him how well off a man can be if he makes
use of all the things that nature provides. I never saw the
time when the Chief could not use what he had at hand to
make what he needed.

To get back to our picnic, by noon we had worked up
right hearty appetites, so we cleared a spot in the sun by a
big spruce and built a warming fire and had our victuals. I
never thought venison steak could taste so good. It had been
hanging frozen since last fall, and, broiled over the glowing
coals at the edge of the fire, it was that tender we didn't need
a knife to cut it. I had some boiled potatoes all ready to fry
with onion rings and baking powder biscuits that I had
baked that morning. They were touched with the frost, but
that made no difference; in fact I think they tasted better
for it. What with some strawberry jam that Hank's sister
sent up for Christmas, and plenty of steaming tea, we did
ourselves pretty well. Then when the Chief had sliced some
chips from his plug of tobacco and got his pipe fired up and
smelling right fragrant, we hit the trail for Otter Stream.
There were lots of wolf tracks around, so we figured they
were after the deer which are in their yards in the heavy
spruce.

While we were looking over the beaver pond we talked
about other creatures living under the ice. For one thing, I
happen to know there are some very nice brook trout in
that cold water. There are lots of other things too, including
frogs and turtles asleep in the bottom mud. The fish don't
lack for food now. Lots of small critters that live in the
water keep going in the winter, and the fish think they're
pretty good eating.

Most insects die off in the fall, leaving their eggs to carry
on their kind, but it's surprising how many stay alive
through the winter. Some of the spiders, for example, don't
sleep so soundly and on a warm day you can see them occa-
sionally out on the snow. The fishing worms we dig in the

spring have burrowed down below the frost line and are snoozing the winter away. The ants are in snug underground homes well supplied with food. You would hardly believe that so delicate a thing as a butterfly could live through very cold weather, but several kinds find shelter under logs or in rock crevices or sometimes in the cracks of old buildings. That is why once in a while during an extra warm day in a January thaw you may see a small butterfly flying about. And sometimes we see those black and tan wooly bear caterpillars roaming about over the snow. Of course most butterflies and moths do not come out until spring. They winter as pupa or eggs and when the warm spring days come they break out of their cocoons as beautiful winged insects or hatch out of the eggs as caterpillars.

Now that the snow is deep, a big crew is hard at work cutting timber some twenty miles north of Cache Lake. It is the nearest thing to an old-time lumber operation you will find these days. Most of the lumberjacks know their way about, but once in a while one of them gets lost. There was a fellow named Sam—I forget his last name—who was working with a crew up in the country west of Hawk Lake some years ago. One February day when quitting time came the men in Sam's crew piled on a sled heading for camp, but Sam had forgotten his axe, so he jumped off and went back over the brow of a ridge to pick it up, figuring that the boys had seen him leave the sled. He wasn't away more than a few minutes, but when he came back the sled had gone. Then Sam's troubles began. First of all, the country was new to him, and furthermore it was laced with sled tracks where they had been hauling logs. He picked out one track he was sure belonged to the sled that he should have been on, and started out, shouting once in a while in the hope that they would hear and wait for him.

Finally Sam decided he was on the wrong trail, so he backtracked and picked out another line of runner marks

You'll find Mourning Cloaks gathering around your sap buckets in early spring.

Cecropia and Promethea moth coccoons. Pick them in the winter, and watch them come out in the spring. If you get a female Promethea, you'll be surprised!

Sam let panic grab hold of him

and followed them for a while. He walked and walked, staggering through the deep snow, but he saw no sign of the camp. All the while he was yelling his head off, but never an answer came. Sam was in a fix and no mistake, for by that time night had settled down and the sky was overcast. Even if the night had been clear and he could have seen the North Star it would not have done him any good, for he had no idea where he was.

By that time Sam was scared plumb to death and did the worst thing a man can do when he's lost—he let panic grab hold of him. He remembered stories about wolves trailing a man and there were plenty of them around that section, for he could hear them howling. Lumberjacks believed the rattle of a piece of trace chain would keep them away and Sam wished he had one, but he should have known better about wolves attacking a man. Worse than that, the temperature had dropped away below zero and Sam had used his last match to light his pipe just before quitting time. There he was, no way of making a fire and the weather sharpening every hour. Then he started to run. First he would follow one sled track and when another crossed it he would take that one without knowing he had changed direction, for there hadn't been any snow for several days and most of the tracks looked pretty fresh. Every once in a while he would fall, and finally he was so tired he wanted to lie down and go to sleep, but he knew better than to do that, and somehow he kept going.

Well, to get to the end of the story, early in the morning when it was still dark, Sam staggered into a camp. He thought he had made his own, but found out he was in another twelve miles away. His feet were frostbitten, two of his fingers were frozen, and they had quite a time getting him straightened out. Essence of ginger helped, they tell me. Most men would have died, but Sam was strong and rugged and that's the only thing that carried him through.

Getting lost is something that can happen to anybody and it's important that a man know how to find his way around and keep track of the landmarks wherever he goes all the time. I'm so used to keeping a landmark in sight that when I go to a city the first thing I do is spot a tall building or maybe a monument or tree in a park to keep me located. That's what any woodsman would do because he depends upon observing everything as he goes along and building a chain of reference points by which he locates himself.

Everybody who goes into strange country should carry a compass. To be sure, most woodsmen never use them and that's all right if you know your territory. The Chief doesn't need a compass in any country, but the old Indian was born and bred in the wilderness and everything he sees as he travels trails and waterways is part of a picture of the country as a whole. And if he meets a man on the trail he is not backward about getting all the information he can about conditions ahead.

Many a man who owns a compass doesn't really understand how to use it. We all know that the needle points to the magnetic North, which is different from the true North. Thus there is a variation to take into account if you want to follow an accurate course. This variation is either east or west of true North according to your position on the continent and it changes every year. Before starting into the woods find out the compass variation for that location and ask how it should be used in your readings. This is very important when you are laying out a course on a map. If, however, you simply want to reach some landmark you take a compass sight and follow it without bothering about the variation. Check the compass direction every few minutes to make sure you are on the course, for your landmark may be out of sight much of the time.

These are the 32 COMPASS POINTS – the half-points in between are called N½E, NNE½N, NNE½E, NE½N, NE½E, ENE½N etc.

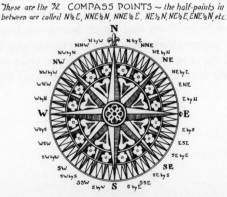

When I go through strange country I always note which way the streams flow, where the hills are, and if I have to skirt around the end of a lake I make sure to locate a landmark on the other side that I will be able to see when I get there. I keep as near the shore as I can, but once in a while you have to go back into the woods to avoid beaver works or a swamp. Such detours may take you out of sight of the lake, and in twisting and turning you can quickly lose all sense of direction. That is a time when a compass helps. Sometimes I break off branches of bushes, leaving them dangling, which shows the way I have come. It's surprising how quickly the eye will note a limb hanging in an unnatural position.

In using a compass a man is apt to forget that the needle is deflected by iron or steel, so it is important when making a reading to put it on the ground or on a stump a few feet away and read the directions from a distance; otherwise your axe or your pocketknife or any other piece of metal such as a frying pan, may throw it off and send you in the wrong direction.

The greatest mistake a man can make is to get suspicious of his compass and decide that it is not taking him on the right course. Unless a compass is so badly out of order that it won't swing freely on its pivot it is better to follow its direction than run the risk of getting lost.

With most things in life I do not believe in looking backwards, but a hindsight when you are working through new country is sometimes the best way of getting ahead, especially if you are not sure that you are going in the right direction and may have to turn back. It is a good thing to look back every little while and pick out a landmark, for trails have a way of blinding out in the middle of nowhere. And you are usually surprised to see that the country behind looks entirely different from that which lies ahead. I remember taking a man on a canoe trip once and on the way back we followed the same route by which we had gone in, yet he insisted we were in new territory until I showed him that

by looking back he would see the land as he viewed it when
we came up the river. He never forgot that experience.

Blazes or other marks of travel are signs to watch for. I
recall a young fellow going into a black spruce swamp and
he thought he was doing the right thing when he blazed a
tree every once in a while on the side of the trunk facing
him as he walked along. When he turned around to come
home the blaze marks were all on the opposite sides of the
trees and if, when he started out, he hadn't located himself
a dead pine on a hill for a landmark he might have been lost.
That was I when I was young and green!

One of the foolish mistakes that a man makes—and it happens often—is to leave camp without telling his friends that
he is going and in what direction. If you get lost that dou-
bles your trouble, for nobody knows where to look for you.

My grandfather, who was a seafaring man, used to say
that any man who went out in a boat without a supply of
fresh water was a fool. The same thing holds good in the
woods in a different way. You can nearly always get water
in the north woods, but a man who starts out without
matches in his pocket in something that will keep them dry,
and a strong knife, or maybe a hand axe, may be trailing
trouble. As a matter of fact, if you are moving about where
food is scarce or in a season when there are no berries, it is a
good idea to have a snack of something in your pocket.

Going out.....

... and coming back!

Knowing something about distance and how to measure
it is a great help in wilderness travel, for there are times
when it is vital to know how far it is from one place to
another. After you have lived in the woods for a while you
learn to judge distance fairly accurately and can measure it
by keeping track of the number of paces it takes to get to a
certain place. My pace is thirty inches and I have learned to
measure distance by counting my paces without finding it
tiring. You can also get a rough check on the distance you
cover by timing yourself. Unless you are carrying a heavy
pack you can walk along a good trail at an average of from
two and a half to three miles an hour. Traveling on a familiar

trail in easy country an old-timer might do a shade better. But on a long trip the tendency is to slow down as you tire toward the end of it.

Once when I wanted to make a rough map of a section of country I made myself a measuring wheel from an old barrel hoop and mounted it between the forks of a light sapling. Knowing its circumference, all I had to do was to roll the wheel over the ground, counting its revolutions every time a nail on one of the spokes snapped a little strip of wood fastened to the forks. I still have that wheel and in winter I sometimes hook it to the back of the dog sled to measure a trip. Some day I'm going to get a counter and hook it to the wheel so it will register distance automatically.

If you have no compass, wind and sun can help to keep directions straight. And there are other signs in nature which are generally good, but which should never be relied upon alone as accurate because they vary with the country. The Chief told me when I came in here young that a man always ought to know the way of the "main wind," by which he meant the prevailing wind, wherever he is. At Cache Lake, it is the west wind. So knowing the winds can help as long as you keep in mind that winds have a way of changing.

When you can see it, the sun is a good guide, for you know without fail it moves in the general direction of east to west. But there are plenty of times when you don't see the sun for days. At night when it is clear there is the North Star to guide you, and that friendly sign, which marks the true North, never changes position. You have probably

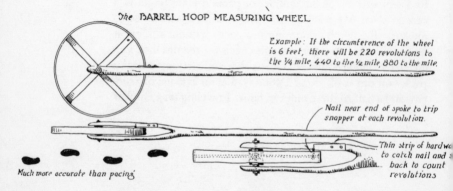

The BARREL HOOP MEASURING WHEEL

Example: If the circumference of the wheel is 6 feet, there will be 220 revolutions to the 1/4 mile, 440 to the 1/2 mile, 880 to the mile.

Nail near end of spoke to trip snapper at each revolution.

Thin strip of hardwood to catch nail and snap back to count revolutions

Much more accurate than pacing.

heard before that a watch makes a good compass. When the sun is shining you point the hour hand—the little one—to the sun, and South will be halfway between the hour hand and the figure twelve.

When you get down to hardpan, the whole business of living in the wilderness, finding your way about, and avoiding the dangers, is much a matter of common sense and getting the habit of observing everything closely. If you have common sense, which is the same thing as good judgment, you don't often get into trouble, and every time you do get into trouble you learn something about common sense the hard way.

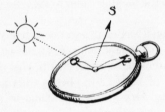

FEBRUARY

The Stars and the Silence

Wolves are on the move now, for when the snow is deep food is hard to get and they are hungry and savage. We hear them at Cache Lake, but not as much as further north in the Thunder Lake country, where the Chief has a trap line. I usually go along with him and while he looks to his traps I strike across to the logging camp to see how the cutting is going.

Fire burned over part of this section a few years ago and left a desolate and lonely ridge covered with the white skeletons of standing dead trees. That is what they call dry-ki, a shortening of "dry-kill timber"—trees killed by fire, but still standing. Dry-ki has also come to mean timber killed by the backwater when they raise the level of the lakes for lumbering. We call the place the Graveyard and it is the kind of country wolves like, for it borders on a swamp where the deer winter. If wolves can drive a deer out into the jackpots of tangled timber and slash they usually get it.

One night when we made camp half a day north of Cache Lake the big gray critters began their howling in the hills where Lost Chief Stream runs through the Graveyard country. Now, there is nothing friendly in the howl of a wolf, yet I find something strangely beautiful in his quavering song, especially on a still cold night. If a man is given to feeling lonely in the woods the howling of a wolf can bring it on about as fast as anything, but I'm not bothered that way. At first there was only one wolf, but he made himself

heard all right. Soon another started, then a third and fourth joined in, and their chorus came to us strong and clear on a breeze that barely slanted the smoke of our fire.

Well we knew that the deer and the moose for miles around that night were hearing the wolf-song and moving closer together, listening uneasily and searching the air with lifted heads and quivering nostrils for a trace of the scent they dread more than any other. Along the creeks the white hares stopped nibbling the bark of tender saplings and scurried for cover, and a mouse hunting for seeds among the dead weeds on top of the snow would dive into his hole under a stump. Only the lynx, crouching on the limb of a spruce in wait for a rabbit, would pay no attention.

Chief Tibeash, sitting on his blankets on a deep bed of balsam boughs by the fire, grunted in disgust and began cutting little chips from a plug of black tobacco. Rolling them in his palm with the heel of his brown hand, he filled his pipe and reached for a glowing ember. He listened to the wolves for a long time and frowned when one of them, having stopped for a few minutes, began howling again just like a man joining a quartet at the wrong place in the song.

What bothered the Chief was that the wolves were in his trapping territory and might cost him some fine skins. As it was the weather had been colder than usual with a spell of twenty below zero or lower for ten days without a break. A long stretch of cold weather during the short days of mid-winter is likely as not to keep the animals pretty close to home with the result that the trapper's catch may drop off.

I asked the Chief if he had ever known a wolf to attack a man. He had heard of many such attacks, he said, but none were true so far as he could find out. He agreed that wolves will trail you and sometimes circle a camp for hours, but more from curiosity than anything else, he thinks. You hear them all winter, but mighty seldom actually see the animals.

Some people would have you believe that wolves run in large packs. According to what I know, and the Chief agrees, six or seven would be a large number to see together.

Springs from behind and hamstrings it

Four or five is more common and often they are all members of the same family—father, mother, and several one- or two-year-olds. But even three wolves can make a noise that sounds like ten, which probably accounts for some of the yarns you hear.

Born in April or early May, young wolves romp and play with all the fun of dog puppies. The old folks feed them faithfully, but it's not long before they begin to teach the youngsters to hunt for themselves. Smart critters, they are, too. Working as a team, wolves will soon bring down a deer if the snow is deep, but with good footing a deer can usually outrun them. Sometimes a wolf will go for the throat, throwing the deer head over heels. Another way is for one or two wolves to run close to the deer's head to keep its attention while another springs from behind and hamstrings it by cutting the tendon in the hind leg. After that a deer hasn't a chance.

I would say that most wolves weigh somewhere between seventy and eighty pounds, though quite a few go up to a hundred and thirty or more, and they average about two feet high at the shoulder. Mostly they are a mixture of brown and gray in color, but some are a creamy white, while others are what you might call black.

We were camping well north of Faraway See Hill and the stars looked down on us like the sparkling eyes of millions of curious children. The Aurora Borealis, or Northern Lights, slashed the northern sky into thin bands of rose and yellow and ghostly green that reached from the earth high among the stars. They were always moving, suddenly rushing across the sky, rising and falling, then fading to a dim glow only to flare up again to flow across the night, a wide river of rippling light. The Chief said it reminded him of the young people he used to watch in his boyhood when they danced in the light of the fires against the dark forest. And the soft swishing noise you hear when the lights are strong was like the sound of their deerskin clothes as they moved about. The old man likes to watch the northern

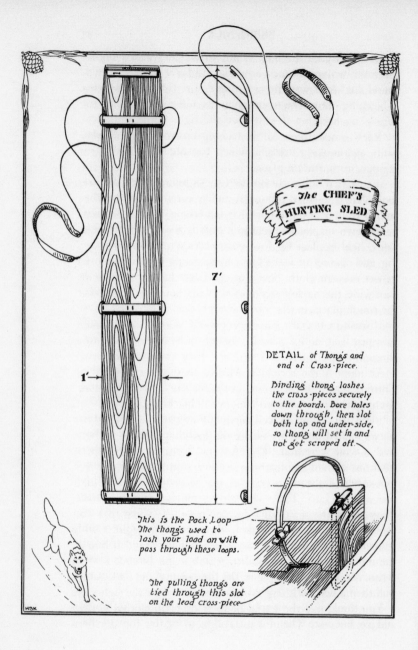

7'

1'

The CHIEF'S HUNTING SLED

DETAIL of Thongs and end of Cross-piece.

Binding thong lashes the cross-pieces securely to the boards. Bore holes down through, then slot both top and under-side, so thong will set in and not get scraped off.

This is the Pack Loop The thongs used to lash your load on with pass through these loops.

The pulling thongs are tied through this slot on the lead cross-piece

HDK

lights and says it must be rainbows dancing in the night. Even the wolves stopped howling and for a while the only sound we heard was the cracking of the frost in the trees.

Sleeping out in the open when the temperature is below zero is no hardship if you have the right outfit and stick by a few simple rules. All we had with us was our blankets, grub, and cooking utensils, which consisted of a pail, frying pan, cups, and tin plates.

We carried our outfit on the Chief's hunting sled, which looks like a narrow toboggan and is common among the Indian trappers of the north. It is nothing more than two hand-hewn maple, ash, or birch boards about half an inch thick, held in place by four crosspieces with rawhide lashing, and curved up at the front by steaming over a slow fire in wet moss or cloth. Seven or eight feet long and about a foot wide, this narrow sled is so flexible it seems to flow over the rough places in the trail and easily snakes between trees and brush in heavily wooded country. There's not a nail or a peg in it, and the load is lashed on by thongs running through loops fastened to the ends of the crosspieces.

Although dogs are often hitched to hunting sleds, the Chief never takes them out on the trap line. They disturb the game, leave a scent that makes the wild things extra cautious for a long time, and sometimes get into the traps. So we hauled the sled with a long double moosehide thong with a wide section at the loop to put over the forehead to spell our shoulders once in a while—same idea as a tump line. There are more ways than one of using your head in the woods. The Chief taught me years ago that the first thing to do when you make camp is to turn your sled or toboggan on its side if loaded, or on end if empty, so the runners won't freeze to the snow and will be free of frost in the morning. It is a good idea to scrape the runners clean when you stop for the night, for there is nothing harder to pull than a sled with frosted runners.

You think of sleds or toboggans being used only on snow and ice, but once when I was traveling along the shore of the

St. Lawrence River close to where it widens to meet the sea I saw people sliding down the high sandy cliffs on toboggans and skis. The beach was very narrow and when they hit the bottom the toboggan skimmed out on the water quite a way. I have heard of people sliding and skiing on dry grass, too. When I was young I took one of my mother's best big trays to slide down a hill under the tall pines where the ground was covered several inches deep with dry and slippery needles. It was grand sport.

We spent two nights on the trail to the Chief's cabin on Thunder Lake, circling wide to cover part of his trap line on the way. The first day out we crossed a black spruce swamp and saw signs that deer and moose had been feeding on the cedar tips. The paths in their yards are not packed down like most trails, but are a series of large holes formed when they step in the same places as they move back and forth. On the edge of the swamps we came on the trail of a fox and followed it to the base of a big spruce where it had pounced on a partridge sleeping under the snow. A few scattered feathers and a bright red stain told the story of the never-ending battle for life in the forest. If snow falls after a partridge dives into the white cover its hiding place is fairly secure; otherwise it leaves a sign and scent on the surface.

As usual in winter travel we followed the waterways whenever we could, for the going on lakes and rivers is easier than in the woods where the drifts pile up, and we took turns breaking trail. Darkness comes early in the north country's short winter days and about four o'clock the Chief headed into a stand of big spruce on the south side of a ridge. As long as I have been in the big woods I have never gotten over the way the old Chief goes about making himself comfortable under all conditions, winter or summer. A good woodsman has patience. He realizes he can't change nature nor hurry her. He doesn't fret because a river runs the wrong way for his journey, doesn't cuss over being wind-bound for days on an island in a big lake. He knows he can't lower the hills to make a portage easier, and in winter he won't try to fight a blizzard. He learns early that rushing does not often get you where you are going any faster than taking it quietly. Wise in the ways of the woods, he realizes that often the longest way is the shortest. He never takes any more steps than he needs to, and he knows just where to sink his axe to bring down a tree with the least number of strokes. In the far away cities they call that efficiency and teach men to do things with the fewest motions. Up here they have no name for it, but just watch a good woodsman pick up a canoe and walk away with it and you will know what I'm driving at. And what's more, you'll probably learn to live longer.

The place the Chief had chosen for a camp site was in the middle of a little opening surrounded by big shaggy trees, and I knew he had found just what he wanted when he took off his snowshoes and used one of them like a shovel to clear a place for our camp.

On many another winter's night we have slept with nothing but the sky for a roof and the trees of the forest for walls, but that night the Chief thought there was a chance of the wind springing up, so we had made just enough of a shelter to catch any drifting snow which would quickly form a cover on the balsam thatching.

I have made a winter camp by cutting away the low branches from a thick spruce to form snug sleeping quarters under the tree, but there's always the chance that dry snow will sift down through the branches if the wind makes up. What's more, the fire is likely to melt snow clinging to the tree and soak everything.

For winter sleeping in the open there is nothing to equal a rabbitskin robe. One robe is equal to at least two blankets and it insulates you from the cold in the way that nature devised for the wild things—by trapping the air in the fur. One method of making a skin robe is to begin cutting the rabbitskin in a circle in a continuous strip about three-quarters of an inch wide. In that way you get a piece several feet long from a single skin. If a strip is too short you sew it to the end of another. The next step is to twist the the strips around thin hide thongs until they form what looks like a fur covered rope. These pieces are then woven into a robe about four feet wide and eight feet long. You want them wide enough to roll in and plenty long enough so your head can be covered. Some Indians make their robes of flat strips cut lengthwise of the skin and then sewed end to end. The edges are held by a binding of strong cotton cloth. Rabbitskin robes are hard to get now, for few are made, the Indians preferring to buy blankets.

The only disadvantage of a rabbitskin robe is that it sheds hair from the day it is made until it wears out. I got tired of waking up with my nose and mouth full of rabbit fur, so I sewed my robe between two strong cotton sheets, which ended the trouble and, I believe, made the robe warmer than ever.

The largest blanket that can be found is none too big for winter camping, for rolling in your blanket is the only way to be sure of keeping covered while you sleep, unless you use a sleeping bag. The blankets you lie on should be spread out flat and those in which you will roll are pulled up far enough to cover your head. Then with the top blankets spread out flat over you, lift your legs stiffly from the hips and fold one side of the blankets and then the other beneath your legs. Then no matter which way you turn in your sleep you will wind yourself tight in your covering. The sides of

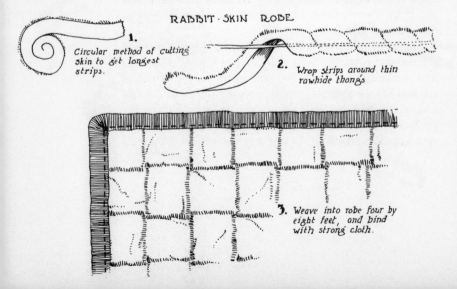

RABBIT·SKIN ROBE

1. Circular method of cutting skin to get longest strips.

2. Wrap strips around thin rawhide thongs

3. Weave into robe four by eight feet, and bind with strong cloth.

the blankets beneath you can then be folded over and fastened on top with big horse-blanket pins if you need extra warmth. Sleeping bags are also fine for camping in cold weather, but I started rolling in blankets and skin robes when I first came into this country and I will always be partial to them.

The first thought on making a winter camp is firewood and plenty of it, for if a storm comes in the night and you have to go out and hunt fuel you may have a bad time of it. The wise thing is to get in enough to last you until daylight, come what may. And it is a good idea to put some dry birch bark and small dead limbs under cover close at hand to start the fire quickly.

Your axe is your most valuable tool in the woods. In cold weather you have to be careful of it, for in temperatures far below zero metal gets so brittle it may chip. Once in a while you find an axe with such a high temper that it is as brittle as a stick of candy. The only cure for that is to heat the head to a dull red and then plunge it into a can of oil. I've seen the Chief use bear grease, but any heavy oil will serve. It should be done with care and outdoors in case the oil catches fire. That treatment softens the metal and prevents chipping in low temperatures. Another thing to remember is to keep your rifle away from heat in cold weather. It is best to leave it outside your camp while on the trail. When cold metal is suddenly warmed it sweats and the moisture freezes when you take it out in the cold again.

Rolling in a blanket
is really a cinch, once
you get the hang of it.

The fire lighted up the dark forest

While I cut balsam boughs for our bed and as cover for a shelter, the Chief felled several dead trees, for a standing dead tree is drier and makes better firewood than timber that has been lying on the ground. By the time he got back with the first load I had built up a mattress of boughs two feet thick and spread a deerskin robe to keep the cold from striking through. On top of that I laid out the blankets and our rabbitskin robes.

We were both hungry, but on the trail we never start supper until the night's wood supply is stacked handy to the fire, which was already lighting up the dark forest and taking the sting out of the cold air. While the old man finished his chopping I built up a low wall of green birch logs back of the fire to reflect the heat toward our bed and filled the pails with snow to melt for tea water. Ice is better than snow if it is handy. Suddenly the Chief appeared out of the darkness with a shoulder load of logs and gave the word to start supper.

While we sat eating in the good warmth of the campfire we got to talking about food—the right kind of food for the life you are living. We can't understand why some people think that because you live in the woods you can eat anything and always be healthy. True it is that life in the open is all in a man's favor, but I have seen too many woodsmen with "misery in the innards" to know that you can't abuse your stomach without paying a price, be it in the woods or the city.

On the trail when you're working hard you can eat more fats and sweet things than you can when taking life easy. The fact is, you need those energy foods for hard work. Baked beans on the trail are nourishing and give a man staying power, but beans as a regular dish when you are not active will soon make a man wish he had never tried them.

When we are traveling the Chief and I always carry bacon, the mainstay of the woodsman's fare, flour for pan biscuits, bannock, or flapjacks, powdered soups if possible, sugar (brown is most nourishing), rice, which is fine with raisins in it, and maybe some prunes or apricots for variety. We also like dried apples when we can get them, for you need fruit to keep fit. Then with some fish or game in season a man can live well.

The finest meal we had at the Chief's trapping shack was broiled pike, which he had taken late in December and cached in the ice for use on his trips. That's an old and good way of storing fish and meat in the woods in winter. When he caught several dozen fish the Chief chopped a trough in the ice about nine inches deep, laid the fish in it side by side a few inches apart and poured water over them. In no time they were frozen in solid.

When we went down to chop out some fish for supper there were wolf tracks all about the little spruce tree the Chief had stuck in the snow to mark the place, and plenty of signs that they had been scratching, but they couldn't break into the old Indian's refrigerator. We left enough for several meals later on. If you plan to use all the fish at one time, they can be frozen in the original fishing hole, first filling it almost full with broken chunks of ice. The trough method is best when you want to leave part of your catch for later eating. Unless you set up a marker, or take a range on the spot, snow will soon hide your cache and you may never find it again.

The wind does strange things with snow on the open stretches of the lakes. Often it packs the snow almost as hard as sand on a beach, leaving long curving ridges to mark the places where the ice cracks and heaves as it expands when the temperature drops very low. When ice four to five feet thick begins to crack you know about it, for the noise is like many shotguns going off at the same time. Then sometimes you hear a grinding sound like a monster gritting its teeth. The Chief says the lake is just stretching in its sleep. Along the shores where the drifts are deep, the wind sometimes whirls the snow into the form of waves just as if the water breaking on a shore had suddenly frozen.

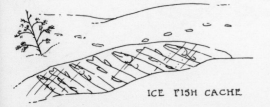

ICE FISH CACHE

Did you ever walk out on a February night in the north when the moon is bright? You can actually read by its light, and the outlines of hills miles away can be clearly seen. Up here there is what is called a dry cold, and even when the temperature drops below zero you can walk out in your shirt sleeves for a look around without even feeling it. That shouldn't fool you though, for you can freeze your nose or ears in a mighty short time and not even know it.

Sometimes you meet a traveler on a winter trail and have to tell him his nose is white. Woodsmen used to think that the best way to thaw a frozen nose or ear was to rub snow on it, but people who have studied frostbite now say that the best thing to do is to warm the frozen part. If it's your nose, warm your hand inside your shirt next to the skin and then cup it around your nose, but don't rub. Warm water is also good for getting the frost out.

I wish you could step out with me and look at the sky one of these February nights. The stars are sparkling blue-white. It makes you think of flashing jewels hanging in beautiful designs on a dark background. Looking to the south the Great Hunter, Orion, seems to be watching Taurus, the Bull, and to the southeast of Orion is Sirius, the big Dog Star. Canis Major, they call him, and he's the brightest of them all. I always like to look at the Big Dipper, part of Ursa Major, the Great Bear constellation, with its pointers lined on Polaris, the North Star, that age-old friend of men who know where to look for a true guide on the trails of the world.

NORTH STAR

I like the Indian idea better. They turned those three stars in the handle of the Big Dipper (that's part of the Big Bear) into hunters.

the way the Greeks t the Big Bear looked see a bear with a long tail?

A OR

The hush of the north woods in winter is often so heavy that you begin to think of it as something more than silence. At times it is like a strange kind of mist just beyond the power of eyes to see, yet so real you want to reach out to push it aside to let sounds come in. The quieter it is the harder you strain your ears without knowing why you're listening. But when the hush is suddenly broken by a sound—the bark of a dog fox far away in the hills, the ring of an axe on frost-hardened birch, or maybe the scream of a lynx—you realize that in the still, clear air the range of your hearing has increased tenfold. The voices of men, the sharp whine of sled runners on dry snow, or the falling of a tree, which seem nearby, may be from five to ten miles away. Quiet enough it is many a night to hear a deer mouse snore.

Sometimes when it is so still you think there's no breeze, the air is actually moving. At such times I can stand in my cabin door and hear the thunder of Indian Chutes fifteen miles away. And I often hear the Chief chopping kindling at his place over on Shining Tree Lake two miles away, and once in a while I hear Hank singing to himself. You have to be careful what you say about your neighbors in the northern winter. What is more, in the clear cold air you can see over greater distances than almost anywhere else. A hill that looks to be three miles away may be twenty miles distant.

On my way back from the Chief's not long ago I saw a great horned owl sweep down through the pines and disappear across the lake. It is the largest and most powerful of its kind and a savage killer. The snowy owl, which often shows up here in the winter, looks larger than the horned owl because it has a much thicker covering of feathers. As a matter of fact it is smaller and weighs less.

A Snowy Owl looks to be as big as a Horned Owl, but he isn't. It's just feathers. And ever see either owl without his feathers? You wouldn't believe it could possibly be the same bird!

These night hunters have to work hard for their food this time of the year, for the field mice, their favorite fare, are safe in their tunnels deep under the snow. They eat almost any small animal, such as rabbits and the like, not to mention grouse and other birds if they can get them. The horned owl even eats skunks, but I never heard of the snowy fellows going that far. When the lemmings, which look something like a mole, are scarce in the Arctic, the snowy owls head south in search of better hunting grounds. Sometimes they even go into big cities where there are usually plenty of rats and mice. I often wonder what a snowy owl would think about the way human beings jam themselves into one place where, if somebody didn't bring in their food everyday, they would not know what to do to keep from starving. I have seen many of the big white birds, so I suspect this is one of those years when, for some reason nobody understands, the lemmings are scarce. The same thing happens with rabbits every so often, and then the wolves, foxes, and other meat-eating animals, as well as the owls, go far afield in search of new food supplies.

The great horned owl nests late in February and often the mother sits on her nest, which is usually the old home of a hawk or a crow, through zero temperatures and driving snow. The young are covered with a cream-colored fuzz when they hatch and need to be kept warm so they spend most of their time under their mother's wings. Owls gulp their food whole and later on after it has digested they spit out fur and bones in neatly rolled pellets. You can often spot a horned owl's nest by finding those little pellets under a large tree in a lonely part of the woods.

You may think I'm jumping the gun a mite, but, be that as it may, after the middle of February my mind just naturally turns to thoughts of fishing. You are right, spring is a long way off, but I can't help it and so I either tie myself some flies, take apart my reels and oil them, or read fishing stories.

This year I made a rod and you'd be surprised to know what it was before I started. Well, this is the way it all began. Last summer a couple of young fellows came up for a vacation and brought along some fencing foils to have a little fun, both being pretty good at the sport. They were old foils and when my friends left they gave them to me, thinking Hank and I might try it this winter. I didn't say anything, but I knew that the only kind of fencing Hank and I will ever do is with an axe around our garden to keep the deer away from the beans. Until recently those foils have been standing in the corner, then just for fun I picked one up and began whipping that fine steel blade around. Suddenly an idea came to me. There right in my hand was the makings of a fine bait rod!

From that time on I couldn't rest until I had the thing worked out. First I filed off the end of the handle where it was riveted outside the pommel, the little knob on the end, and then slipped off the hollow grip and the guard. I found that the handle end of the blade was slightly curved, so I hammered it straight very carefully and then filed it round to fit the handle socket of my regular bait rod. By that time I was getting mighty excited, for I could see the idea was promising.

The blade of a foil as it comes is too stiff for fishing purposes, so I decided to take off some of the metal by filing. To make sure of doing a good job I nailed a board edge-up on my bench and cut a groove in it to fit the foil blade snugly. With a pocketknife to score the outline and a narrow chisel to dig out the wood, that was simple. I then laid the blade in the groove and with a fine-toothed file began to thin it down. You have to be careful to file evenly with long, diagonal strokes to keep the proper taper, taking off more at the butt end than near the tip. The idea is to file each side until the blade has just the right whip. That is where you need patience, for you can't hurry it. I worked for several evenings until it seemed just right. Then I cut

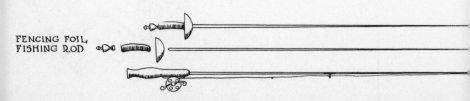

FENCING FOIL, FISHING ROD

the little button off the tip of the blade, fitted an agate tip in its place and wound on a guide about halfway between the tip and the handle.

The night I finished the job it was snowing hard, but early the next morning it was clear and if anybody had seen me out there on snowshoes doing a little plug casting with what was once a fencing foil they would have good reason to think I was out of my mind. But it worked! Yes sir, I could send that plug fifty feet as nice as you please and just where I wanted to drop it, too. When I started making the rod I figured it would be good only for trolling, but a few casts convinced me it would also be fine for bait casting. As a matter of fact, I tried it on light plugs and then reeled in a five-pound stick of wood as a test and it handled nicely.

Speaking of making things reminds me to tell you that Hank has been carving animal tracks lately. He just takes blocks of white pine, draws the outline of the track which he copies from the casts he has made from real tracks, and then carves away. It's surprisingly easy and they certainly make interesting decorations on the wall. All you need is inexpensive carving chisels which you can buy all made up in sets. Bird tracks are just right to practice on. If you have a dog rub a little soot on his paw, press it down on a block and then start hollowing out the impression of his track.

When Hank was over here a while ago he made me a split log shelf for some of my souvenirs. Nothing new about the idea, but somehow it always pleases me to see how such a shelf fits into the rough log wall. Simple as can be, yet strong and useful. Looks especially fine if you oil the wood.

I wouldn't have you think I am given to bragging, but all in all my cabin is snug and has a fit-to-live-in look. By the table where I read in the evening I have a big barrel chair, softened with turkey-red cushions made by my sister, and it is cut to fit me and tilted for comfort. The only trouble with these chairs, as you usually see them, is that they stand too straight and tire your back after a while. I remedied that fault by screwing two tapered birch strips to the bottom. This gives the chair a comfortable tilt and at the same time prevents it from going over backwards. Very pleasant it is to sit there on a winter's night when the wind is fingering at the cabin windows and listen to the kettle singing to itself over the slow fire. Once in a while it seems to doze and then wakes up and starts again on a high key that brings the dogs' heads off the floor to see if there is a mouse about.

Wherever men boil water the song of the kettle is a song of peace and contentment and home. It always takes me back to the warm kitchen in an old farmhouse where after supper my grandmother would sit by the table and read to me from *Swiss Family Robinson*. The singing of the kettle was always part of it and once in a while when she stopped for a moment you would hear a beetle working under the bark in a stick of stovewood in the box close by. And after a while I would hear her saying, "My land! I do believe you've been asleep all the time I read to you." Then I'd go upstairs and make haste to get into the billowing folds of a deep feather bed.

MARCH

Strong Winds in the Sugar Bush

Down in the swamps where the black spruce and cedar have sheltered the moose and deer through the long winter, the damp snow is crisscrossed with tracks, for the animals are moving out of their yards by day, returning to the safety of thick cover when darkness comes. Twigs and bark and cedar tips no longer satisfy their gnawing hunger for green food, particularly the tender water plants they will find in the lakes later on. Lean and restless, they range toward the hills, eagerly reaching for the reddening maple buds and pawing the snow in search of new shoots. The bucks are shedding their horns now and soon they will roam the woods alone, leaving the does to family cares.

It is not spring yet, not by three feet of snow and a lake full of ice. And high winds as cold and damp as a dog's nose and just as searching, whine through the woods. Yet there is something in the air that stirs the blood and you can't help lifting your eyes to the sky to look and listen for the first geese, although you well know they will not arrive until the lakes show open water. The moose-birds are livelier now and doing a lot of talking among themselves, and the first of the tree sparrows have shown up.

Another sign of the slowly changing season is the chatter of red squirrels in the maple tops. They are getting ready to build nests for their families and are making an awful fuss about it. I can't say that I like the little critters, for they rob birds' nests and often kill the young. But they are spunky rascals and you can't help admiring them in a way.

Slowly, very slowly, nature is waking up from the long winter sleep. Even now the sap is rising in the trees to nourish the buds and I have already seen bear tracks at the south end of the lake. The young coons will be arriving soon and the first thing you know I will be out listening for the best and finest of all spring sounds, the song of the peepers in the bogs. To be sure, we are still melting ice for our water, but it won't be long until my spring is open and I can again take that pleasant walk in the morning to get a pail of clear, cold water.

The minute I spotted squirrels in the sugar maples I knew the sap had started, so I told Hank and the Chief that we should get going. They hiked over the next day and we started tapping the trees and putting in the little wooden pipes—spiles, we call them—to guide the sap into our pails. The Indians used alder because the pithy center can be pushed out easily and it makes very good spiles. They gathered the sap in bark utensils and before they could get metal pots the syrup was made in bark or wooden containers by dropping hot stones into the sap until all the water evaporated. The Chief says they sometimes let the sap freeze and in that way the water separated from the pure syrup. That's why the little golden drops on the end of an icicle of maple sap are so sweet and the squirrels know it well.

We collect the sap in cooking pots, pails, and even tomato cans. When the sap is running freely you get from two to three gallons a day from a good tree. But it takes anywhere from four to six gallons of sap to make a pound of sugar and thirty or more to produce a gallon of syrup.

Sap runs best on a warm, sunny day after a frosty night with a chilling northwest wind. Sugar maples are very sensitive to weather changes and the flow of sap slows down

Indian

White Man
—some folks use lids to keep out snow and dirt, but they're not necessary.

Here are a few kinds of metal spiles that are used in the woods.

with strong winds and changes in temperature, such as an extra warm day or a freezing night. Sap starts flowing earlier on the south and east sides of a tree than on the north and west. Some old-timers say to tap a tree on the north side to get the longest run. The best syrup is made from sap gathered soon after it begins running. Late sap has a peculiar woody taste, but otherwise it is good sweetening.

Sugar maples are not the only trees that give sap, for you can get a good sugar or syrup from other trees. Not all of them yield as much sap as the maples, and some of them, especially the shagbark hickory, are hard to get started, but if you can get a hickory to give up its sap you have got the makings of very fine syrup.

The sap of the black walnut tree, the silver maple, red maple, black birch and the sycamore makes syrup. It is interesting to try it, but unless you strike it right usually you don't get enough to make it worth-while.

Soon after we started getting sap the three of us had a sugaring-off party. We took some of the boiling syrup and dropped little pools of it on the snow. In no time it was maple candy, sticky to be sure, but mighty toothsome. Hank made us some doughnuts to go with the sugar and we had a fine time. I might say, too, that Hank's doughnuts are about the best I ever ate, for they are dry and mealy without a trace of grease. He says the secret is to keep the fat at just the right temperature. Hank also brought along a jar of pickles his sister sent him, for after eating a lot of sugar you crave something sour.

We make most of our sap into sugar, which keeps better than syrup, and rare good eating it is, especially if you drop a chunk into hot boiled rice. We make a few gallons of syrup apiece and store it in jars in a cool, dark place. Heat molds it.

Working out among the maples we saw many of the birds that stay around here most of the winter. This is a good time

The essentials for a real Sugaring-Off......

....Doughnuts,

...Pickles, Snow, ... and, of course, Maple Sugar!

to study them, for being a little short of food they come close to your house if you put out something for them to eat. Just now they are not as shy as they will be later on when they begin nesting. With only a few birds about, you quickly learn to recognize them. To my way of thinking, it is more satisfactory to learn everything you can about a few than to know very little about many.

Now is the right time to build birdhouses, and Hank and I have already started ours. It's a fine way of keeping these friends close by and we take particular pains to make the kind that please the birds we like to have nesting in our woods. I am always sure to have a family of house wrens and usually bluebirds. Birds are choosey and know just what they want in the way of a home, so you must build your boxes the right shape and size before they show any interest in starting housekeeping. Having birds for neighbors is more than a pleasure, for they help to keep down insect pests that ruin your garden.

Before March is over I get out my tackle to inspect the rods and oil the reels against the day when I can use them. It's a good idea to check the wrappings on the guides and make sure all joints are in good condition. I lent my fly-tying vise to a friend last fall thinking I wouldn't want to use it for a while, but I could not resist the temptation to tie a few flies. First I tried my big bench vise, but that was too clumsy for small trout hooks, so I did a little thinking and came up with a fly vise made of a long three-eighths inch bolt and a wing nut that works surprisingly well.

I first slotted the bolt with a hacksaw to a depth of about an inch and a half and then, after screwing on the nut with the wings down, I pried open the jaw slot slightly, inserted a small nail about half an inch from the end and then pressed the jaws together again in the bench vise. This leaves a slight bulge in the bolt and when the wing nut is turned up the

WREN HOUSE

Removable top ——>

Hook ——

Nail to hook over——>

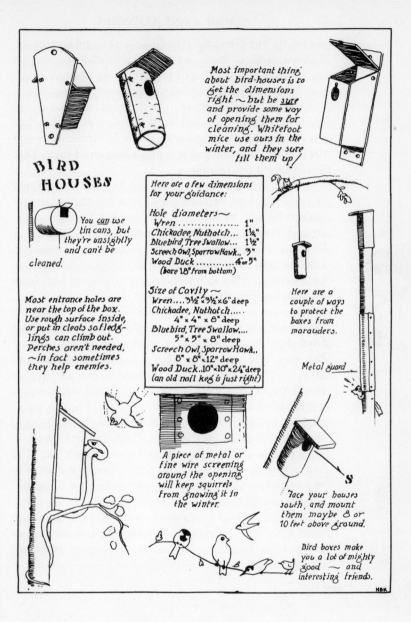

Most important thing about bird-houses is to get the dimensions right ~ but be *sure* and provide some way of opening them for cleaning. Whitefoot mice use ours in the winter, and they sure fill them up!

BIRD HOUSES

You *can* use tin cans, but they're unsightly and can't be cleaned.

Most entrance holes are near the top of the box. Use rough surface inside, or put in cleats so fledglings can climb out. Perches aren't needed, ~ in fact sometimes they help enemies.

Here are a few dimensions for your guidance:

Hole diameters ~
Wren . . . . 1"
Chickadee, Nuthatch . . . 1¼"
Bluebird, Tree Swallow . . . 1½"
Screech Owl, Sparrow Hawk . . 3"
Wood Duck . . . . 4 or 5"
(bore 18" from bottom)

Size of Cavity ~
Wren . . . . 3½" x 3½" x 6" deep
Chickadee, Nuthatch . . . . .
    4" x 4" x 8" deep
Bluebird, Tree Swallow . . . .
    5" x 5" x 8" deep
Screech Owl, Sparrow Hawk . .
    8" x 8" x 12" deep
Wood Duck . . 10" x 10" x 24" deep
(an old nail keg is just right)

Here are a couple of ways to protect the boxes from marauders.

Metal guard

A piece of metal or fine wire screening around the opening will keep squirrels from gnawing it in the winter.

Face your houses south, and mount them maybe 8 or 10 feet above ground.

Bird boxes make you a lot of mighty good ~ and interesting friends.

HBK

jaws of the vise clamp tightly. To finish the job I tapered the jaws with a file to leave plenty of clearance for working on the smallest hooks. I don't know anything so small in the making that makes a man feel so big as tying a trout fly.

The bolt I used happened to be threaded from end to end so I fastened it to my bench with two nuts. If a fellow had a bolt threaded at one end only, he could file the other end flat on four sides and wedge it into a hole on a bench. That would keep it from swinging.

A bobbin for your spool of silk can be made from a scrap of fairly stiff wire, bending the sides so that they fit snugly against the sides of the spool. By pressing the ends of the crossed wires beneath the spool it turns freely. Whether it be an axe or a pair of hackle pliers, I favor the best equipment I can buy, but I also enjoy those little emergencies when you have to make a tool that will serve your purpose well from the odds and ends that come to hand.

The snow is wet and heavy and you no longer hear the sharp crunch that snowshoes make and the whine that comes from sled runners on the dry, cold snow of January and February. The ice on the lakes is already getting old and gray, which is a sign to keep on shore. When we have no choice but to cross weak ice in the spring we cut ourselves a green birch sapling about ten feet long and hold it across the body in front of us. The idea is that if you break through, the pole will catch on the edge of the hole and give you something to hang on to and help you to climb out. The best way of saving yourself, if you go through the ice, is to move slowly and flatten out as much as possible to distribute your weight.

During the winter the lakes are our highways, but at this time of the year no man who thinks much of his dogs or horses takes them on the old ice. In logging operations

FLY-TYING
BOBBIN

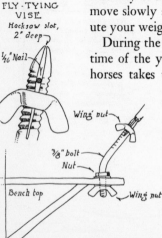

FLY-TYING
VISE.
Hacksaw slot,
2" deep
1/16" Nail
Wing nut
3/8" bolt
Nut
Bench top
Wing nut

years ago I saw many fine horses go through in the spring and the way the teamsters fought to get them out showed how much they loved the animals. Neither man nor beast can last long in ice-cold water so the job had to be done in a hurry if it was to be done at all and nobody shirked. They would slash the harness with an axe and use ropes and chains, risking their lives trying to pull the animals out.

Every once in a while we like to go ice fishing, and although it is pretty late the Chief was over not long ago and we went out on the heavy ice in the cove north of the cabin where a little brook comes in, and cut two holes through thirty inches of ice. All we had was a couple of short saplings with six feet of line and bass hooks baited with small chunks of fat pork. We got a dozen speckled trout, which you seldom get in winter fishing anywhere else but in the north, and a four-pound lake trout, as well as several pickerel.

Part of the fun is finding a sheltered place in the woods on the shore and cooking the fish right then and there. They never taste so sweet and in the winter the flesh is very firm and white. Over on Shining Tree Lake the Chief has a little fish house on runners that he skids out on the ice where he can fish sheltered from the biting wind.

During a spell of weather Hank and the Chief came over, as they often do, to work with me for company's sake on small indoor jobs that go so well with easy talking. Hank made himself a new moosehide sheath for his hunting knife, fastening the side with copper rivets, which don't take the edge off the blade. I worked on a bread knife made of an old hacksaw blade of the heavy duty type used in machine shops. It is about an inch wide and thick enough not to bend when you slice. But the smaller blade used in a hand frame will also work very well.

The handle is made of two sections of maple or birch the insides of which are slotted just enough for a tight fit when the blade is laid between them in plenty of waterproof glue. I then riveted the end of the handle, using the hole provided

SHEATH

Belt
loop

Snap   'A'

The entire sheath is cut from one piece of leather. Fold the belt loop over the back and rivet at "A." Fold sheath over front and then rivet along edge. Be sure and make a very careful paper pattern first.

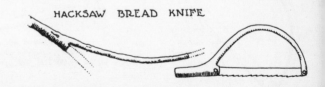

HACKSAW BREAD KNIFE

in the saw and then fastened the inside end of the handle with two small brass screws, one on each side of the blade. A brass ferule or a lashing of copper or brass wire over the screws is a good idea for extra strength. I put an edge on my blade with a coarse stone, making sure to have it sharp without cutting down on the size of the teeth. That knife slices hot bread as nicely as you please without tearing it.

While I'm on the subject of saws, an old friend of mine carries a thin bucksaw blade coiled in a round tin box with a couple of bolts and wing nuts to go with it. When he wants a bucksaw all he has to do is to pull out the blade and cut a limber sapling. After slotting the ends and making holes for the bolts he bends the sapling bow to the blade and is ready to go to work.

All this time the Chief was busy repairing a runner on my sled. I always admire the way he makes use of what comes to hand when he needs a special tool. That time he wanted to make a hole of exactly the right size for the thong that lashes the runner to the body legs. He got just what he wanted by filing sharp grooves in the four flat sides of the point on a six-inch finishing nail. I don't know any finer sight than to watch a man with skill in his hands shaping wood to his needs.

One night while the Chief and Hank were with me I began rummaging through the old chest under my bunk where I keep all my treasured things. Near the bottom I found a little varnished birch log about six inches long and two thick. It is split in half, hinged, and the center hollowed out to hold a set of jackstraws carved from birch. Nicest work of its kind I ever saw. An old woodsman made them for my mother away back before I was born. There are forty pieces in the set including an axe, hammer, guitar, ladder, plow, sawhorse, a peavey like lumberjacks use on the rivers, and two balls in a cage. Not one of them is over five inches long and the handles are no bigger than a toothpick, yet every detail is per-

PORTABLE
BUCK-SAW

~in
the
tin box

— and in
the sapling
frame.

Here's one of our
nail drills, with the point
shown on the left, enlarged.

fect, even to the teeth in the bucksaw blade. Scratched on
the bark of the log box in a dim scrawl is the inscription:
Bûchette de Noël—1880, which means "Christmas Log."

Every once in a while in the woods, especially toward
spring, a man starts craving various kinds of foods that he
knows there is not a chance in the world of getting. Mostly
it is for something sweet, because working in the woods you
burn up energy rapidly, which brings on a natural craving
for sugar. In the city you are just as likely as not to be hankering for venison steak, broiled trout fresh from the water,
or maybe a bowl of fresh-picked raspberries.

The Chief, Hank, and I have a "hankering meal" every so
often, and you would be surprised what a lot of fun you can
have in just talking about what you would eat if you could
get your wish. One night Hank happened to mention that
he would give almost anything for a good plate of fried oys-
ters with tartar sauce. That started us going! The Chief,
who always enters into it with a twinkle in his eyes, said he
would give a lot for a slab of roast beef which he always
orders in the little eating place out at the settlement. By that
time I was drooling with the thought of a big plate of vanilla
ice cream with hot butterscotch sauce poured over it. That
sort of talk always whets our appetites, and we ended up
with a fine supper of some of the trout we caught through
the ice, hot biscuits, and Indian pudding made from a recipe
I worked out myself. This is how I make it:

I take four cups of evaporated milk, which I heat to the
scalding point and then stir in a half cup of corn meal, white
or yellow, mixed with two tablespoons of flour; two-thirds
cup dark molasses; a half cup of venison suet cut very fine;
a half teaspoonful of ginger and the same amount of cinnamon, and a teaspoonful of salt. This mixture I cook on the
stove a half hour or so until it gets thick, and then I turn it
into a baking pan for the oven. I pour over the top of the
pudding a cup of cold milk, just letting it stay on the top and
not stirring in. This I set in the oven and let it cook from
two to three hours. Served hot with chunks of maple sugar it

is a grand dish. If you have some cream to pour over it, all the better.

The morning after we finished sugaring we were sitting by the stove smoking and drinking a second cup of coffee when Wolf began scratching a flea behind his ear. The steady thumping of his leg on the floor caught Hank's ear and he remarked that it sounded like a drum. That is the way Hank gets ideas and I knew then what he had in mind. Sure enough, before long he rubbed a little bacon fat on the bucksaw blade and went down by the lake to look over a big hollow cedar that fell in the big wind last fall. When he came back he had a nice piece of cedar about twenty inches long and ten wide. As the Chief knows a lot about such things, Hank asked him how the Indians made their drums and the old man was glad to help. He took my long chisel and mallet and showed Hank just how to chip down and smooth the inside of the hollow log. When he finished the wall was not more than an even three-quarters of an inch thick all around. The thinner the wall, the better the boom. Almost any hollow dry log will make a drum. Cedar or basswood are just right, and remembering the old hollow trees in my grandfather's orchard, I asked the Chief how about a piece of apple wood? He said it ought to be fine.

Hank cut off the ends of his drum log nice and square so it would sit up straight and also make it easier to stretch the heads on evenly. After that he rounded and smoothed the outside edge on both ends of the log with a file and sandpaper so the heads would not chafe through. Chief Tibeash gave Hank pieces of untanned deer hide, that is rawhide, for the drum heads. They are put on wet, for as the skin dries and shrinks it gets tighter than a greenhorn's nerves when he meets a bear.

THE DRUM

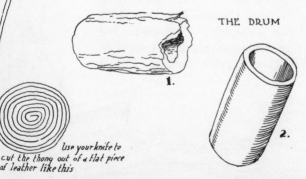

Use your knife to cut the thong out of a flat piece of leather like this

1.

2.

3.

...... and here's the Drum

The Chief said a man he took fishing last year told him
his boy had used an old piece of automobile tube for a head
and had made a pretty good drum by stretching it over the
ends of a water pail with the bottom cut out. All you need
to beat a drum is a stick with a ball-shaped wad of cotton
cloth wound tightly around the end. Then tie on a final
covering of soft leather cut from an old glove. Drums are old
and wonderful instruments.

When the drum was dry the Chief tried it out. At first he
was just thumping easy like, but in a minute a faraway look
came into his gray eyes. Somehow you felt he was looking
back out of time. His lips tightened, and the beat of the drum
grew louder and louder until the cabin was filled with the
throbbing rhythm of an Indian war dance. It was a strange,
wild sound and we couldn't take our eyes off his wrinkled
brown hands which seemed hardly to move. Suddenly he
stopped, the faraway look faded away and then he was the
old Chief Tibeash we had always known. I asked him who
taught him to beat a drum like that and he just shook his
head.

"No man taught me," he answered. "It is the way my people made their drums talk many, many years before I was
born. It has been sleeping up here." He touched his head and
I understood what he meant. Just born in him, it was.

Hank wanted to paint some Indian designs on the side of
his drum so the next morning the Chief and I snowshoed over
to Hank's cabin where he had some special kind of color he
was set on using.

As we traveled up over the long rise that lies just west of
Beaver Tail Lake, we picked up the trail of a snowshoe rabbit going in our general direction. At first the tracks went
along in a straight line, but suddenly we saw that it had
made a wild jump to one side and then started running in
long leaps, zigzagging as it went. It's easy for a woodsman
to read that story. And sure enough the tracks ended at a
spot where the snow had been tossed about for several feet.
At one place we made out the dim outline of large wing tips,

and found a little tuft of white fur. An owl, probably a big snowy owl, or perhaps one of those Labrador horned marauders, had been hunting. Savage birds those fellows are, and some of them have a wingspread of five feet and more. I have even seen them swoop down at Wolf, but they know better than to get too close to his sharp white fangs. Well, that's the way nature is, and I guess it is all part of a plan of life.

Because this is the time of year when your footgear gets soaked in the damp snow, the best thing to do with wet moccasins when you come in is to take a flat chip or the back of your knife and scrape out all the moisture you can, then stuff them with bent birch twigs to hold them open for drying. Keep them back from the stove so they won't get hard. Slow drying is best for leather of any kind. I have seen many moccasins and snowshoes ruined by drying them too close to the fire.

The Chief tells me he has seen quite a few moose tracks sharp and clear in the snow along the lake shore near his cabin. Moose are queer critters. They seem to enjoy a touch of civilization and like as not you will find more moose a few miles out of a settlement up in this country than you will in the deep woods miles from anywhere. That reminds me of the days when I was prospecting and used to go to a mining town every once in a while for supplies. There was a fellow who lived a few miles out of the camp who found a bull moose calf which he fed and tamed and later broke to harness. He used to drive into town with that moose hauling him in a buggy and it just about stopped everything when he arrived. That was all right at first, but after about two years the attention went to the fellow's head. He got to be quite a show-off, making it a practice to drive in on Saturday nights and to hitch the moose to the rail of the board sidewalk. Then he would just sit around smoking a big cigar and enjoy the stares of the miners, for there is always a crowd in a mining camp on Saturday night.

It is all part of a plan of life

After a while some of the boys got sick of this showing off and one fall day they hatched themselves a plot. One of them was a moose hunter and on a Saturday night he went back in the woods not far off the road where this fellow drove by with the moose. It just happened that when our friend was driving home a cow moose began calling from the woods near the road. It was a quiet evening and the air was sharp, so the sound carried clean and clear.

What happened after that we heard from the man who had owned the moose. It seemed that he was going along right smart and everything was fine until that moosecall came. Then something happened—he wasn't sure just what —but all of a sudden he found himself lying under a spruce by the roadside and his moose was going into the bush, buggy and all, at a terrible rate. He never saw that moose again, although he did trace down what was left of the buggy, piece by piece, but for a year or more after that hunters said that they saw a moose with some tattered harness on it roaming the woods.

It is about time I got busy on my small canoe, the one I generally cache on Shining Tree Lake. Nothing much wrong, but it needs some touching up. There's a gouge on the bottom where I struck a rock coming down the rapids last fall. I sent away for a can of that good waterproof glue they use in boat yards and I'll set a thin piece of wood in the cut to bring it flush. Sometimes I use the soft wood that you buy in cans, for when it hardens it takes a good finish. It is best for a deep cut, where you can tamp it tight. I finish it off with paint or varnish when it's bone dry.

When the Indians build birch bark canoes they make the seams tight with a pitch made of one part grease and ten parts spruce gum. Bacon fat will do for the grease and pure spruce gum warmed in hot water can be used to patch a small hole in a pinch. But it's not a bad idea to carry a small can of white lead in your pack for just such emergencies.

If the canvas on a canoe tears and you don't get at it right away the water works in under it and starts trouble, so when

HBK

A moose with tattered harness

you make repairs be sure the canvas around the tear is glued securely to the wood. Once in a while a cut is so bad you have to make a patch of canvas or other cloth to cover the hole after it has been filled in with white lead or gum. Patches of that kind may be rough and ought to be replaced when there is a chance to do a good job.

Taking good care of a canoe has a lot to do with its life. You never see a good woodsman drive a canoe ashore bow on, which puts a sudden strain on the keel, especially if you are carrying a heavy load. Of course when the water is rough there are times when you have no choice about landing, but the right way is to come in broadside to the shore. A canoe should be turned on its side on shore and laid in a shady place where it won't get too much sun.

I have owned several birch bark canoes and they are fine craft, but they spring a leak when you least expect it and are easily damaged. The seams and rough edges make for a lot of friction, and bark canoes are not as easy to handle in a wind as other types.

I have often watched Indians making their birch bark canoes. They soak the birch bark in water for a day to get it soft so it will bend without splitting, and then sew it together with watap threads made from the roots of cedar and spruce gathered in the spring. They soak the ash ribs, too, and form them to the shape they want by holding them down with rocks. Not many are made these days.

With the lake at my door, taking a bath in the woods in summer is a simple and pleasant event, but in winter when you usually have to climb into a washtub, it can be a major operation. But I have a simpler method and I recommend it above all others for cleanliness and refreshment.

Years ago a Finnish miner who told me about using fireflies for light in mines, showed me how the people in his country take steam baths the year round. So when I came to Cache Lake I built a little log shack about four feet square and seven feet high with the sides chinked tight and a small ventilating hole on one side close to the roof. The bathhouse is set over a shallow pit and the floor is a light movable grating made by nailing saplings a few inches apart on two cleats. An old piece of canvas serves as a door.

When you want a steam bath you build a big fire close to the shack and throw in good-sized stones to heat until they are just about red hot. The rocks are then shoveled into the bathhouse pit and the floor grating dropped into place. For a bath you take a pail of water into the shack and pour it, a dipperful at a time, on the hot rocks and in a few seconds you are bathed in clouds of hot vapor.

After about fifteen minutes of that treatment you could wrestle with a bear and win. We take steam baths all winter no matter what the temperature without any bad effects. When I step out of the bath shack I take a quick rub down with snow and then make a run for the cabin. I had always believed that going into cold air after a hot bath was dangerous, but my Finnish friend convinced me there was nothing to that theory as long as you rub down with cold water or snow right after the steaming.

Steam baths are nothing new in the north country, for the Indian medicine men used the same method for treating sickness. The Chief says they built small birch bark lodges for steam treatments and the old medicine men made a great mystery of the magic healing power of the white vapor. The idea of taking a steam bath just for the sake of cleanliness was new to the Chief, but when I built my shack he gave up his washtub and took to steam with great enjoyment.

The moon is almost full. One night when I went out to sniff the weather I saw something that pleased me. Near the place where I buried the bones of the smoked fish we had for dinner I saw a skunk ambling along. I suppose people might wonder what thrill there is in seeing a skunk. Well, it's because they are a sign that spring is on the way. It is not here, mind you, but coming, maybe next month, maybe later, according to the way winter gives up. When the skunks wake up from their long sleep it is a good sign. The Indians sometimes call it Skoo-kum Pesim, the Skunk Month, and no disrespect intended. I'm fond of the little critters, for you can depend on a skunk to mind his own business as long as you mind yours, which is fair enough.

That moonlight night, clear and quiet, reminded me of other spring nights when I was a young fellow and came up here in the summer to work as a surveyor on a new railroad they were running through the northern forest. That was when I learned about Side Hill Grazers. You have probably heard of them; maybe you have even hunted them. I did when I first came up here and I had the fun of taking many others on hunts. Of course these strange and rare beasts, which have legs longer on one side than on the other so that they can walk along the side of a hill and browse in an upright position, can be hunted only at night.

Whenever a fellow new to the north arrived one of the first things we did was to take him on a grazer hunt. The slopes of the deep cuts where the railroad went through the hills were perfect grazer country. Before we started on a hunt we would always tell the new man that these beasts were very ferocious and that the only way to capture them was to grab the legs on the long, or downhill side, and give them a quick twist to throw them off balance. Once you did that they were helpless.

We always sent scouts ahead and then we would post our victim high on the side of a gravel slope and leave him in the darkness thinking of the tales he had heard about these terrible animals. Then when we were sure he had waited long enough to be scared plumb to death, someone would jump down the bank or start rocks rolling down. About that time one of the boys would let out an unearthly howl and another one would sneak up on our hunter and grab him. He always thought the end had come when that happened. Then everybody went back to camp feeling that the fun had been worth all the climbing.

It was a different kind of hunt that I went on with the

Chief many years ago. He was after a bear and besides the Chief and myself there were two young Crees who had a great respect for the Chief. We walked for miles following the trail of a bear until the Chief signaled that we were getting close. There we stopped and the Chief made a speech to the bear, explaining that he would not take his life if he did not need his fur for warmth and the grease for his people. He said he was very sorry that the bear's fur was valuable, that it would have been much better if the bear had been a porcupine, in which case he would not have been hunting him. Then he motioned us to stay where we were and he went ahead. A few minutes later we heard the crack of his .38-55 Winchester up on a ridge, and when no second shot came we were sure the Chief was successful.

After he had dressed the bear, he cut off the top of a young spruce, trimmed off the side limbs, and carefully set the animal's head on top of the bare pole. He was talking in Cree when he did it, but I could make out that he was telling the bear's ancestors what a fine critter this fellow was and that it was an honor to have him join them.

That is how the Chief feels about the wild things and hunting them, for the best Indians never kill except when they need food or fur. I have seen the Chief pass many a deer and moose without a thought of shooting them because he didn't need meat at the time. If everybody had the same idea about hunting we wouldn't need any fish and game laws.

When the Chief kills a moose he ties the antlers to a tree, generally at the mouth of a creek, just to make sure that the spirit of the animal is not offended. Where the narrows opens up into Snow Goose Lake you can see moose antlers hanging in a dead tamarack facing to the south.

I woke up one night and heard a sound that made me glad to lie and listen. At first it was the flinty picking of sleet on the window near the foot of my bunk, but in a little time it softened to a steady wet whispering. I knew then that the first thawing rain of March had come, for the wind was from the south, and by daylight the snow, pocked with little holes where the water dripped from the eaves, had settled some four inches.

I have seen a lot of rain in my day and there is more to it than just water falling from the sky, for by reading about the weather and keeping watch I found there are many kinds of rain. There is the fine, misty rain of spring and fall, the heavy thundershowers of July, and the steady rain that beats down for days at a time when a big storm is passing over. You can be pretty certain that rain made up of small drops is falling from low-lying clouds, but if it comes in large drops then it has probably come from high up, maybe four to nine miles. In that case the raindrops start out as snow or hard frozen pellets, growing as they fall through heavy clouds, and melting when they come into warmer air near the earth. I figure a sudden summer thunderstorm has the largest drops of any kind of storm in these parts.

I learned away back how to measure the size of raindrops by letting them fall for just a few seconds into a pie plate loosely filled to the top with flour. After you have caught your raindrops you put the pan aside until the drops soak up flour and finally harden. Then you lift them out very gently and what you have is a good cast of the drops just as they were when they struck. Surprising what a difference you can see by comparing the casts of raindrops from all kinds of storms. You can do the same thing with dry plaster of Paris.

Later in the spring I'll be hearing the quiet whispering of fine rain on the new leaves. Sometimes a light night breeze playing in the tree tops will make just about the same

Sugar Maple

Silver Maple

Red Maple

Black Birch

Sycamore

Black Walnut or Butternut (leaves almost the same.)

Shagbark Hickory

sound and fool me into thinking it is raining. I enjoy watching the summer shower dapple the lake into a million circles and enjoy listening to the rain slanting into the water with the sweeping sound of the broom on my cabin floor.

The man who has never walked in the woods and smelled rain and felt it on his face has missed something indescribable. But best of all I like the sound of rain playing on the roof at night about the time I am dropping off to sleep.

APRIL

Thundering Ice and Black Water

THE BREAK-UP has come and the ice is out of Cache Lake!
It started early one morning and when I woke up and heard
a muffled rumbling sound coming through the darkness
from the head of the lake I knew what it meant. There is
no mistaking the thunder of ice going out. Chief Tibeash
and Hank heard it, too, and when they came over we went
up to the carry to watch the sight that next to the geese
coming north means more to us than anything else that
happens in early spring.

Just above the rapids where Lost Chief Stream gets into
the Manitoupeepagee River, the ice jammed on the rocks
and the water flooded over the banks and rushed down
through the woods in a frothing torrent that kept us up on
the ridge. It was not long, though, before the jam broke and
great blocks of ice, some as big as a wagon bed, came thundering down the main stream. You wouldn't know there
were any rapids then, just tossing gray ice riding water
black and cold and powerful.

The ice on the rivers never freezes as thick as on the lakes,
where the water is quiet, so it is the first to go out. Sun and
warm south winds and the battering of the ice coming down
the streams are needed to start the heavy stuff out of the
lakes. By sundown that day the ice at the head of Cache
Lake was beginning to heave and break.

I never have quite understood it, but the news of the ice
going out of a river spreads like no other information in the

woods. Once I was at a settlement when an Indian came in and told us that that morning the ice had started out of the mouth of the river which was two hundred miles away. I asked him how he knew and he just shrugged and said, "I know!" I made a note of that date and found later that it had gone out on the very morning he had told us.

I knew it wouldn't be long after the ice went out until the geese would be coming over. And sure enough, I heard them! The night was still and clear, the stars were sparkling like splintered crystal, and the cool white moon was loafing high over Snow Goose Lake when it came—that wonderful sound all men of the woods wait for every year—the hoarse honking of the big gray Canada geese. In clear weather they often fly right through the night and just hearing them talking among themselves up there in the friendly darkness does me a world of good. You can be sure there was a wise old gander at the point of that great flight wedge leading them on to the lonely salt marshes that stretch along the low shores of James Bay.

Although the ice has gone out and signs of spring are multiplying, there is still plenty of snow back in the woods where the sun can't reach it. It is no longer the soft white coat of winter, for now it is gray and heavy. Under the conifers, where the partridges, grosbeaks, siskins, and cross-bills have been feeding, the drifts are sprinkled with the brown scales of cones and tiny chips of bark, twigs, and broken buds. But, unlike the dirty snow of city streets, mixed with soot and cinders and the sodden refuse of civilization, our snow is clean. If you dig down in the shadow close to the north side of a big tree you find the snow still dry and granular, which is one way the Indians know the direction of north in winter storms.

Down in the little marshy place by the spring the first green and purple hoods of the skunk cabbage are showing. After looking at snow since last November, they are beautiful to me. I walked along the shore of the lake and saw deer and moose tracks in the soft earth near the narrows. That's

HBK

That great flight wedge leading to the lonely salt marshes

where they swim across in their travels back and forth between the ridges in the summer.

The sight of fresh tracks started me thinking of the days when I first came up here and got a lot of fun making casts of the tracks of wild animals. It is the best way to study and learn to know their footprints. Spring is a good time to make casts, for the ground is wet and makes nice clear prints, especially if you can find them in clay. All you need is some plaster of Paris mixed about as thick as heavy cream. The right way to mix it is to put cold water in a tin can and then slowly sprinkle in the plaster until the water disappears and it looks like cream. Start by making a little fence of cardboard around a track, pushing it into the mud carefully. Then pour the plaster in very gently and leave it alone for half an hour or so. Don't try lifting it before it sets hard. Take it home and let it dry out. Then unwrap the cardboard, wash off the mud, and you'll have an exact pattern of the animal's track.

The next step is to make a cast from the pattern, for what you are really after is a track just as the animal left it in the earth. First you coat the pattern with soap softened in hot water. Now wrap another piece of cardboard around it, first soaping the inside wall, and then pour in the plaster. Be sure to let it dry for several hours. Finally unwrap the cardboard, separate the casts, and there is the finished footprint.

With a little practice you can make fine prints and start a collection. If you want to try something special you can lay out some soft mud or clay at night with some bait in the center. You ought to have tracks by morning. For practice you can begin with a cat or dog.

While you are out looking for tracks you will see many other things of interest. Soon I'll start looking for the marsh marigold with blossoms the color of country butter, and the first violets too. I seldom pick wild flowers for I would rather see them blooming just where they grow. There would be lots more mayflowers and lady's-slippers if people

Makes a
very in-
teresting
collection.

Find a good
clean track......

STING A TRACK

2. Put a cardboard
mold around it,.....

3. Pour in plaster and
let it set,.......

4. After cleaning and soaping, wrap
it in another mold and cast.

had not pulled them up by the roots until they are seen in only a few places now. Another pretty flower, although its perfume isn't so pleasant, is the wake-robin. Trillium is another name for it.

Bird's-foot Violet

Watch for the white flowers of the bloodroot that fold up at night, and the hepatica with its beautiful pale blue, pinkish or white blossoms. Learn to enjoy your flowers where they are. Picking wild flowers makes me think of kidnaping—taking them away from their natural homes and all the things they need from the earth. Generally the flowers that come in April are small, growing close to the earth as if to be ready to duck back in if it gets too cold. Later on when the weather is warm they grow taller.

When I was a boy I loved to wander along the brooks and streams where life is very active in the spring. Some of the fish are spawning and the turtles are sure to be out sunning themselves on logs and rocks on warm days. The snakes are also moving about. In truth, very few snakes are poisonous, and there are none of that kind up here. I never kill snakes for they help in keeping down the mice and other rodents that damage our garden and get in the house.

Trillium, or Wake Robin

There is plenty of life in the woods now, although you do not see much unless you know just where to look. The young skunks are in their burrows and the squirrels are busy tending to their new families. So are the mink, which make homes for their little fellows in hollow logs. There are not as many otter up here as there used to be, but there are still some. They keep their babies in well-hidden places under banks or roots. The lynx are also busy with family cares. Their kittens mew just like the household kind and are just as playful.

Hepatica

With the first stretch of warm days in April the eggs of some of the hardy insects begin to hatch and you soon hear them humming around in the quiet of the twilight hours. The beetles and the bark-borers begin to appear now, and little mounds of soil show that the hard-working ants are busy. If you watch you will notice quite a few moths and butterflies about, but they are mostly the small dull-colored kind. The beautiful large butterflies won't be seen until the weather is much warmer. I have already seen a queen yellowjacket flying around under the eaves of the cabin. She is looking for a place to start a nest, I expect. Later this month the bumblebee queen will be doing the same thing. You usually see her fly close to the ground watching for a likely spot for a nest, which may be in an old mouse nest or in a hole in the ground. I have already seen a ladybird beetle—the little red fellow with black spots on his back—walking across the sill of the window after his long winter sleep.

Back in the days when they cut big timber up here, the river crews had to wait for the lake ice to clear before the spring log drive could begin. Once it started no power on earth could stop that wild trip of the big logs down the streams into the rivers, across lakes, over falls, and through rocky gorges to the sawmills many miles away. Not so much of that now and much of it is pulp logs too light to keep up a muskrat.

Red Squirrel

I can look back to the days when the rivermen rode logs two feet or more across the butt. You could hear the logs coming for miles, for when they formed jams, which was often, there was excitement aplenty and more than any man's share of danger or death. Those big sticks would toss around like straws in a wind and pile up in a tangle the like of which I can't describe. Breaking jams was risky work.

Right up above the carry I have seen men out under the downstream wall of a jam looking for the key log that held back thousands of tons of timber. Working with peaveys and pike poles, they always found it. Once the piece was loosened the jam broke with a rush of flying sticks, and every man raced for his life. If there was clear water and no logs between them and the river banks, they had to run ahead of the breaking jam. Sure-footed as cats, they leaped from one log to another until the jam had settled and spread out on the stream. Then if the water ahead was steady going they rode the logs as long as they were running free.

Come what might, I never saw a riverman who wasn't ready to go out on the logs when the cry, "She's a-holdin'" or "She's a-jammin'," went up. They would race out and try to break away the logs before they built up to a real jam. Some died doing it, but thought of going over the Long Portage never held them back. No place for a timid heart or a weak back.

When peaveys and poles failed to break the jam they would dynamite it. Usually somebody on the bank would throw a stick of explosive fifty feet or so across open water and the boss standing among the logs would catch it. He would tie the dynamite to the end of a long pole, light the fuse and poke it down in the tangle of timber, and shout, "Fire! Fire!" Every mother's son would hike for the bank and wait behind trees and rocks for the blast that hurled logs hefting a ton or more high in the air in a cloud of white smoke and flying spray.

Once the logs began to move, the crew rushed out on the river yelling, "Now she hauls!" or "There she pulls!" and "Walk her! Back on her, boys!" Night and day as long as the drive was on every man was wet through. They would stand in the ice-cold water up to the waist pushing logs into the current, yet seldom did I ever hear of anyone being sick. What they wore for underwear was heavy wool, which is what you want for wet work.

Speaking of blasting jams, I remember the time I had been at one lumber camp for over a week before I found out that what the boss pulled out of a box under my bunk every morning was the day's supply of dynamite. And me a steady smoker!

Looking back on it I believe my best memory of the great river drives is the picture of thousands of logs lying

Lying motionless in the dead water

motionless in the dead water below the rapids on a warm
May evening. At that time of day when the breeze dropped,
the sweet smell of rock-scarred pine and spruce came strong
and fresh through the thin mist that gathered almost as soon
as the sun got off the water. Then the men would stop to
eat, and in the quiet you would hear whip-poor-wills calling
or maybe an owl back in the darkening woods. Good days,
they were.

Taking logs through fast water was only part of the drive,
for booms had to be stretched across bays and coves to keep
the timber on its course, and on the big lakes the logs were
gathered in "bag-booms," big loops made of logs chained
end to end, and towed by small steamboats or pushed by
a favoring wind to the outlet stream. And all the while men
in "pointers" or bateaux, big boats with high pointed ends,
moved about picking up drivers, working logs off the rocks,
or breaking up "wings" which formed when a bunch of logs
took a notion to start off by themselves. And the rear crews,
"sackers" they called them, followed the main drive, clearing logs off the banks and shallow places.

Life in the lumber camps was simple. The food was
plentiful and good or the men left. They were pretty sure
to get corned beef and salt codfish, sometimes tripe and
plenty of baked beans with pork, dried apples stewed, molasses, fruit preserves and cookies, cake and pie. Any cook
who couldn't turn out good hot biscuits and all the pies the
men could eat was in for trouble, which meant the tote road
for him.

When the drive started, the cookees—fellows who helped
the cook and waited on table—followed the crews, serving
four meals a day. They got thick pea soup, beans, ginger
cookies and sweet cake always, and tea strong enough to
float an axe. Some of the cooks were pretty fussy in camp
and made the men take off their hats, wash their hands, and
slick their hair before sitting down on the benches at long
board tables piled with victuals. Meals were eaten in silence,
a rule that headed off arguments that might end with flying

fists and feet. Using feet in a fight was fair and square in a lumber camp battle, and many a man's face showed the punctures of the calks in some other man's boots.

Almost every camp had a cat. No one seemed to know where it came from, but I can tell you an old-time logging cat was as independent as a pig on ice and lived the life of Riley. It helped to keep wood mice out of the oatmeal barrel, which was where it often slept. I heard of one cat that would follow the spring drive with the cook's outfit and at the end travel back to camp to live wild until the crew came in to start cutting at the end of summer. Another cat I knew always took a seat on the first load when the contracting teamster started hauling supplies to the camps in September. Yes, those tote road cats lived well, and gave the camps a homelike touch.

Every time I think of cats I recall a story old Billy McDonald used to tell. He was foreman at my father's camps and a rare storyteller. Often when the men were sitting around the big drum stove drying their clothes, someone would prime Billy to start a yarn. One of his best was about a famous camp cat. It seems that the old-timers in the logging camps would tell the green hands stories of strange and terrible doings in the woods, and sometimes the talk would work around to the devil and his visits to lonely camps. Usually they were tales of Paul Bunyan flavor but altered to suit the occasion. Billy told about one cold January night when Lucifer appeared and demanded a man. The old-timers played up to that and there was an awful goings on over which one of the new men would be given to the devil to carry away. Finally when they'd had their fun somebody grabbed the camp cat, a black one, tossed it to Satan and told him to hit the trail. Nobody said a word except a man by the name of Victor who leaped toward the door and tried to save the cat, but the devil disappeared into the stormy darkness with the feline yowling like a banshee. Then the men broke down and howled themselves hoarse.

Billy didn't remember exactly what time it was, but he

TOTE-ROAD CAT, REX

thought it was about three o'clock in the morning when there was a strange noise at the door. The cook, who was turning out to start breakfast, opened the door and let out a yell that brought all the men out of their bunks. What they saw froze them where they stood. Coming through the door was a black cat, the very same they had thrown to the Evil One, but now it was as big as a bear. Its eyes were burning red, and its tail, as big as a man's arm, was waving savagely. The beast went from one man to another. sniffing and growling, and you could hear them sucking in their breath with terror. Then the cat walked over to Victor and began purring—Billy said it was as loud as a donkey engine. It seemed to be trying to get him to follow, so Victor got together his outfit, picked up his rifle, and the cat led him away into the dark woods. Nobody moved or said a word.

Weeks went by, but no sign or word of Victor and for reasons of their own the logging people made no attempt to find him. Then late one Saturday he turned up looking well-fed and satisfied. The whole camp ran out to meet him and rushed right back when they saw Victor riding a sled load of fine furs pulled by the huge black cat. As soon as the animal saw them it began to spit and snarl, and they hit the bunkhouse doors like a log jam.

Everybody treated Victor with great respect and some of the men even took off their hats when he came in. He told them he and the cat were living in an abandoned trapper's cabin on Wolverine Lake and that he was on his way to the settlement to sell his furs. As Billy told it, Victor said that after he went away with the cat that night, it led him straight to the trapping cabin. Then after he had set things to rights and got a fire going the cat went out. Daybreak was a long time coming and Victor was beginning to get worried, when finally away off to the west he heard something and soon he saw a bull moose coming toward him on the tear with the big black cat riding him. Yes, sir, that cat was cradled snug-like between his antlers and it was holding the animal's ears with its paws just like he was driving a horse. He brought the moose right to the door and then jumped off so Victor could shoot it.

That was just the beginning, for from then on the giant feline went hunting everyday and brought back prime fur animals. All Victor had to do was to sit in the cabin and work on the skins of martin, fisher, mink, and lynx, which the cat brought in slung over his shoulder as proud as could be. Once it came back with a full-grown wolf and another time it dug a bear out of his wash and drove him right to the cabin.

According to Billy, there wasn't much truck with the devil around the camp the rest of that winter. Victor, so the story goes, got rich with the aid of the big cat, married, and settled down on the west branch of the Shinkwak River, taking teaming contracts once in a while just for the fun of it, the cat riding beside him and purring all the time.

During the usual April rainy spell I put in some time getting things fixed up for the summer. I made myself a new table from three boards, two pieces of split birch log, and some seasoned birch saplings for legs. I plan to make some benches the same way to go with it. That will mean company won't have to sit on the nail keg. The only tricky part is to bore the holes in the logs at the proper angle so that the legs will set just right. The best way is to lay the pieces on the floor, make a wooden templet or guide of the angle, and use it to start each hole.

While I was working on the bench Hank came over and got an idea that he would try his hand at making some candle holders out of tin cans. You've probably seen some of them before. They come in handy and a candle is a pretty safe light to have in a house, especially if you have to carry it around at night, which is not safe to do with a kerosene lamp.

TIN CAN LAMPS

The bean can lamp

Tin cans make good lanterns too.

...and you can cut your lamps in fancy shapes if you want to.

SPLIT-LOG TABLE & BENCH

What is more, a candle is almost certain to go out if it drops on the floor. I save the ends of all burned candles, melt them up and pour them into a jelly glass, first setting a wick of string in the glass by tying the top to a twig that rests on the rim of the glass. This kind of candle lasts a long time.

TUMBLER CANDLE

Birch bark candle mold

Hank sometimes makes his own candles by molding them in the bark slipped off a small decayed birch sapling. You often see birch rotting on the ground in dark places in the woods and if it has been there long enough the soft wood can be pushed out, leaving a nice mold for a candle. You make a little wooden plug with a hole in the center to hold the wick in place. Stick the plug in the bottom of the birch tube, tighten up on the string, and tie it to a twig across the top. Then all you have to do is pour in your melted wax and when it's hard run a sharp knife down the side and strip off the bark. A piece of bark about hoe-handle thick and four inches long is easy to clean out and makes a candle of the right size.

When I first came up to this country I worked for a while in a mine and I still have my miner's candlestick and a very handy thing it is. One end is sharpened so that I can stick it into a wall, and there is also a little hook to hang it on my hatband leaving my hands free to work. They are not used much since the gas lamps came in, but I find it useful and it keeps the memories of my mining days green.

For a long time I had been wanting a bellows to quicken up my fire once in a while. It is a very handy thing to have around for various purposes. So during a stormy spell I got to work and made one. Mine has extra long handles so that I don't have to stoop when I use it.

The main part of the bellows forming the air chamber is eight inches wide by twelve inches long and the handles are two feet long. I had saved a nice piece of pine board which I planed down to half an inch thick so the bellows would be light to handle. For the nozzle I used an old .38-55 rifle cartridge with the head filed off. It is just about the right size, the wide end being fitted into the block at the point of the bellows.

In the lower board I bored an inch and a quarter hole for the intake valve. The valve flap is made of a small block of wood faced with a piece of soft leather about a quarter of an inch larger than the hole with room enough left on one side to tack it to the inside of the board. Across the block is tacked loosely another little strip of leather, so that the flap can rise about a quarter of an inch. The idea is that when the boards are pulled apart, air is sucked in, but when they are pushed together the air forces the leather flap tight against the intake hole.

On the bottom board is nailed a little block about two inches long with a hole bored through it to hold the nozzle. Now, before you hinge the top board to the block with a strong piece of leather, you have to put springs between the boards to keep them separated. I used two slender pieces of willow, curving them around and tacking the ends down to the lower board near the point of the bellows. With that done you are ready to hinge the top board and fit the leather sides. For this you will need some soft pliable leather. I used soft smoked deerskin, but the sheepskin chamois that you can buy would work very well. To get the shape of your leather the best thing to do is to prop the two boards apart where you figure they would be as wide open as you would want them, and then fit a paper pattern around them and trim it until it is just right, leaving plenty of room at the pointed end for tacking around the block.

By using a pattern you don't run the danger of spoiling your leather, for the job of fitting is a little tricky. I found that the best way is to tack the leather on with the tacks part way in until you are sure it fits, expecially around the handles

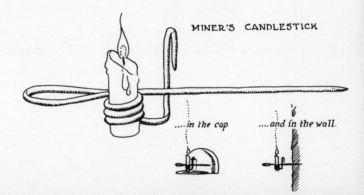

MINER'S CANDLESTICK

....in the cap.   ....and in the wall.

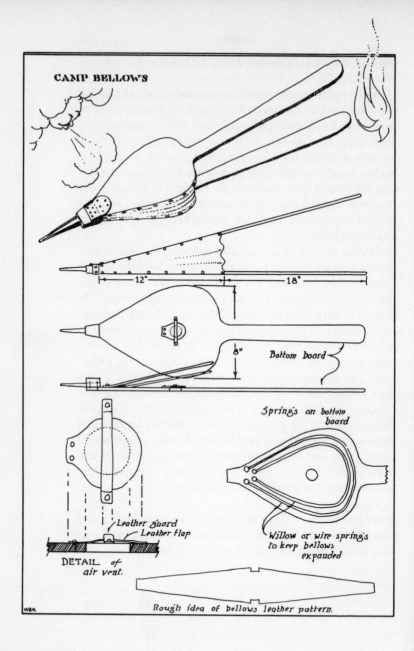

CAMP BELLOWS

12"

18"

8"

Bottom board

Springs on bottom board

Leather guard
Leather flap

DETAIL of air vent.

Willow or wire springs to keep bellows expanded

Rough idea of bellows leather pattern.

HBK

where you have to notch it. When it is all laid on you can drive the tacks home and then cover the edges with a binding strip of rawhide which not only protects the leather but helps keep it airtight. There should also be a binding strip where the leather fits around the point of the bellows.

Aside from brightening up my fire in no time at all, I use the bellows when I ready up my house to blow dust and crumbs out of the floor cracks where it's hard to get at them with the kind of home-made broom I make.

A while back the Chief told me about a fine litter of husky pups owned by an Indian who lives on Otter Stream, so I went up to look them over and brought one back, for old Wolf needs help on the sled and by next winter the young one should be able to pull his weight. Being given to barter when the trading is right, I took along an extra bucksaw and after some palavering back and forth, and with a plug of tobacco thrown in, I got the puppy. He's a smart little fellow with a black cap, ears and back. The rest of him is almost white.

He seems to like his new home and it took me only a few days to name him. Every time I moved he would pounce at my feet to grab my shoelaces or the bottom of my pants. I tripped over him so much I said suddenly one morning, "Young fellow, your name is Tripper!" That's a good name because he'll soon tire of tripping me and when he grows up and is a fine sled dog he will be taking many trips.

Tripper is about the size of a ground hog now and has all the signs of the true husky. His fluffy little tail curls close over his back and when his pointed ears stand up to listen hard he looks like a small wolf. I've got to thin him down because he's too fat now. It's comical to see him try to chase my tame deer mouse. Once he tripped over a root and fell head over apple cart, sat up looking sort of foolish and then started trailing the mouse again.

Old Wolf doesn't quite know what to make of the young one, but he is patient when the pup pulls his tail, gnaws his ears, and tries to chew off his feet. Just once Wolf growled and Tripper, knowing what that meant, ambled off to play with a piece of deer horn I gave him. He gnaws on that horn by the hour, which is fine for his teeth.

In the fall I'll begin training the pup for his job as a sled dog. You never break them to the sled until they are six months old and strong. Before that age you can ruin their strength and spirit. About midsummer I'll make him a simple deerskin harness and let him play around pulling a little piece of spruce sapling weighing just a few ounces. That will make it easier for him to get used to the feel of the regular harness when he takes his place behind Wolf. And Wolf will not let him forget who is the leader and the boss, and Tripper, being next the sled, will have to learn the wheel dog's special job.

I am certain to have a spell of seed-catalogue fever which generally comes on without warning at the end of one of those April days when the air is soft and warm and the pleasant smell of the earth comes through the windows in the evening. I am never so far away from civilization that I can't get a seed catalogue, and for thirty years I have been trying to solve the mystery of how to produce the kind of tomatoes that grow on the covers of the seed catalogues. I do pretty well, but I have never quite made the grade. I wonder if anyone ever has.

My catalogue comes to me from the air, for my friend, the pilot of the company's plane, knows how much I count on it and he always brings it in. If landing conditions don't favor him he comes in low over the lake and drops it where it is sure to fall in a clear place. I get my seeds the same way.

When it comes to tomatoes, which, raw or cooked, go well with almost everything, I have my own ideas. One is to plant them deep so that they will carry through dry spells without any trouble. I set mine half the depth of the stalk when they reach the transplanting stage. To protect them from cutworms I then make collars of strips of tar paper about three inches deep, leaving about an inch of collar above the ground. Some say not to stake your tomatoes, but I hate to see them lying on the ground, so I hitch mine to little birch branches and once they get started they take good care of themselves without much tying up. Although it will be a while yet before I get my garden under way I enjoy just thinking of pale green lettuce and pea vines bright against the rich black soil of my patch down by the lake. It was part of a little bog until I drained it; now it grows wonderful vegetables.

Up on higher ground where the soil is mixed with sand and well drained, I plant my potatoes early in June, for I depend on the late crop to put away for the winter. We grow very fine potatoes here in the woods and they have a flavor all their own, especially when baked in the ashes of a campfire. There is quite a trick to cut seed potatoes, for you get a better yield if you cut them so that you get the eyes on the flower end and in the middle instead of the stem end where the potato was attached to the plant. When the time comes to harvest the crop we have to watch for sudden cold rains which make potatoes soggy. Another thing is that if potatoes lie in the sunlight for any length of time after digging they turn green and are not much good. For keeping through the winter, potatoes should be stored in a dark dry place where the air circulates freely, but they must always be protected against freezing.

Rhubarb is one of the plants that I couldn't do without, for nothing that comes from the garden in spring is so refreshing as stewed rhubarb, hot or cold, and if you have a little cream to pour over it and some hot biscuits to go along, you have a dish fit for any man. If you have no cream, evaporated milk goes very well. The right way to cook rhubarb is to simmer it slowly for about half an hour in a covered pot with just enough water to cover the bottom. Young stalks do not have to be peeled and cook up to a fine pink color. You need enough sugar to bring out the flavor.

I also grow fine carrots, beets; cabbage, and green beans, and I never fail to have herbs to flavor my cooking.

One of the troubles with gardens in the woods is to keep

the deer out of them. There is hardly a fence you can put up that the critters won't jump, but Wolf sleeps outdoors all summer and deer don't get very close before he scares them off.

I don't limit myself to vegetables for I'm more than passing fond of flowers and the color they give a place in summer. Along the south side of the cabin close to the wall I grow hollyhocks, deep red and rich yellow, and some white ones. Out in front I have several rows of sweet peas where I can see them from the porch and in the evening when the west wind stirs gently their scent comes to my window. Close by I always have a bed of nasturtiums, which do well here and are rich in color. I tried those beautiful bright blue morning glories for two or three years but didn't have very good luck. Then a fellow told me that the seeds are flint-hard and should be nicked with a file and then soaked. That solved the mystery of why so many of my seeds failed to come up, so now I put them in a dish of water until they germinate and then plant them at once with the sprout straight up. If I want early blossoms I start the seeds in trays indoors with collars of tar paper around each one so that it can be transplanted without disturbing it very much. And for the birds I plant sunflowers all about the place, for the seeds make wonderful winter bird food, especially for chickadees. I always store away a plentiful supply. Once I discovered the endless pleasure of raising flowers I look forward to it every year. I don't know anything akin to the excitement of going through a seed catalogue and discovering new strains to try my hand at.

Almost every evening now that the days are warming I listen to the frogs in the swamp. Most people know the song of the peepers, but not one out of ten has ever seen one. It is hard to believe that a frog not more than an inch long can have such a big voice. They are fawn or brownish color, and have a cross on their backs. When they sing their

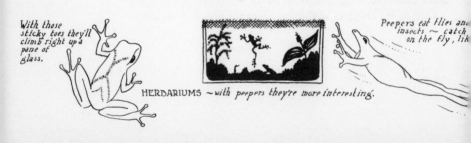

With those sticky toes they'll climb right up a pane of glass.

HERBARIUMS ~ with peepers they're more interesting.

Peepers eat flies and insects ~ catch on the fly, lik

throats swell out almost as big as they are themselves. They are tree frogs or hylas, and they have little sticky discs on their toes for climbing through the shrubs and grass when they are hunting for insects. Like all frogs, they go to pools and ponds in the spring to lay their eggs. They are hard to find, but at night you can locate them with a little patience. Flashlights don't seem to bother them much, and, if you stand still for a while where they are singing, it won't be long before you spot one of those round throats like a little toy balloon. They make nice pets if you keep them in a glass fish bowl or small tank with some moss and woods plants. The top has to be covered with a screen, or you won't have them very long. They eat flies and most kinds of small insects, and they will sing for you, too. Pleasant neighbors.

May is like a wide-eyed fawn

The Green Tide Flows North

WHEN MAY comes to the north country it reminds me of a fawn walking out of the woods alone for the first time, wide-eyed and uncertain about what to do next. A timid month is May, and not sure of itself, for though the days may be warm, the nights are often sharp with frost and sometimes windowpane ice comes on the coves. Once in a while we have a snow flurry—"robin snow," we call it.

Out in the shady place back of my cabin snow still lies under a shaggy spruce like a dingy white collar on a man who needs a hair cut. Spring is gaining, to be sure, but the tattered white patches in the woods on the north slopes of the Cache Lake hills show that winter is not leaving without a fight. In places the ice in the ground is like black flint, but where the sun strikes down through the branches water is running under the matted needles like a frightened little critter trying to get away without being seen or heard. Once it makes its way into the open, though, the trickle picks up strength and talks out loud to itself as it snakes through the moss and stones. Then, free at last from the thongs of winter, it hustles on down the hill to the lake, leaping over the ledges, ducking under logs and racing with all the excitement of a brand new brook. That's how May shows up at Cache Lake.

When I came to the big woods years ago I used to get letters from a friend down south. In the spring when the ice on the lake was gray and just starting to honeycomb and

I was still poking wood in the stove to keep warm, he would write that where he was summer had come. The trees were all dressed in new leaves and he was picking lettuce from his kitchen garden. Once, I remember, he wrote that a mocking-bird was singing in a dogwood tree and the scent of honey-suckle and the drowsy droning of bees came to him through the open window. But here the wet, soggy snow of late winter still lingered in the forest.

Coming to me from time to time, first by rail and then by the hand of some trapper or prospector who passed my way, those letters started me thinking of spring as something more than just a time of the year. I began to think that if I could rise high in the sky and had eyes that could see a thousand miles or more to the south and as far east and west, I would look down upon a mighty tide of fresh new leaves bursting from brown shields, meadows covered with new grass and bright with the color of wild flowers. That would be spring on her journey out of the south, a tide of plant life moving into the valleys, spreading along the rivers and around the lakes, and rising up and over the hills to ripple quietly across the gray flat lands. A wonderful sight!

But that was not all I pictured, for behind the edge of the land's green flood and high in the sky I would see another tide—millions of migrating birds of every size and color moving in a straight, strong current of hurrying wings from their wintering places hundreds, perhaps thousands, of miles away. Out of the tropics they would come, flying across the Gulf of Mexico or from island to island in the blue Caribbean, picking up others from the bayous and rice fields of Louisiana, from the swamps of Florida, the pine forests of North Carolina and the waters of Currituck Sound and Chesapeake Bay, all driven by a common instinct toward their nesting places in the north. Some would stop along the way; others would fly on, sweeping across the Great Lakes or winging up the Atlantic Coast until they looked down upon the lonely Barren Lands and the bleak waters of the Arctic Ocean north of Canada.

And so it was I came to think of spring and autumn as two great tides rising and ebbing, one bright northing green, the other a crimson and gold flood that begins to flow toward the south when the clear crisp nights of late September give the signal to start.

All nature is now wide awake and alert, and neither frost nor a late flurry of snow will change her plans for long. Our season is short and summer, hot from hurrying, comes bustling along to get on with the business of growing things. All of a sudden the leaves are out, the tender plants that hid during the cool weather push up through the dark earth without fear, flowers unfold and soon the seeds begin to form.

From the doorway of my cabin at this time of year I can see a swamp maple, red against the dark wall of the forest across the narrows between Cache and Snow Goose Lakes. The tops of the birches make a feathery pattern against a sky that only May can show, and down by the water's edge where the tracks of deer are sharp in the sand, a pair of black ducks are pretty sure to be sunning themselves. Their nest is probably in the marshy place across the cove.

The crest of the tide of wings reaches Cache Lake this month. One day all is quiet and then some morning the woods are filled with song and birds are feeding all about. I like them all, but somehow I think I listen hardest for the notes of the first eastern song sparrow. While the flight is at its height I give all the time I can to watching for the travelers that stop off for a snack on their way still farther north. It is worth getting up before the sun lifts over Hunting Wolf Ridge to catch just a glimpse of a fox sparrow and hear his morning song. He may not end his journey until he has found a mate in the wild lake country of Labrador or maybe over Hudson Bay way. And on warm evenings in the twilight I can hear the beautiful silvery chorus of the vesper sparrows. Sometimes they are called ground birds or grass finches.

I recall that when I was a boy I stood in the moonlight on

a spring night and heard the faint chirpings of birds high above me. That was when I learned for the first time that migrating birds fly mostly during the night and stop to rest and feed by day. Storms or head winds may delay them for a day or so at a time, but if the weather is fine they gather in great numbers at twilight, talking among themselves, and then as if by signal they lift into the sky, circle, and head away on their course. Some of the small birds make their long night flights at heights of a mile or more and all follow well-established sky trails year in and year out.

The food needed by those millions of traveling birds is one of nature's big problems, which accounts for the fact that most of the birds keep behind the front of the spring tide line. If they arrive in the north too early there is no food for them. First the plants must grow to produce seeds for the seed eaters and the insects must hatch. The birds that can find food despite cold and even snow, start north far ahead of the first sign of spring and a few extra tough fellows spend all winter with me.

Almost any evening at twilight when not even a leaf stirs and the lake lies like a dark mirror, I will hear my first wood thrush singing back in the thickets. Later when darkness comes and the water turns to silver in the light of the full moon, the whip-poor-will begins calling from the ridge over toward Hank's place. I can make a fairly good imitation of the call so I sometimes try to bring them a little closer.

It is about this time of spring that the white-footed mice are raising their first young. They will have two or maybe three more families before snow flies again. And the bats are busy with small ones too. Speaking of young, I have seen the first baby rabbits of the year out by the path to the spring.

With the water high and spread out over the marshes, the pike and pickerel are spawning in the shallows and if other fish didn't eat many of the millions of eggs they lay, there wouldn't be much fishing for any of us. The pike and pickerel are killers and the less of them the better for the game fish. I might also mention that the bass and the sunfish are making their nests in the sand in warm clear water near the shore. The male fans out the sand with his fins to form a hollow, then drives the female in to spawn. He guards the nest with great devotion, swimming back and forth over it, and woe it is to any other fish that comes near.

Every spring Hank and I go up to the beaver dam on Otter Stream to see how they've wintered. It is a caution how a few small animals can build a dam strong enough to control the waters of a large pond even when the spring freshets throw all their weight against it.

Beavers work just like human engineers, for some of their dams have rounded fronts while others are straight across. Now, an engineer would build a rounded front where he wanted to hold back a lot of deep water and maybe take care of quick floods. The straight dams are for quiet places where there is not much danger of extra pressure. Whether the beavers know the difference, I can't tell you, but they build both kinds of dams and somehow I have a notion they have a pretty good idea of what they want in the kind of places they build.

I did quite a bit of whittling during the winter and the things I made include a brown bear—the kind you find in Alaska—a black duck, and a doe. However, there is nothing just like sitting out on a warm May morning and carving a piece of fragrant white pine. It must be dry so it won't crack, and as clear of knots as can be found. Spruce carves nicely, too.

I have enjoyed whittling ever since I was a boy and have learned a few things that help to make it easier. As a matter of fact, once you get started it is not hard, and it is one of the pleasantest things you can do. Take a duck, for example.

The sunfish are nesting

NO TRESPASSING

The Industry of the Beavers of Canada.

(from "The Beauties of Nature and Art" published in London, 1774)

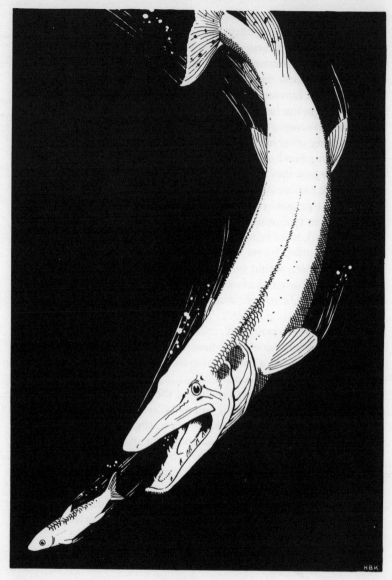

The pike are killers

The grain should run lengthwise with the body so that the head and bill can be carved without having them break off. That is important, and the same rule holds true in carving a bear. The feet of a bear are important in making him look what he is, and if the grain is up and down the toes are apt to snap off. Take my word for it and have the grain running lengthwise from nose to tail because the legs are heavy and the snout thick, so there is not much danger of breaking them off. Now when it comes to carving a deer, horse, ox or such animals, the grain should run up and down in line with the legs, which are slender, and need a lot of fine work.

Most whittlers make the mistake of trying to carve with a dull knife. I keep a good whetstone right beside me and about every fifteen minutes I freshen up the edge and then hone it on a piece of leather or the sole of my shoe. What I want is a razor edge that will cut across the grain almost as smoothly as it does along it.

In carving an animal, getting it blocked out in the rough form of the beast is half the battle. If you can't see the animal in real life, pictures help a lot. Learn to draw outlines and then shape up the heavier parts, leaving slender legs, ears and tails to the last. Some tools that help a lot in carving are a coping or jig saw, a sharp rasp, a good medium-coarse half-round file about ten inches long, a small rat-tail file, and the best quality pocketknife you can find. With those tools and plenty of sandpaper to finish off, you have everything you need to carve the finest pieces. Some carvings look best if you leave the knife marks as they are without any sanding, but this finish requires more skill for sandpaper rubs off many mistakes.

In carving a bear some folks like a smooth finish. I prefer to show the fur. That can be done by using the edge of a

Rasp,

File,

and Knife,

and,

of course, a Coping Saw.

These are the only essential tools for wood-carving.

Oil stone

Sharpen your knife with a rotary motion ~edge should have a bevel like this, not this

file or making fine knife cuts to get the little marks running the way the hair does. The effect, to my way of thinking, is very lifelike. It's just a matter of how you look at it.

In case you want to try some whittling, don't make your animal too big. A bear four and a half inches long and three inches high at the shoulder is plenty of work for any man. What is more, it is not always easy to come by good, dry carving wood. Up here I use white pine, spruce, and some birch, but there are other woods that are fine for carving. Apple wood is always treasured by experienced whittlers, and pear and cherry and mahogany are very choice, too. You can finish carvings with wax or rub them with boiled linseed oil. I'm partial to a little beeswax rubbed on with the palm of the hand, which warms the surface and gives a nice polish.

As soon as I get around to it I'm going to carve an otter out of a piece of white hawthorne that was sent to me by a friend. It seems that he had a tree that had to be cut down and knowing it was a beautiful wood he had it sawed up in chunks and dried very slowly so it didn't check. It's extra fine grained and almost white. Once I carved a piece of white holly, which is just about as precious as gold, and I have always wanted to glue thin strips of dark wood and white holly together to make a block for carving a zebra. I figure that would be something to have.

Now that summer is coming on I am busy making a small saddle-pack for Tripper. Wolf has been helping me carry loads in the summer for several years, so I figured Tripper should carry his share this summer. By saddle-pack I mean little canvas bags laced to a wide strap of canvas or hide that can be tied around the dog just back of his shoulders, so he can help to lug supplies. It is necessary to be careful about overloading a dog, although I have known some big fellows to carry as much as twenty pounds. Ten is load enough, and the trick is to be sure that the weight is balanced on each side of the dog so the saddle won't slip one way or the other.

Grain this way   Grain this way

BLACK DUCK

KODIAK BEAR

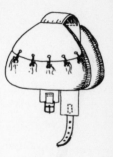

I still laugh over the time years ago when I had a big dog named Nipper who loved to chase rabbits. We were on a trip and in Nipper's saddlebags were several pounds of white beans in paper bags. That was a mistake in the first place—no paper bags in the woods. All of a sudden Nipper spotted a rabbit on the trail ahead of us, and away he went. The flaps on the saddlebags got loose, the bags broke, and old Nipper sowed white beans all over the north country, or that's what it seemed like to me. I spent half a day picking up individual beans, because they were precious food. I was thankful they were white.

It is getting on to the time when we will be out in the woods more, so I have been looking over my outfit and one of the things I made is a new sheath for my hand axe. For years I have used one made of heavy moosehide, but this time I decided to try something new. I got my friend the pilot to bring me in a sheet of sixteenth-inch aluminum from which I shaped a sheath the like of which has never been seen in these parts. It is no heavier than the old leather one and to my way of thinking it gives much better protection. Aluminum shapes easily and my sheath is simple to make once you cut a cardboard pattern to the size of your axe. It goes together with four rivets and has slots on the open side to hold it in place with a thong.

I'll still use the heavy leather sheath for the large axe, for it has a copper insert on the blade side to keep the edge from cutting into the leather. It is nothing more than a strip of thin copper that fits about halfway up the inside of the sheath with small holes to lace it snug along the upper edges. Being soft metal, copper never dulls the edge of the axe and is a very effective guard without adding much weight to the sheath.

Although it is chiefly for home use, another thing I made is a long-handled bacon turner fashioned from an old kitchen fork. It is just the thing to keep your hand out of reach

METAL
AXE
SHEATH

WHITE-TAILED DEER

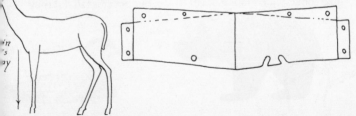

of the hot fat when it splatters from a pan. All I did was to file off the rivets on the fork handle and replace the handle with one sixteen inches long. I used maple and rubbed it down with boiled linseed oil. It's the most useful thing to have around the kitchen you ever did see, and it is good for meat cakes and the like, too.

We have been talking about having an "eat-out" soon, which recalls a little grill I once saw up in northern Canada. Just two horseshoes joined by two rods welded to the sides of the shoes. Mighty fine for broiling or holding a pot over a picnic fire, but too heavy to carry on a trip where weight counts.

Every year about this time I make a trip up river to see what's going on at the bear den on Skeleton Ridge. There has been a bear family in that den off and on for many years. I hiked up to the carry on a nice warm day about the middle of the month and found a good spot on a rise that looks straight across to the ridge and on beyond to Faraway See Hill, standing clear and sharp high above the dark forest. Expecting to see some action, I took along the old spyglass that used to belong to my grandfather who was a seafaring man. Sure enough the first look gave me a chuckle. The old mother bear was sunning herself at the mouth of the den and out in front where the earth was warm the two little cubs were playing. Not much bigger than good-sized ground hogs, they were, and having a good time romping around. Once they got so wild they walked all over their mother's head and quick as a flash she gave them a cuff that sent them rolling over and over. But that didn't bother those young fellows more than a minute. In no time they were at it again and one knocked the other over the edge of the bank and he slid down only to come scrambling up for more.

Standing on their hind legs they boxed and wrestled for a while and then all of a sudden quit that game and started climbing a little pine tree, one nipping at the heels of the fellow above. The way they played out on the end of a limb looked like sudden death to me, but never a fall did they

16"

BACON (or meat cake or sausage etc.) TURNER

The HORSESHOE GRATE

have. After a spell they got tuckered out, scrambled down and curled up in a sunny spot near their mother, one with his little black head on the neck of the other.

On my way home I went down to the river to catch a mess of trout for supper. I nearly always have my rod along at this time of year and never take more than I can eat in a day. I got one two-pound squaretail that made my mouth water. I tap fish on the head when I pull them out, which is the right thing to do.

On the way back to the cabin I spotted a nice patch of cinnamon ferns and picked a hatful for supper. Mighty good food when they are young and tender in the fiddlehead stage. You just boil them with a little salt, the way you cook spinach. I like a touch of hot bacon fat on mine, and a few drops of vinegar. They're good cold, too, for salad.

As soon as I came out into the clearing I saw Hank and Chief Tibeash sitting down by the lake. They had come over to talk about the canoe trip we take every summer so that the Chief can look over the trapping country for next fall. The Chief always likes to be doing something, so while he and Hank waited for me he made a sling stick, a very old Indian game, to show Hank that it was better than a slingshot. It seems the Chief was a champion sling stick shot when he was a boy and the way he can throw a stone with that contraption is something to see.

He started by whittling out a tapering birch stick about two feet long with a tip that is flat on one side and about three quarters of an inch wide. The handle was a little smaller than a broomstick. He told Hank that hickory, ash, or maple make good sticks, but that pine or spruce is too soft. The lighter the stick the better. The Chief cut notches on the narrow edges of the tip and just below made a shallow hollow to hold the stone.

When he finished the handle and smoothed it down with the sharp edge of a scrap of broken glass, he tied a flat moose-hide thong to the notched tip and made a loop on the end just opposite where he would hold the stick. To load the sling the Chief put a small stone in the hollow under the thong at the tip, holding the loop down with the thumb of his throwing hand. He then swung the stick back over his shoulder in much the same way a fisherman handles a bait rod in casting. At the end of the cast when his arm came up high he let go the thong and the stone sailed far out on the lake.

The Chief says you can use sling sticks to shoot arrows, too. The only change is to tie about ten inches of strong cord with a knot in the end to the loop. The arrows are exactly the same as you use with a bow, except that you cut a little notch in the shaft about six inches below the head to catch the knotted string. To shoot arrows you throw from the side at hip height, holding the end of the arrow with the left hand and pulling it back hard before snapping the stick forward with the right.

While the Chief was working on his stick, Hank sat on a log twisting grass blades. I couldn't make out what he was up to for a while, but soon he got down on his hands and knees and began crawling around with his nose to the ground and holding something to his eye. It seems that when he was young he used to twist a grass blade into a little loop just big enough to hold a drop of water, which makes a fairly good magnifying glass. Hank claims a drop of dew, which is sure to be clear and clean, makes the best kind. The loop should be about an eighth of an inch in diameter. If you don't get just the right amount of water in the drop it produces the opposite effect of a magnifying glass and makes everything look very small. I think a paper clip twisted up to a loop would make a good one.

Getting back to that canoe trip I mentioned before I got off the trail talking sling sticks, we generally go when the black flies and mosquitoes thin out. Before we start this

SLING
STICK

With a knotted cord the Sling Stick shoots a notched arrow. Get plenty of room to practice in ~ especially at first

Here's the way the Chief throws a stone. He gets amazing distance, too.

year I have to make myself a new stern paddle. Canoe paddles are just like shoes—they work best when they fit right, and I like to make my own. Spruce is best for open lake work where you have plenty of water, but maple or ash are the woods for rapids and shallow water where you may hit rocks. The best length for a stern paddle is the height of your shoulder, and for the bow one that comes up to your eye level. Because you steer with the stern paddle it helps to have the blade a little wider than the bow paddle. The lighter they are the better, because in steady traveling a good canoeman dips his paddle about twenty-five times a minute and that is over 1,500 strokes an hour. When you are working like that for hours at a stretch just an ounce in weight makes a big difference. I have a favorite spruce stern paddle that weighs just fourteen ounces and I have worked it all day without being tired at sundown.

Paddles remind me of people: some of them are stiff and don't seem to want to help a fellow, but others are light and lively and bend just enough to give you that extra thrust at the end of the stroke. A good one slides out of the water as quietly and smoothly as a beaver. Paddles can be light yet very strong if you know how to shape them. The section of the handle where it joins the shoulder of the blade is a spot that takes a lot of punishing strain. That is why you should carry the thickness of the shaft part way down the center of the blade, tapering off gradually toward the edges. This gives strength in the center and at the same time lets the blade cut the water cleanly.

I have seen men paddle as though they were trying to churn the lake into a froth. A good canoeman leaves only a smooth oily whirl of water and a wake that dies out quickly. He hardly makes a sound. He keeps his right arm fairly straight and stiff, with the left arm slightly bent, and swings his body forward on the driving stroke, which gives power that can't be got any other way.

What I'm trying to say is that you make your body from the waist up do most of the work, using the arms almost

PAPER CLIP
MICROSCOPE
—and you'd be
surprised what you
can see with this
simple gadget

GRASS MICROSCOPE

—of
course it's
enlarged a bit

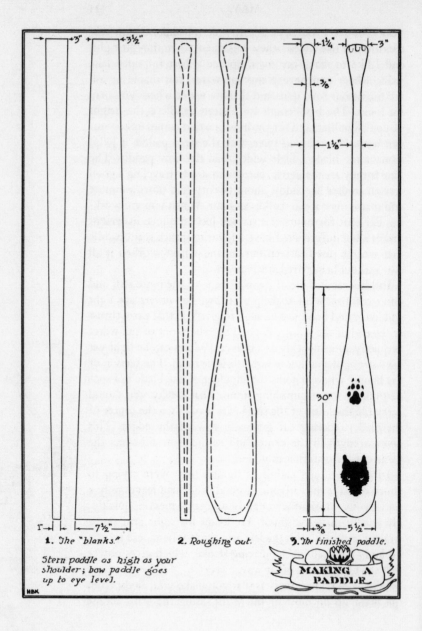

3" 3½"

1¼" 3"

⅜"

1⅛"

30"

1" 7½"

⅜" 5½"

1. The "blanks."

2. Roughing out.

3. The finished paddle.

Stern paddle as high as your
shoulder; bow paddle goes
up to eye level.

MAKING A
PADDLE

HBK

as if they were fixed brackets to hold the paddle in the right position. If there is no canoe handy you can practice by sitting on a log or box. The short Indian stroke is the secret of handling a canoe with the least labor.

A spruce board that has a good straight grain and is free of knots is the right stock for a light paddle. Have it plenty long, eight inches wide and near the bottom about two inches thick so you will have lots of room to work. Lay out the shape of the paddle and set the proper measurement for length according to who is to use it. Then saw out the rough outline, leaving room on all sides for finishing to the right size. A vise is a help and a drawknife makes the job a downright pleasure. You can finish off with a small plane and then sandpaper to a glass-smooth surface. It can't be too smooth, for a fine finish makes for easy paddling. Then varnish with two coats of spar varnish, using very fine sandpaper between coats when the first is two days dry. If you follow that plan you will have a good paddle, and if it is maple it ought not to weigh more than two pounds.

Just a word about caring for paddles. Don't abuse them by pushing against rocks or the bottom, which spoils the clean, thin edge that means so much for quiet and powerful paddling. Always have an extra paddle for you can't tell when one will break. In rough water, shallow streams, or rapids use your maple paddle. Spruce is not tough enough for that kind of work. And don't leave your paddles lying in the sun. Just remember a good workman has the right kind of tool for each job and if he loves his work he'll take good care of his tools. That's the idea with paddles, too. I almost forgot to say that I like the way some Indians cut little grooves in the handle to fit the three middle fingers, which gives a firm grip. I have one paddle I decorated with the tracks of moose and wolf, and another that has a drawing of an unmapped lake.

I got so interested talking to Hank and the Chief about our trip that after they left I began going over my gear, checking on supplies and the like. I guess I don't have to tell you that the most important thing in the woods is having something to start a fire with. Matches are the first thing I think of and how to keep them dry is the next. Of course at home, here in the cabin, I keep them in covered tin cans so the mice can't get at them and start a fire. In the woods you can carry them in tightly corked bottles, which is all right except that the glass is apt to break. The best trick I know is to waterproof the matches. The way to do it is to melt up old candle stubs or wax in a can set in boiling water so the melted wax won't catch fire, and pour the liquid wax over layer after layer of matches in their box until finally the matches are sealed in a cake of wax. After that you could drop them in the snow or the lake and still have good dry matches to be dug out when you need them most. Being waxed they burn longer and are fine in a wind or wet weather. But they ought to be kept in a covered tin even on the trail, for if there is anything mice, squirrels and chipmunks love, it's wax.

Sitting around the campfire one night while I cooked some biscuits we got to talking about a fine outdoor oven I learned to build, when I was a young fellow, on the north shore of the St. Lawrence River. Many of the French people who live in that part of the country like the old ways of doing things and some still bake their bread in outdoor ovens.

The French Canadian ovens, made of clay or mortar on a foundation of stone or cedar logs, are built waist-high for easy working. On top of the foundation they make a floor of the same clay or mortar that is used for the roof of the oven. Being several inches thick, the floor can be laid on a log foundation without danger of fire damage, though I figure a stone is best and not so likely to sag and crack the oven.

After the floor is dry you are ready to begin work on the

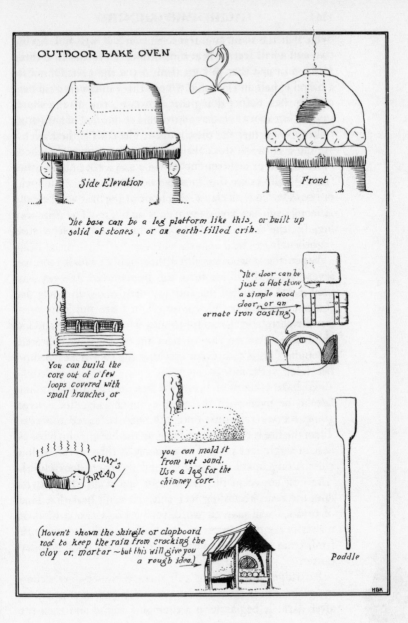

OUTDOOR BAKE OVEN

Side Elevation

Front

The base can be a log platform like this, or built up solid of stones, or an earth-filled crib.

The door can be just a flat stone, a simple wood door, or an ornate iron casting

You can build the core out of a few loops covered with small branches, or

THAT'S BREAD!

you can mold it from wet sand. Use a log for the chimney core.

(Haven't shown the shingle or clapboard roof to keep the rain from cracking the clay or mortar ~ but this will give you a rough idea.)

Paddle

HBK

oven, which is about four feet long, two feet high and maybe two and a half feet wide at the bottom. To form the arched roof you can either pile up sand to the right shape or cut a barrel in half and lay on the mortar to a thickness of about eight inches. Before doing that, however, you place a short smooth log about as big as a stovepipe at one end of the form to keep an opening for the chimney. The ends of these ovens are closed in with thick walls of mortar, leaving an arched or oblong door eighteen inches wide and a foot high at the front. While in use this door can be closed with a flat rock or board sealed with clay so that none of the heat will be lost. A fancy oven can have an iron door on hinges. The chimney log, by the way, is pulled out while the mortar is still slightly soft.

When the mortar has dried thoroughly, which requires several days, the inside form can be removed. If sand was used it can be pulled out through the door with a hoe. In the case of a half barrel, you just light a fire and let it burn out the barrel, being careful to start with a small fire and let the barrel catch on slowly after the wood is well heated through. This is to prevent cracking the roof if any dampness is left in the mortar.

To bake a batch of bread the first step is to start a hot fire in the oven with the chimney open. The fire is kept going for several hours until the oven is heated through. Then the fire is raked out and in goes the bread, which bakes best in single-loaf pans. The chimney is then sealed with a close fitting board or flat stone and the oven door closed. The heat stored in the heavy floor and walls of the oven does the rest. According to Hank you can't beat that kind of bread. I will take his word, for he knows good food. It makes my mouth water to think of a thick brown crust fresh from a hot loaf and spread thick with good country butter.

Partridges—the Indians call them Ben-asee—are drumming and I hear them almost every day and now and then after dark. It begins with a thumping sound and then the drumming begins, slowly at first, then faster and faster, until it becomes a strange rolling beat. The sound is made by the quick motion of the wings against the air and it's a wonderful sight to watch a cock partridge standing on a mossy log in dappled sunlight with his tail spread wide and low, his head high and the ruff lifted, flashing his wings in the wild drumming ceremony. One of the strange things about partridge drumming is that it fools the best of woodsmen. Often when you go straight to the place where you think the sound starts you find that it is either to one side or the other, and like as not much farther away than you thought.

The best partridge country around here is close to Jumping Sand Spring, which is just off the trail on the way to the settlement. Chief Tibeash showed it to me years ago and I never fail to stop by that clear cold spring on my trips out. The Indians have used it for generations and the great canoe birch that rises above the spring is covered with messages and marks they left on their travels.

When you come to a stand of pine where the trail joins an old tote road along which pale green grass grows between two red lines of dry pine spills that have settled in the shallowed ruts, you are near Jumping Sand Spring. I never have known what it is about a spring that makes a man want to keep its location to himself. Maybe it's just because he wants to feel that it is his own. But that's the way it is with most of them, so the path to Jumping Sand Spring has no blaze to mark it. You know it by an old pine, where you turn sharp left, and walk down a short slope into a clearing where the fireweed blooms in August. Right there you are more than likely to flush a partridge, be it spring or fall, for the cover is right for them and the feeding is to their liking. Standing there by the spring where the woods thin out toward a swamp, you can look west across Caterwaul Creek to Lobstick Hill, which is close to the portage to Megusee Lake. It is fine country.

JUNE

Soft Twilights and Fireflies

Pipsissewa – the young leaves make good nibbling

DAWN is the best hour of a summer day and every now and then I get up early and walk to the rise back of the cabin to watch the sun ride up over the edge of the dark forest that stretches mile after mile to the eastward. The air at daybreak is as cool and sweet as spring water and is fragrant of the earth—the good strong smells of wet and rotting wood, balsam and spruce, and the aromatic scent of bracken drenched with dew. And like as not I catch the faint sweetness of pipsissewa blossoms and come on shinleaf flowers, the lily-of-the-valley of the deep woods, nodding on their slender stalks.

By the time I get to the top of the ridge the gray light of the false dawn has passed and the shadows, like the night animals, are seeking the dark places of the woods to hide until twilight comes again. Soon the sky is flooded with color and little clouds float low over the broken line of the tree tops.

Ever since I was a boy I have enjoyed shaping clouds into pictures. One morning recently, as I watched the day breaking, the golden sky took the form of a lake and the little dark cloud streaks were canoes—the big six-fathom birch bark canoes of the fur brigade that every spring long, long ago glided past the shore of Cache Lake. It took eight to ten *voyageurs* to paddle those big fellows and their high bows were painted with pictures of animals and birds. They could carry three tons of freight apiece. Chief

128

Tibeash says the crews would paddle steadily for about two hours singing songs of the great north country, and then rest for one smoke.

The bowman was the most important member of the crew and the steersman came second. Once they had been chosen for the coveted place the bowmen had the right to choose their crews. Rivalry was strong among the canoes of the fur brigade and often the men would grease the bottoms of their craft with pork fat to make them run faster. When the wind was favorable spruce masts were lashed to the bow gunwales and tarpaulins or blankets rigged for sails and then for a few hours the men would lie back and rest while the canoes sped along. When the wind failed or changed, the crew went back to work and the rhythmic thumping of the paddle shafts against the gunwales broke the stillness of the north.

Coming up to a portage they always started a race to the landing place and the water was lashed to a white froth by flashing paddles as the fleet sped like a great brown wedge toward the shore. The canoes were never beached, but were unloaded while still floating in shallow water so that the bottoms would not be damaged, and not until they were empty were they lifted out. Each crew had a supply of birch bark, pitch, and spruce roots to close leaking seams or mend tears in the hulls.

At night the *voyageurs* camped on the shore, eating huge amounts of bannock and fried pork washed down with strong tea. In fair weather they wouldn't bother with tents but just rolled in their blankets on deep beds of balsam boughs. Long before daylight their breakfast fires would be going and the brigade was on its way by sun up. About ten o'clock they usually stopped for a tin of tea and a rest. Those were good days!

June is a great family month in the big woods. The Indians call it Wawe Pesim, the Egg Moon, for this is the height of the nesting season and the birds are wearing their most colorful feathers and singing their sweetest songs.

Shin-leaf

There is a great difference between the songs of the birds in June and their calls in other months. As for plummage, some of the most brilliantly colored males will not even look like the same birds next winter.

The young animals are big enough to go out with the old folks now, and I have already seen a family of skunks, the mother leading the way followed by five little fellows about the size of small kittens. Skunks make good pets, just as gentle as can be if you get them young enough and don't scare them while they are getting used to you.

Over by Snow Goose Lake not long ago I saw four fox pups in front of their burrow. Nice little fellows they were and full of mischief. Most of the time they were playing with feathers that were left from their meals, for right now they depend on food their parents bring them but pretty soon they will begin to hunt their own as nature planned.

The little black pincushion children of the porcupine are now about six weeks old and the old ones have come down from their perches in the trees and now spend a lot of time in the meadows feeding on new grass. At night they often go down to the shores of the ponds to eat the tender young shoots of the arrow plant and lilies. The young muskrats are still keeping pretty close to the houses though the mothers may let them out to look around on warm days. They will soon be swimming and learning the ways of muskrat life. The baby weasels and minks are already going out with their mothers to learn the ways of these savage little hunters. I hate to think of the number of birds' nests they will rob as they hunt day and night, for they never seem to get enough.

Soon after I got up one morning I noticed a wood thrush carrying a good-sized shred of birch bark to a bush just outside my cabin. After a while the bird came back with another piece of bark and placed it a mite distant from the other. Well, by nightfall that thrush had started building a nest between the two pieces of birch bark, and by the next afternoon the job was finished. I was curious about the pieces of birch bark beside the nest, so during early evening when the birds were away I went out and lifted them off the limb and dropped them on the ground. To my everlasting surprise, when I got up the next morning the pieces of bark were back on the limb beside the nest. I can't for the life of me understand why the birds wanted them there, but I didn't touch them again. It is a privilege to have a pair of wood thrushes build their nest beside my cabin.

The robins break the dawn for me these days and a mighty pleasant way to be wakened it is. Almost always the next thing I hear is a phoebe bird, and then like as not a big flicker begins to drum on a dead birch limb up on the ridge. What's more he has to talk about his job and I can tell you there's no sleeping once he starts.

One of the pleasant things about June is watching the bull bats gliding about in the still air at twilight. I envy them, it looks so easy. Though their common name is nighthawk, they are really not hawks at all, but much more like whip-poor-wills and about the same size, though their wings are pointed and their tail forked. Some folks call them mosquito hawks, pork-and-beans bird, burnt-land bird, or chimney bats. In flight you can tell them from whip-poor-wills by the white spots on the underside of their wings. They tell me some of these birds go as far north as the Arctic Ocean in the summer and then winter in South America. Like whip-poor-wills, they have very big mouths which open wide to scoop up insects.

The nighthawks lay their eggs on bare ground and, surprising as it may seem, often raise a family on the flat gravel roofs of city buildings. Maybe you have heard them on a quiet evening making a booming sound which is caused by air rushing through the feathers of their wings when they dive or turn quickly. They only make that sound during the breeding season. Their eggs look for all the world like pieces of gravel and even the little birds are so protected by color that they might be just little bits of rock or moss. Nighthawks spend the sunny part of the day resting on the ground or maybe on a rocky place, but come evening you will see them in the sky.

On still, warm evenings the darkness is filled with hundreds of tiny twinkling lights as the lightning bugs fly about in the open places and along the shore, but not so much over the water. It is one of the sights of summer I never tire of watching. The light of the firefly, which is really a beetle, has no heat and is one of nature's many mysteries. Most people don't know that the eggs of the firefly and its grub, which we call a glowworm, give off a steady light.

Some years ago I worked with a Finnish miner who told me that in the old days in his country the only light the miners had in the underground workings was made by fireflies which they caught and put in bottles. He said their kind gave off more light than ours. Later I tried out the idea when I went into an old mining tunnel. At first I didn't think much of the lightning-bug lantern, but as my eyes got used to the darkness I found it quite a help. In certain parts of South America natives tie little nets filled with fireflies around their ankles to light their way on the dark damp jungle trails.

The Chief and I have been fishing a stream that runs into the Manitoupeepagee half a day's travel north and our luck was good, so we had all the fried brook trout we could eat. The black flies and mosquitoes are pretty bad right now, but we don't mind them much.

Coming over the Cache Lake carry on the way back we were talking about the best way of getting a canoe on your shoulders with the least work. It is a knack that once learned is never forgotten. Take hold of the canoe about five feet back from the end and give a quick lift, keeping your arms straight and stiff. As it goes up swing it over until the canoe is right above your head and then walk your hands down the gunwales until you are under the paddles where she will balance just right on your shoulders. And be sure the paddles are lashed tight to the thwarts. I have seen some nasty falls

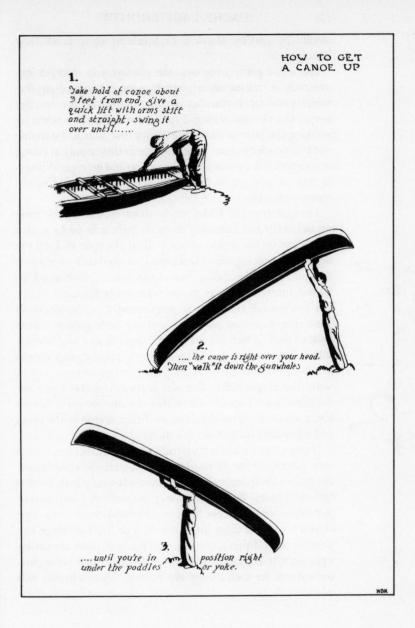

HOW TO GET
A CANOE UP

1.
Take hold of canoe about 3 feet from end, give a quick lift with arms stiff and straight, swing it over until......

2.
.... the canoe is right over your head. Then "walk" it down the gunwhales

3.
.... until you're in position right under the paddles or yoke.

HBK

caused by paddles slipping or breaking away from their lashings.

Once you get moving over the portage you soon get into the way of taking short steps that have a sort of rhythm which prevents the paddles jarring too hard on the shoulder bones. If a portage is long, I spell myself once in a while by hooking the bow of the canoe over a low limb and stepping out from under to rest. That trick saves the trouble of lifting it up again. There was a day when I would go right through without a stop just to be able to say I could do it. I've got more sense now.

On our trip the Chief made some spoons by cleaning mussel shells and fastening them on little split sticks with a notch cut on the inside of one half of the split to keep the shell from slipping out. He scraped off the black coating on the outside of the shells, wound the handles with string to hold them tight, and the spoons were ready for use.

I don't think there is any prettier sight in the woods in June than a mother partridge and her little golden brown balls of fluff, which are not much bigger than a hickory nut when they are hatched. The mother builds her nest on the ground and while she is hatching the pale brown eggs marked with darker spots of brown, she is always on the watch for enemies. Some people believe that the mother gives out no scent while she is on the nest, so if that is true when foxes and other enemies find her it is mostly by accident.

If you come on the hen partridge and her little ones, which may number from six to fifteen, or sometimes a few more, she gives a sharp little cluck and instantly every little golden ball disappears. If all our young ones obeyed like young partridges we would not have much trouble with them. Try as you will, once those little fellows hide it is just about impossible to find them, even though some of them are sitting right on top of dead brown leaves, because their color protects them. At such a time the mother, always brave, will

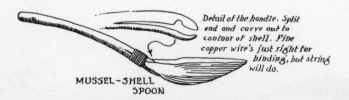

Detail of the handle. Split end and carve out to contour of shell. Fine copper wire's just right for binding, but string will do.

MUSSEL~SHELL
SPOON

flutter in front of you, pretending that she has a broken wing, dragging herself along with the hope that you will follow and be drawn away from her babies.

During a spring rain storm and at night, when the air may be chilly, the little ones snuggle under their mother's warm wings. In about two weeks young partridges begin to flutter into the air for short distances and by the time they are a month or six weeks old they can get off the ground in a hurry and fly quite a distance. In midsummer on warm dry days you see partridges in sunny places on an old tote road where they love to take dust baths. In the early spring they eat many insects and some vegetable foods, but later they turn to fruits and seeds. In winter the birds can stand very low temperatures and live on buds and even bits of bark.

These warm days the dogs spend a lot of time in the lake. Wolf just paddles at the edge, but Tripper has turned into a loon hound. Every time he sees one he starts swimming after it. The birds seem to enjoy it and they dive when the dog gets near. That always puzzles Tripper and you can almost see the smile on old Wolf's face as he watches from the shore. He is old enough to know you can't catch a loon that way.

I noticed a turtle sunning itself on a rock in the lake one day, so I got myself a piece of pine and whittled one just like it, but only an inch and a half long. I colored it with a mixture of roofing tar and kerosene, which makes a very good wood stain. You can wipe the stain on with a piece of cloth if you have no brush, and rub it off when you get just the shade you want. This kind of stain penetrates wood quickly, so if you want a light color wipe it off a few minutes after applying. You can get it as dark as you like by repeating the coats or by adding more tar to the kerosene. When I finished my turtle I glued it on a small piece of rock which gave it a lifelike appearance and made it useful as a paperweight.

Carving a turtle is not all I have been doing lately, for I made myself a horn to signal Hank at his cabin. It all started

when Hank's mother sent me an old buffalo horn that she found stored away in the attic in their home down in the city. Knowing us, she figured we were pretty sure to put it to some good use. Well, it didn't take me long to get to work. It made me sad to think of the days when hundreds of thousands of those big shaggy brown fellows roamed the western plains. Too bad they were killed off, although there are still a few left in the national parks. It just goes to show the need for laws to give the wild things a chance and at the same time let hunters have their share.

Making a horn is not very difficult, for all you have to do is cut the tip off about three inches from the point and then bore a hole so that the tip when reversed will fit into the horn to make a mouthpiece. Of course if a fellow had a regular bugle mouthpiece it would be even easier, but I like the idea of using what I had at hand. The wide end of the tip must be hollowed out so you can use your tongue to help make the right sounds. The tip is solid and it takes a little care and some patience to drill a hole through it. Once that is done a file helps to shape it into a mouthpiece. When I was finished I polished the horn by scraping it with a piece of broken glass, then I rubbed it down with fine sandpaper, and finally burnished it with a little chunk of soft pine covered with candle wax. I filed little grooves around the horn near each end to hold a rawhide thong in place.

Hank came over the day I finished the horn and found me practicing. He said all the critters in the woods must think some new animal with a terrible voice had come to the big woods, but I am proud of the sounds I make, and I am getting better all the time. The sounds all depend on the way you fit your lips into the mouthpiece and how you use your tongue to make different notes. Hank wanted me to try it some quiet evening to see if he could hear it at his cabin, which, as you know, is on Beaver Tail Lake, two miles away. He said he would try to signal me with his drum or fire a

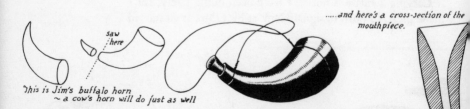

.....and here's a cross-section of the mouthpiece.

This is Jim's buffalo horn
~ a cow's horn will do just as well

saw here

shot from his gun if he heard it. Well, sir, at twilight one evening when the woods were as quiet as a sleeping mouse, I let loose several good strong blasts on the old horn and waited. I almost jumped out of my britches when I heard the faint thumping of Hank's drum answering me. We kept on signaling until I ran out of wind. I figure we can work out regular signals like three blasts for "Pie. Come and get it!"

As I have said before, Hank's a great fellow for building things, and now he has an idea to make one of those long wooden horns boatmen used on the rivers out west years ago. Mighty powerful and nice sounding they were, I hear.

Now that I have that horn finished, I have to get my camping outfit out and go over everything to make sure it is in good shape for a trip I am going on with the Chief and Hank in August. One thing I am right proud of is my old frying pan which has a square brass socket handle into which you can slip a long sapling and so cook away from the smoke and heat of the fire. The best kind of pan for camping is the common sheet type which is lighter and quicker heating than the cast iron ones. If you want to make one all you have to do is saw off the handle four inches from the rim and then rivet on a socket one inch square and four inches long. Copper or brass is best, and be sure to use flat-headed rivets so the sapling handle will slip in easily. A pan with such a short handle takes up very little room and certainly is handy for cooking.

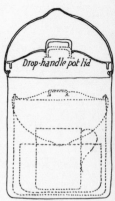

Drop-handle pot lid

NESTED COOKING KIT
~bend bail to keep pail hanging straight on stick over fire.

I like to travel light enough so that, if the portage is short, I can carry the canoe and my pack over in one trip. All the cooking and eating tools I need are my frying pan, two tin pails, a tin bowl and a cup that all nest into each other. There is also a tin plate, a large and a small spoon, and a knife and fork. That is all any man needs except a good sheath knife for cutting bacon, cleaning fish, and such like. And I make sure the handles on my pails are riveted or hooked on.

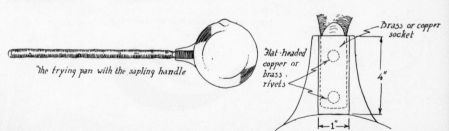

The frying pan with the sapling handle

Brass or copper socket

Flat-headed copper or brass rivets

4"

1"

I can carry the canoe over in one trip

Soldered handle-lugs melt off and drop your meal into the fire. If you can't get any other kind, melt the lugs off, punch holes through the pail just below the rim, and fit the handle hooks through them. I almost forgot to say that I always keep a quart can with a top that clinches on for my bacon fat. That is important, for fat is mighty good to fry fish in, to make biscuits, and for many other things. I keep every drop, for it is nourishing food in the woods, and you can't make good flapjacks without it. I keep coffee, tea, and pepper in tight cans, too. No need for a coffee pot. A pail is just as good and a sight easier to clean.

Maybe you have other ideas, but I like to carry most of my grub in little canvas sacks. I'm not much of a needle-worker, but every man in the woods has to learn to sew on buttons and stitch up rips in his clothes, so I knew how to sew up some canvas bags for beans, prunes, apricots, oatmeal, sugar, rice, and raisins. They are about fourteen inches long and nine inches wide with bigger ones for the flour and sugar, but everyone has his own ideas on size. I dip the bags in melted candle wax, then slosh them in hot water to take out the extra wax. That treatment helps to keep out the dampness. I sew deer-hide thongs near the tops to tie them up. Cord or cotton tape would do, or a leather shoelace. Don't forget they have to be hung or packed in pails in camp, so mice and squirrels won't get at them. They love the wax as well as the contents.

I am reminded to tell you about the needles I carry in my packsack just in case I snag my pants. I can use any of those needles to find my way if I ever lose my compass. I have a magnet and I rub the needles across the open end before I start on a trip. All you have to do to use one as a compass is to grease it slightly with a little bacon fat or rub it across a candle and then, holding it in a looped grass blade, lower it very quietly into a puddle of water. It will at once swing in a North-South line, but what you want to be sure of is to test the needles by your compass before you leave so you will know which end points North. Or if you have no

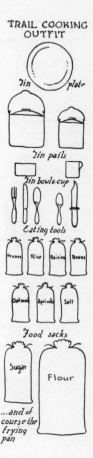

TRAIL COOKING OUTFIT

Tin   plate

Tin pails

Tin bowl & cup

Eating tools

Prunes Rice Raisins Beans

Oatmeal Apricots Salt

Food sacks

Sugar   Flour

...and of course the frying pan

*When you magnetize
needles always do
them in the same
direction so you
won't get mixed
up later*

*Lower the
needle in with
a blade of grass*

compass handy you could check it by the North Star, which is easily found by sighting along the up-and-down stars on the end of the Great Dipper. The North Star points to the earth's North Pole, which is not exactly the same as the North Magnetic Pole to which the compass needle points. But for all general purposes that will be close enough. Don't put the needle in water in a metal pail for then it will be influenced by the metal. It is better to make a very small pool about the size of a cup at the edge of a lake or brook, and after placing the needle in it stand back just as you do with a compass so your knife or any other metal on you won't disturb it.

Just to amuse himself Hank magnetized his hunting knife and, tying a thread to it at a point where it would balance, suspended it from the thread. For a while the knife revolved and finally came to rest with the blade pointing North as Hank proved with his compass. We agreed it was a good idea but it takes too long for the knife to come to rest to be any good except in an emergency.

As a matter of fact if a fellow didn't have a magnet in the woods there is a way of making one if you can get hold of a bar of steel. It must be steel, not iron. An old piece of drill steel or a good-sized file would do. The only other tool you need is a hammer. The idea is to line up the steel bar with the earth's magnetic field, which is North, or that is close enough. You can get that easily by sighting on the Pole Star. Then, keeping the bar lined up with the North, set one end down on something solid and, holding the other end up at an angle corresponding to the latitude for your location, strike it several hard blows with the hammer. Just to give you an example if you live in the vicinity of forty-five degrees north latitude you would hold the steel up at a forty-five degree angle. The hammering lines up the steel with the earth's magnetic field and so magnetizes the bar. Once that is done you have a permanent bar magnet for magnetizing needles.

And there is still another way of magnetizing a needle.

*To make a
PERMANENT
BAR
MAGNET*

*47°
(approx)* →North

*Align steel rod or bar (not iron)
with earth's magnetic field, by pointing
to North Star ~ due north, pointing up at an
elevation corresponding with latitude (Cache
Lake 47°, NewYork City 42°, Florida 20°)*

If you have a wet or dry battery and a coil of fine wire made of about 100 turns, you simply insert the needle in the coil and hook the two ends to the battery for a few seconds and the job is done. As a matter of fact, if you have an odd piece of copper and a piece of zinc, a glass jar or crock, and a little caustic soda, you can make a fine wet battery. You make up a solution of one part by weight of caustic soda to four parts of water and then suspend the plates by wires in the solution from wooden rods. The copper plate is the positive pole and the zinc plate is the negative side.

If you magnetize a bar by the hammering method it is interesting to suspend it on a string so that it just balances, and you will find that the north pole of the bar will slowly swing to the North.

While he was visiting us one time, Mr. Beedee made a compass from nothing but a little round pill box, a pin, and an empty .22 caliber cartridge, with the transparent covering from a cigarette package for a top. The cartridge was used for the bearing for the pointer, so he sharpened a nail, wrapped paper around it until it exactly fitted the cartridge, and tapped it lightly to get a little indentation in the center of the cap so that it would balance nicely on a pin which was fastened to the center of the pill box with a few drops of glue. He bent the pin near the head to form a little base so that it would hold firmly when it was glued down. Then he took a magnetized needle and fastened it to the top of the cartridge with a drop of the tar that I use for patching my roof. Glue would do just as well. We all gathered around when he tested it and sure enough the needle swung straight to the North.

I made one for myself, making the case of half an inch of birch bark from a decayed sapling about two inches in diameter from which I could clean the soft wood just as we do for making candle molds. The little circle of birch bark

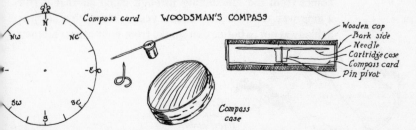

Compass card   WOODSMAN'S COMPASS

Wooden cap
Bark side
Needle
Cartridge case
Compass card
Pin pivot

Compass case

about half an inch high was glued on a flat piece of bark and when it was dry I trimmed it to the shape of the circle.

You can also make a compass by using an old safety razor blade instead of a needle for the pointer. The bearing which revolves on the pin is half an inch of lead pencil with a small hole drilled into the lead about an eighth of an inch from the end. The piece of pencil is then whittled to fit the middle opening in the razor blade and then twisted to hold between the edges.

All this talk about compasses gets me to thinking about the weather and I wonder what we would do without it. It is my belief that in addition to giving us our lakes and streams, the forests and the crops, the weather has done more than any one thing in nature to help men to make friends. Some folks are naturally quiet and many are shy and do not seem to know how to get going with other people, but once you get them started by talking about the weather they are pretty sure to open up. It is just like driving a wedge into a log that is hard to split. A man may have no opinion on politics or what the world is coming to, but he is pretty sure to have an opinion on the weather. For, be it sunshine, rain, a blizzard, or a hurricane, the weather means something to every living one of us.

I met one of my best and oldest friends on a train and our friendship began when he glanced out the window and said, "That sky's a weather breeder or I'm no judge of what looks like a mare's tail!" And I met another fellow, who writes me to this very day, when we made camp close to one another on the shore of a lake, and got to talking about weather signs.

The Chief warns that it is risky to put your faith in any one sign. The thing to do is to watch several signs and see how they check up. Take a yellow sunset, for example. That is pretty often a sign of a storm, because the color comes from the sun shining through damp air that is still a long way off. When you see a yellow sunset you are just as likely as not to notice that smoke from your cabin chimney

Greased
needle in
small puddle

drops down toward the ground instead of rising, the reason being that when the atmospheric pressure begins to fall smoke finds it hard to rise. And if there is a ring around the moon on the night of a yellow sunset you can be pretty sure rain is on the way. If the ring is fairly clear in outline the rain may not reach you for a day, but if it is a soft or misty circle it will not be long coming.

Another sign that may mean stormy weather is that earthy, rainy smell you sometimes notice before a storm, especially near a muddy pond or marshy place. Some of this odor, which at times is very unpleasant, is caused by marsh gas escaping from the mud at the bottom of the pond, where it is formed by rotting vegetation. This gas is most likely to bubble up from the bottom when the atmospheric pressure is low as it usually is before a storm. When the pressure is high and the weather clear most of the gas is held at the bottom. When I was a boy I would row out on a pond and drive a pole into the bottom and touch a match to the gas when it came to the top in the form of bubbles. Makes quite a flare for a second or so. In addition to the gas, low atmospheric pressure has a tendency to keep odors close to the ground, which accounts for all kinds of strong woods scents, including the musky smell of animals just before a spell of bad weather.

Everybody knows that old saying:

> A rainbow in the morning
>   Is the shepherd's warning;
> A rainbow at night
>   Is the sailor's delight.

And it makes sense, for a morning rainbow is caused by the light of the rising sun striking wet clouds to the west, which may mean wet weather is heading your way. But a rainbow at night reverses the direction and the setting sun shines on clouds to the east, which if the prevailing wind in your section is from the west, should mean the stormy area has passed by.

Thunderstorms don't occur as often here as they do in

some parts of the country, but when they do they are generally rip snorters, and if we are outdoors we think the wisest thing to do is to take to shelter. For myself, I don't care to be out on an open lake in a canoe in a thunderstorm, for aside from the heavy seas that the squalls kick up, you may be a target for lightning. I have been told that it is not a good idea to stand in an open place, such as a beach or a clearing, where you are the highest thing above the ground for some distance around.

If I am on the water I generally see it coming in time to get ashore, pull the canoe up into heavy cover and get under it. The Chief has a belief that you are safe under a big birch and he will make for one every time if there is a tree handy. I have seen some birches struck by lightning, but not nearly as many as I have pines, which the "fire from the sky," as the Chief calls it, seems to head for. If I am up on a rocky ridge where there are not many trees I make sure to get down on the side of the slope and away from any high pinnacles of rock that might tempt the lightning. But it is all a gamble and the chances of getting struck by lightning are pretty small.

I suppose you know that a mackerel sky, the kind with streaks or rippling lines like the markings on a mackerel, is pretty sure to mean that rain will come your way within a day's time. And if the clouds stream out in thin, curving lines that folks call "mares' tails" the rainstorm may be only half a day away and is likely to last quite a spell.

A mackerel swimming across a mackerel sky

We have a lot of herring gulls up here on our lakes and the Chief told me long ago that they are apt to stay on the water or sit on the rocks when a storm is coming. I asked about that and a weatherman told me it might be because it is harder for a bird to fly when the barometric pressure is low than during a high pressure spell. And sitting gulls and ducks just about always face the wind, and even when the breeze is so light it is hard to tell the direction, you can make sure by watching the water birds.

When the Chief is planning a trip he is pretty sure to go

Herring gull starting out for day's work.

out and look at the grass just before he turns in for the
night. If there is no sign of dew he knows that clouds are
making up and that the weather may take a wet turn. But
if the night is calm and clear and the stars show, there is
pretty sure to be a good dew and that with other signs is
likely to mean a good day to come.

To most people dew is just the moisture on the grass that
soaks your feet when you go out early in the day. I have
asked many a man how the dew forms and it is surprising
how few know. Matter of fact, dew is moisture that comes
from the air, the ground, and many plants, that condenses
when the earth, rocks, trees, and plants begin to cool off
by radiating or giving up the heat stored in them by the sun.

A good example of how dew forms is to fill a glass with
cold water on a warm day and pretty soon it begins to
"sweat," which is just the same way dew forms by warm
moist air condensing on a cold object. Some plants seem to
be able to throw off heat better than others. Those with
soft, fuzzy leaves, such as the mullein plant, which is covered
with a growth of very fine vegetable hairs, cools quickly
and that is why you find a heavy coat of dew on the soft
leaves.

Most people do not know that a dewdrop is a little mirror
and if you take the trouble to get up some morning and get
down on your knees, whether you get wet or not, you will
see on the crystal surface of each drop the image of nearby
trees and even the clouds. Of course the picture is upside
down, but that does not matter, and just to look at it is a
sight worth getting up for.

While you are at it, watch for the beautiful pattern of
the dewdrops on cobwebs, and note the way the drops form
on the horizontal threads of the spider's web while the small
vertical threads hold practically no dew. The dewdrops
on a spider's web remind me of pearls strung on a fine silk
thread.

I like to look at the dew forms on grass blades, too. These
drops are particularly fine for reflecting images. The point

June is one of our best months

of the blade of grass often holds one large drop with smaller ones arranged in perfect spacing along the sharp edge of the blade.

A flower garden on a morning when the dew is heavy gives up its fragrance in a way that you don't seem to find at any other time, and if you keep your eyes open you may find a caterpillar sleeping on a stalk with every hair on its back topped by a tiny dewdrop.

Getting back to weather signs, it has been my observation that when clouds are riding high in the sky, which means little moisture, the weather is pretty sure to be fine. And I might say that when clouds in general begin to disappear it is a sign the moisture is evaporating in dry air and that the weather will be good.

In my part of the country the west wind is what we call the fair one. An easterly, especially in the fall and winter, may bring a change in the weather, as does a warm southerly wind with falling pressure. The north wind is our cool wind. Knowing what to expect from the winds and observing other signs make a combination for fairly accurate weather forecasting.

You do not have to worry about much bad weather in June, for it is one of our best months and everything is so fresh and clean you like to be about in the woods as much as you can. The first of the Indian families that spend the summer on Snow Goose Lake has passed down in their birch canoe and I was glad to see them again. The mother was in the bow and just back of her, with a puppy in her arms, was a little girl called Nanugayna, which means "a small star." Back near his father and working hard with a short paddle, was my friend, a boy named Neebeeshshay, which is Cree for "wind blown leaves." But I never can say his name, so I just call him David, and he likes it. I will be going down to visit them when they get settled.

JULY

The Moose Are in the Lakes

THE BIG WOODS are hot and dry and quiet these days, for we have come to summer's halfway mark and nature is pausing for a rest on the portage from spring to fall. The rains are past, the growing season is over, and now come the dog days when Sirius, the Dog Star, rises and sets with the sun.

The days of July are long and sunny and even the winds seem too lazy to blow, which gives all the insect pests a chance to make life miserable for man and beast. The moose and the deer are in the quiet coves and backwaters of the streams trying to escape the tormenting winged pests, which make them lose some of their fear of man. Paddling through the narrows from Snow Goose Lake with Chief Tibeash recently we came on seven moose up to their necks in the water and in no mood to get out of the way of our canoe. Not until the Chief whacked his cupped hands together to make a report like a gun did they plunge back toward shore where they watched us pass and quickly returned to the cool protection of the mud and water where juicy lily roots helped to make them forget their misery. No, sir, you are never quite sure of the mind of a moose in fly time. It is best to give him the right of way. The antlers of the deer and moose are out of the velvet stage now and are growing hard and strong.

There's no mistaking a July evening. Often the sun sets in a blaze of red and heat waves dance over the open rocky places. In the hush of twilight when the smoke rises in a

Two moose in fly-time.

slow, wavering streak you can hear the solemn croaking of the herons flying across to some night feeding place. The air is filled with the hum of the mosquitoes and you can hear the crazy laugh of a loon echoing in the hills.

To be sure, July has its good points, but if anyone asked me which month could best be spared if summer had to be shortened, I think I would say July. The Indians call it Aupascen o Pesim, the Month When the Birds Cast Their Feathers. They are lucky to be molting during the hot days. This month brings the worst insect pests of the year, the common black fly, the mosquito, and the midge, or no-see-um, as the Indians call them. The black fly is small enough, but the midge is still smaller and you can't see either one of them coming. You just feel them. There is one good thing about black flies: they go to bed early and as soon as the sun sets they disappear. But the midge and the mosquito are sleepless and bloodthirsty pests.

Head nets are some help, but mosquito netting is too coarse to keep out the black flies. If you use a net it must be of cheesecloth, which is pretty hot around your head on a warm day. I rely on plenty of fly dope and my favorite is made of about three ounces of pine tar, three ounces of vaseline, and one ounce of citronella. Mix it thoroughly in a can set in boiling water, and then put it in small cans or wide-mouthed bottles. The vaseline, being thick, helps to keep the dope on your face longer than the liquid types and is easier to carry. One fellow I know adds a little camphor to make the dope that much more hateful to the insects. I have used bear grease in place of the vaseline in a pinch, but it is apt to get rancid and unpleasant in warm weather. Another dope I have used is made of pine tar with olive oil taking the place of vaseline, and one ounce of pennyroyal. Pine tar is too harsh for the skin of some folks, in which case the citronella and pennyroyal will have to do. When camphor is used it should be dissolved in grain alcohol before mixing with the rest of the ingredients.

When you turn in at night you want to make sure that

your tent is free of insects. There is only one thing to do about mosquitoes, and that is to chase them and swat them. Likely as not you will find the midges on the front of the tent down near the bottom while the black flies are at the top where it is lighter and warmer. But what is better than swatting is a D.D.T. bomb filled with a gas that clears a tent of insects in no time. To be sure it is just another piece of gear to carry, but one of those bombs is worth a lot in good sleep free of bugs that bite.

The Snowy Tree-Cricket is some-times called the Temperature Cricket.

You hear people say that at this time of year it is so hot that even the birds haven't got enough energy to sing. Maybe there is a little truth in that, but the main reason they are quiet is that all the excitement of the mating season and nest building is over. I suspect, too, that while the young ones are still inexperienced about keeping out of trouble the old folks are not anxious to let anyone know where the family is feeding. You hear them singing a little early in the morning or in the evening, but the fine rich songs of May and June are gone and as a matter of fact, you don't see very much of the birds these days, for they keep to the shade of the deep woods and spend quite a lot of time close to the waterways.

Although most of the tree swallows have raised their families, we still find a few nesting, sometimes in a knothole or in an abandoned woodpecker's nest. Their nests are usually made of straw and feathers. Tree swallows do not depend entirely on insects for living, because they can also eat berries, which few other swallows like. On pleasant days you see them darting about in the warm air, especially toward evening, but if it cools off quickly they will suddenly disappear and won't be seen again until the weather warms up. From what I have observed at such times they go into the woods or the hills where they are sheltered from cool air.

We also see cedar waxwings—some call them cedar or cherry birds—nesting this month, and if you put out little shreds of cloth or string where they can find it you can be pretty sure that it will be woven into their nests. They also like the soft outer bark of grapevines and cedar trees and line their nests with very fine roots.

Outside my window in the hush of the evening I can hear a tree cricket chirping. Its full name is the snowy tree cricket. Only the males chirp and one of the interesting things about them is that you can tell the temperature from their song. Just count the number of chirps per minute, subtract forty, divide the result by four, add fifty, and the result will be the temperature within a degree or so. If you don't believe me, try it yourself and you will be convinced.

Tiger
Swallowtail

Now is the season when you see a great many butterflies, and it is mighty interesting to walk through a grassy place in a clearing and watch them rise up and flutter away in the quiet air; and at night the moths come by the hundreds drawn by the light in the window.

I wonder if you have ever noticed that the butterflies seem to dress to suit the season in which they fly? In the spring before the leaves come out and the woods are still drab and colorless, most of the butterflies are the dark-winged kind marked with some brown and black. Often you will find them when patches of snow are still on the ground. When the skunk cabbage sprouts and the timid violets show their flowers, you will see small blue butter-flies, while later when the woods have put on the full bright dress of spring, the big swallow tails come with colors that gleam like brushed metal, and others with stripes and belts of bright colors flutter through the woods. In the clearings the little white and yellow butterflies appear, and all about the woods are the small ones with warm brown and black wings. When the summer sun is highest and all the blossoms are out you will notice that the butterflies flying then often show copper colors and spotted patterns with black and red to catch the eye and suggest that autumn is on the way. Then there are others with spots that look like polished silver on the lower side of the wings, while some show peacock's eyes. The color of the moths usually suggests the darkness in which they fly, although you often see the little

Black
Swallowtail

Spicebush
Swallowtail

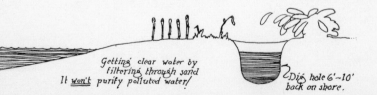

Direction of
current

Hitch rope
on side of
thwart
nearest
puller

white and yellow butterflies fluttering at the lighted window.

There is no greater pleasure than studying butterflies and the best way is to get yourself a book with accurately colored illustrations so that you can learn to know each one. You don't have to go far to find butterflies, for some love the shady places where brooks flow quietly, and others the hillsides. The forest meadows where the wild flowers look to the sun are the favorite place of many.

Two young fellows came through on a canoe trip and stopped by Hank's while I was there one day, and as it was close to sundown we asked them to pitch their tent close by and spend the evening with us. Mighty nice boys they were, and interested in learning all they could about woodcraft, especially about handling a canoe. Seems they had quite a tussle getting up some of the streams and had forgotten to bring along any line for "tracking," which is what we call hauling a canoe up fast water.

What you do is hitch your rope on the forward or middle thwart and one fellow goes ashore and pulls the canoe up the stream while the other stays in and keeps her off rocks. If you hitch your rope to the bow ring the canoe is pulled toward the shore, which is wrong, but with the rope tied to a thwart the canoe will pull up stream fairly straight and sometimes the current will hold her out without any steering.

Of course you can pole up a stream, too. We use a pole about twelve feet long with an iron spike in the end, but you want to be sure of your balance before you try that.

The choice of method depends, of course, on the kind of stream you are in. Where the current is too swift for poling, tracking is the best way.

These boys were surprised that the water in some of the lakes up here is so brown, and I told them how it gets that way from so much vegetation. Lumbering also turns water brown. Maybe you know the old trick of clearing water when you have to take it from a murky lake by digging

Getting clear water by
filtering through sand
It won't purify polluted water!

Dig hole 6'-10'
back on shore.

a hole back from the shore, maybe six to ten feet. A sandy beach is the best place and when you get down to the water level it filters through and the sand screens out most of the sediment. Bail out the hole several times and soon the water will come in almost clear. Mind you, filtering does not necessarily purify polluted water, which is something a fellow wants to be on the watch for. If you are in doubt the safe thing to do is to boil it. Another method is to put two drops—no more—of iodine to a gallon of water. That kills dangerous germs. If water has an unpleasant taste or smell, drop some charcoal from your fire into it while it is boiling. The charcoal will absorb the objectionable taste.

One of the things I did this summer was to make myself a grass cutter, and I do not mind saying that I am just a mite proud of it. Up here we do not have lawn mowers and could not use them if we had, but just the same the grass in the clearing around the cabin has to be kept down. I took a metal hoop from an old flour barrel and bent it into a triangular shape and set it into a slot sawed in the end of a light dry spruce sapling, where it is held in place by nails driven through and clinched. I filed the bottom blade on both sides until it was very sharp. Then all I had to do was to walk along and swing it back and forth at my side, and down came the tall grass. It is much better than a sickle because I do not have to bend over. The lighter the metal the better because a sort of whipping motion gives best results. A nail keg hoop would be even better than one from a flour barrel, but I had none.

These are days when an afternoon nap is pleasant, and that reminds me of barrel-stave hammocks. Hank made one with hay wire woven in and out between the staves on both sides and in the middle, with loops at the end to hang it. Some bore holes in the ends of the staves and weave the wire through them. Also good sash cord can be used in place of the wire for such a hammock. To my way of thinking this type is more restful than other kinds of hammock where you are doubled up most of the time.

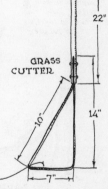

22"

GRASS
CUTTER

10"

14"

File both sides to a
sharp edge

7"

A friend of mine who lived down in the jungles of Brazil for a while brought home one of the hammocks that the people down there use. It is nearly seven feet long and five feet wide, and looks much the same as our old-fashioned woven hammocks. It is the extra width that counts, for the Brazilians sleep in it catty-cornerwise and lie almost as flat as if they were in a bed. These hammocks are hand-woven and some have extra fancy edgings. He says they are very cool for sleeping so I asked him to get me one to try out on hot nights up here.

Hank loves to stretch out in his stave hammock between two pines close to the shore of the lake and watch the young ducks feeding along the lake shore. Some of them are so tame we can feed them by hand. One day a family of mergansers came by, the mother in the lead, with six little fellows paddling along behind and one riding on her back. And in the woods you see other kinds of young, especially the half-grown whiskey jacks and chubby little bluebirds. You can hear them calling to their parents for food; it seems they are always hungry and a young bird often eats more than its own weight in a day. Hank always has his binoculars handy and he lies back as comfortable as you please and studies the birds by the hour.

These long and sultry July days I relish a glass of raspberry shrub, or raspberry vinegar, a mighty fine hot-weather drink. The way I make it is to crush two and a half quarts of raspberries—wild if you can find them for best flavor— and drop them into a quart of good cider vinegar. Some say wine vinegar makes it better. Anyway, you cover the berries and vinegar for about four days, stirring now and then. After that you strain the mixture through a flannel bag, but cotton sheeting will do, and boil the liquid for fifteen minutes. Before you start the boiling, add half a pound of sugar to a pint of liquid. Skim the froth off as it boils and

Wires go over and under each stave, are twisted together in between.

BARREL-STAVE HAMMOCK

Bring wires together into a loop for hanging

With one downy youngster riding on her back

then pour into clean, boiled bottles and cork until you use it. If you want your drink sweeter you can add sugar when you mix. About a tablespoonful of shrub to a glass of cold water is right for most folks. Ice makes it extra nice.

It is getting close to the time for our camping trip, so I have been putting my canoe in top condition for traveling. It is built of cedar strips an inch wide with ribs every three inches and is finished with spar varnish in the natural color of the wood. Best canoe I have ever owned—broad and flat bottomed at the center to carry a heavy load, with a fine clean-cutting bow which is not so high as to catch the wind and make paddling hard. She weighs just seventy-five pounds.

On long trips I always carry a six-foot square of oiled balloon cloth with brass grommets set in the edges. Its main purpose is to give me a leg-o'-mutton sail for the canoe when the wind is right, for I'm not one to paddle all day if a friendly breeze will let me sit back and take it easy. This combination sail and tarpaulin also serves as a waterproof cover for wrapping my blankets while traveling and comes in handy as extra bedding on cool nights. By folding it in half and lacing the grommets along the two edges I get a light duffel bag.

Used as a sail the square is folded diagonally and the sides laced together with a light cord. The peak is fastened to a mast made of a light spruce or balsam sapling by means of a half-hitch so that the sail can be dropped instantly in case of a dangerous squall. I use another very light sapling for a boom and with a length of line for a sheet I can handle the sail nicely. When I'm alone I use the sail only for running before the wind, but if I have a partner with me I get him to hold his paddle over the side to act as a leeboard and while it is impossible to head very close to the wind, long reaches can be taken to work up-wind pretty well. To be sure that

RASPBERRY SHRUB!

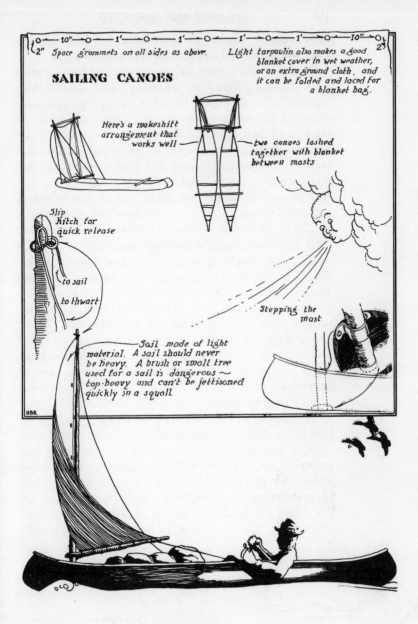

2" Space grommets on all sides as above.

Light tarpaulin also makes a good blanket cover in wet weather, or an extra ground cloth, and it can be folded and laced for a blanket bag.

SAILING CANOES

Here's a makeshift arrangement that works well

two canoes lashed together with blanket between masts

Slip hitch for quick release

to sail

to thwart

Stepping the mast

Sail made of light material. A sail should never be heavy. A brush or small tree used for a sail is dangerous — top-heavy and can't be jettisoned quickly in a squall

HBK

little square is another thing to carry, but it weighs less than two pounds and it never fails to earn its keep.

Once in a while when we are traveling with two canoes and have a long stretch of fair sailing ahead, we lash them together a few feet apart by means of saplings across the stern and the forward thwarts, rig a couple of saplings in the bow of each canoe and hoist my tarpaulin sail full size between them like a square sail. Canoes securely lashed this way are very seaworthy, and it is good sport sitting back taking it easy while the wind carries you along.

If you haven't done much sailing and are new to canoes and north woods waters leave sails alone and stick to your paddle. If you go over in the cold waters of a wilderness lake there is no one to help and you won't last long.

The same thought holds true for outboard motors, which are mighty handy if you can get fuel without too much trouble, but the tendency is to drive them too fast, and in strange waters, particularly in lumbering country, you may smash a canoe on a submerged tree or a "dead man" (wandering water-logged piece of timber) not to mention the rocks that lie just under the water in many shallow lakes. What is more, you will have a chance to see the country better for a good workout with a paddle at a slower pace.

For portaging a canoe I favor a yoke. Paddles can be lashed to the thwarts, which is always good enough, but they are hard on the shoulders. Some woodsmen like the kind of yoke used for carrying pails of water, but my portaging frame is simple—just two pieces of spruce or pine two and one-half inches wide and one and three-quarters inches thick, held apart at the ends by crosspieces to fit on the gunwales. On this frame can be riveted leather or webbing straps four inches wide. The straps must fit loosely to slip them side-

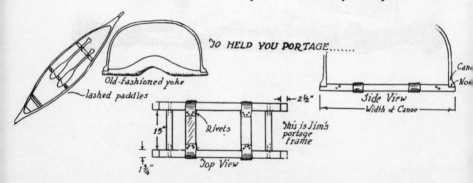

To HELP YOU PORTAGE.......

Old-Fashioned yoke

lashed paddles

Side View
Width of Canoe

2½"

15"

Rivets

This is Jim's portage frame

1¾"

Top View

ways for a comfortable spot on your shoulders. Where the
ends of the frame fit on the gunwales cut a notch three-
quarters of an inch deep, which keeps it from sliding off.
One side of the frame is then lashed to the thwart. For the
shoulder straps I got some discarded machine belting from
a machine shop. It is a fine rig and makes a long portage seem
short.

Another help on a portage is knowing the trick of getting
a heavy packsack on your back. The Chief showed me how
when I first began traveling with him years ago. Put the
packsack at your feet with its back toward you and take hold
of the shoulder straps with both hands. Then bend your
right leg so that you can pull the pack up and rest it on your
knee. The next step is to drop your right shoulder down so
that your right arm can slip through the shoulder strap,
the one on your left as you face the back of the pack. Then
swing your left arm behind you and grasp the other shoulder
strap, give a quick heave, and the pack swings into place on
your back and your left arm slips through its proper strap
with ease. Small as he is, the Chief can still beat Hank and
me at lifting a hundred-pound pack.

One piece of gear I couldn't get along without is a tump
line. Don't know who invented it, but it is about the handiest
thing you can have on the trail and the fellow who thought
of it discovered another way to put your head to work.
Mine is made from two straps of moose rawhide eight feet
long riveted to a headband three inches wide and eighteen
inches long. With a tump line you can carry a load of firewood as easily as you can a blanket roll or pack, and it can
be used to track a canoe up a rapids or lash the load on a sled.

HOW TO LIFT A HEAVY PACK

1. Wrestle the pack up onto your right knee.....

2. then put your right arm through it's strap, grab the other with your left hand, and then heave it onto your back.

3. And now all you have to do is walk away with it!

I have even tied one short on the thwart of a canoe to take some of the weight off my shoulders on a long portage when I had no yoke. You can't afford to be without one.

Food needs careful watching these hot July days and I make good use of the cooler in my spring to keep things fresh. I use a box with several one-inch holes bored in each end and set it in the little stream that flows from the spring so that the water runs through the holes in the box. In the bottom are several large flat stones to hold it down and to set the dishes of food on, for the stones hold the chill of the water and that box is almost as cool as a regular refrigerator. It is in the shade of a big spruce so the sun never hits it. The lid is held down by a heavy stone so the small animals can't get at my victuals, but one night while I was away a bear got in and ate up everything I had. By the way, I keep two small trout in my spring, an old trick to keep the water free of bugs and clean. They are so tame I almost have to push them aside when I dip up a pail of water.

I once had a very practical cold room which I copied from one I saw in a French Canadian village. This kind is built in a hole in the ground six feet deep, six wide, and eight long, has double walls of rough boards separated by two-by-four inch uprights, and the space between the walls is filled with sawdust for insulation. The floor is dirt, and the room is divided in half by a partition of boards with one-inch spaces between them. On the food compartment side are shelves with doors that close to a snug fit, while on the other side ice is stored in the winter, packed down in sawdust. On top there is a board cover with straw, sawdust, and maybe some earth on top of it.

The roof is built on a slant with a door opening into the food room and narrow stairs to go down. The roof next to the door is tight, but the section over the ice is laid up of loose boards like shingles to give free ventilation. Make sure that the partition comes right up to the roof, and it should be double from the top of the shelves up so no warm air will drift through.

Roll your blanket-roll in your Tump Line like this.....and

carry it on the small of your back.

TUMP LINE

3" Head Strap 1½"

15"   8'

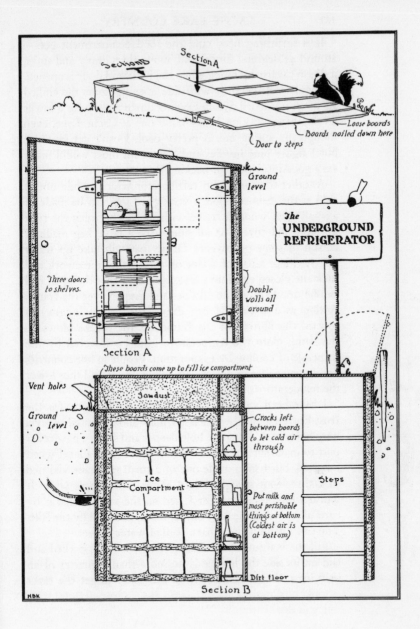

Section B   Section A

Loose boards
Boards nailed down here

Door to steps

Three doors
to shelves.

Ground
level

The
UNDERGROUND
REFRIGERATOR

Double
walls all
around

Section A

These boards come up to fill ice compartment

Vent holes

Sawdust

Ground
level

Cracks left
between boards
to let cold air
through

Ice
Compartment

Steps

Put milk and
most perishable
things at bottom
(Coldest air is
at bottom)

Dirt floor

HBK

Section B

It is surprising how cold the food compartment gets—around 45 degrees! Since cold, moist air is heavy and sinks, it doesn't warm up much when the bulkhead door is opened. In regular refrigerators with side-opening doors the chilled air pours out like a stream heading down a pitch for a lower level. I have a notion I may build one at Cache Lake, even though my spring box is pretty cool. I can't get sawdust, but I figure pine needles and sphagnum moss would make very good insulation for packing the ice.

Another kind of camp refrigerator which, while not as cold as the iceboxes, does a very good job, can be made of a small open wooden frame with shelves between the four uprights and covers on all sides with a large bag made of cotton or some openweave fabric that will take up water evenly. Place a pail of water on top of the framework and tuck the closed end into it in such a way that the open end can be drawn down on all sides and draped over the frame. Acting as a wick, the bag draws the water downwards toward the bottom of the frame. As the breeze blows on the damp cloth the temperature inside is lowered by the principle of cooling by evaporation. People in hot countries use the same idea in porous jars which sweat and thus lower the temperature of the water.

I have been working on my front porch lately, for the frost heaved a corner post last winter and I wanted to level it up before fall. I dug the hole deeper and set in a new cedar post to make sure of a good job. I didn't have a level when I started, but I soon made one of a small medicine vial tied to a three-foot straight board about four inches wide. It worked fine, too, for after I tied on the vial I tested it by carefully placing the edge of the board on a pool by the lake. You can always be sure that a pool of water is level.

Fill the vial just about full so that when it is corked and laid on its side the bubble is no more than a quarter of an inch long. When you put it on the water to get the exact

Rock

Spring

Box

Bank cut out for box

Tin cup on stick

Flat Rock

Holes in end

Spring

Box

THE SPRING COOLER

spot when the bubble is in the middle, get someone to make a mark at the center of the bubble and then later make a scratch with a file to make the mark permanent. You will be surprised how useful a level can be. But remember that the piece of wood you use, whether it is three, four, or five inches wide, must be that same width for its entire length, otherwise it won't give you a true level.

This is a time of year when everyone has to be mighty careful of fire in the big woods. Everything is as dry as tinder and once a fire gets started you are in a fix. A forest fire is a terrible thing to face. I know it firsthand, for once years ago I got caught. First saw signs of it nearly a hundred miles away with smoke billowing to the clouds. That fire was seventy-five miles wide, so there was no way to get around it, and it was coming too fast for me to keep ahead of it. Once they get going in heavy growth, fires generate their own wild gales, and race on at great speed with a deep roaring sound that can be heard miles away.

I happened to know of a lake with a clearing part way around, half a day's travel to the east, so I made for it by way of a portage and got there just in time. The fire was then only a few miles away. Less than half an hour later I was as ready as a man could be in such a fix. I dug a hole in the beach and buried all my outfit, including my coat, watch, and compass. Then I sank the canoe with rocks near shore and sat in the water beside it. I don't mind telling you I was scared plumb to death.

Not long before the fire reached the edge of the lake the animals began to appear, hundreds of rabbits, porcupines, deer and two bears, running for their lives. All except the rabbits and porcupines plunged into the lake and stayed there with their heads just above the water. Then with a frightful roar the fire hit us. I ducked my head over and over again. I could hardly breathe the air was so hot. Then in a flash a great sheet of flame arched over the lake, which, mind you, was half a mile wide, and the air was filled with burning pieces of wood lifted by the great wind. As I ducked

WATER-COOLED REFRIGERATOR

Pan of water

Cloth cover, tied at bottom to keep out flies

again and looked up I saw the deer standing with terror in their eyes. Close beside them were two moose that I hadn't seen before, and not fifty feet away were the bears. The fire was their enemy and they had lost their fear of each other and of me. An hour after the fire leaped across the lake the heat was not so bad, but when I went out to dig up my outfit the sand was still so hot I had to wait for it to cool off. The rabbits were lost, for they were afraid to go into the lake. Little by little the deer, moose, and bears came out of the water and wandered away along the beach frightened and bewildered for the forest was still burning. I had to camp that night right there for the woods were covered with burning trees and I couldn't cross the portage.

That is what a forest fire is like and you can bet I am careful about building my campfire in safe places, such as on a beach or flat rock, and I keep away from any moss or dry sod. That is the worst stuff for carrying a fire underground where it creeps along before you realize it. I use a small fire for cooking—not much bigger than your hand—feeding it dry twigs which make hot flames and don't smoke up your pots. The only time you need a big fire is when the weather is cold or rainy. Before you break camp be sure to wet everything down, scattering the embers carefully so you are sure all hot coals are thoroughly out.

Only a while back I noticed a haze in the air and in a day's time I got the first faint whiff of that smell we all dread. I took a canoe and my pack and started for the timber country to see what was up, but when I was crossing Thunder Lake I spotted the company's plane about the same time that the pilot saw me and he came gliding down to tell me that the fire was west of Bent Pole Lake seventy-five miles northwest of us, and that we were safe unless the wind changed. Airplanes are wonderful things for in an hour he can fly over a section of country it would take us two weeks to cross in a canoe.

On the way back on the Thunder Lake portage I met a prospector on his way up. Somehow when you are on a portage with a pack on your back and you meet a fellow and stop to speak, you just naturally lean forward on your paddles to ease the load of your pack, and so the blades cross between you making what we call "the cross of the north." He was more than glad to get the location of the fire, for he was on a short grub stake and wanted to keep going.

The lightning that is sometimes blamed for starting fires in the woods often comes from the bowl of a pipe, a cigarette, or a glowing match. Any way you look at it, smoking in the woods is dangerous and we make it a practice not to light up when we're traveling. When we want a puff we stop for a rest as the old-timers did and make sure that when we knock out the ashes there are no sparks left to start trouble. Cigarettes are the most dangerous because they smolder for a long time and a fire may not start until you are some distance away. Another reason for not smoking on the trail is that while you are walking or paddling it is bad for your wind. What you need then is plenty of good clean air with lots of oxygen in it.

When I was a youngster in the woods with my Dad one of the things he taught me was to break a match in two before I threw it away. The first time I tried it I burned my fingers and quickly learned why it is a good method of preventing fires, for you can't break a match in two while it is hot.

When you are looking for a camping place, especially during dry spells, pick if possible an open rocky site handy to water. One of the worst battles I had with fire was when I was camping alone and a blaze got started in the dry moss and sod that grows in open evergreen woods. Before I realized it a spark from my fire had got into the moss and worked underground, spreading out in a network and com-

This is the time to watch out for those killers, the Fly Amanitas (2 on left) and the Deadly Amanitas (right.)
They're _really_ deadly!

ing to the surface in a dozen different places. You would hardly believe that I had to work for two hours carrying water from the lake and wetting down every spot that smoked before that fire was out. No sooner would I get one place wet down than another fire would crop up somewhere else. I learned a lesson right there, for I had been burning tamarack which is a wonderful wood in the stove and good for campfires too, but it shoots sparks ten feet without any trouble and you have to watch it every minute.

While we are on the move we try to pick a place for our campfire close to the water's edge so that when we are ready to start on our way all we have to do is to push the whole

fire into the water. Often enough when you wet a fire down and think it is out you may miss a stray ember that gets going later on. If we are on a lake where there are lots of islands, which are mighty pretty anyway, we often choose one for our camp. For one thing the insects are not apt to be so bad out on the water where the wind has a chance to get at them, and another reason is that you feel safer with a fire on an island where at least it can't burn up miles of timber.

If you are in the woods and spot a big fire, make careful note of the direction the smoke is blowing and then if it is headed your way set a course that will take you above or below the fire, whichever is shortest. To run ahead of a forest fire is usually a losing game, for when it really gets up to full power it travels at terrible speed, and as its front widens you don't have time to get out of its path.

Back of my cabin in an open sandy place where the sun strikes down all day, I have built myself a sundial, for it is interesting to watch a shadow mark off the hours, although, as I have said before, we don't live by hours up here. Instead of making a small sundial, I got a clean, straight tamarack about twelve feet long and prepared a location by leveling the ground carefully. That is important if you want accurate time. The pole was set in a hole nearly three feet deep and the earth filled in loosely so that I could swing it down for final adjustment to the proper position. Once that was done I waited until darkness fell and then slanted the pole to the north until, when I sighted along it, the North Star was exactly in line. Then I tamped the earth firmly around the base and made a final check by sighting along the pole to make sure it had not shifted position.

The angle of sight from where you stand to the North Star corresponds to the latitude of your location, so you can also put up a sundial by finding your latitude and setting

The SAPLING SUN-DIAL

Here's the usual
little dial.

the pole at that angle. Just for example, if you live at forty-five degrees north the pointer would be set at an angle of forty-five degrees, but don't forget that in addition to placing it at the proper angle, it must always point North.

The next step is to lay out the hour marks on a circle around the pointer. The simplest method is to drop a plumb bob from the tip of the pointer and drive a stake directly beneath it. If the pole is properly set the shadow of the pole should cover the stake at twelve o'clock, noon. Then with a watch you can mark off each hour by driving a stake in the center of the shadow for every hour that has sunlight enough to cast a shadow.

What got me started making a sundial was one of the signs the Chief left for us when he went on a trip one day. When Hank and I went over to see him we found a little sapling stuck in the ground pointing east, which meant that he had gone across the lake. Right beside it he had marked a rough circle like a clockface and stuck a twig in pointing out from six o'clock. That was his way of telling us the time he left. There was a twig leaning toward the four o'clock mark, so we knew he expected to be back about that time. And it wasn't more than half an hour after that we saw him coming across the lake.

The Chief can't write, but his signs tell a lot. If he is away and wants us to wait for him he will put up little twigs in the shape of a tepee, meaning to make use of his cabin. If he wants to tell us that he has gone for two days he will draw a circle to represent the sun and stick two twigs in the middle, with another outside leaning in the direction he went. If for some reason he didn't want us to follow him he would put two crossed sticks in front of the one showing direction.

Once he left a sign that took me a while to figure out. It was two little logs with a lot of twigs between and a sapling slanting over them. Finally it came to me, for the sapling was just where a pot would be over a fire, which was indicated by the twigs between the logs. Then beside it was the

" Went across lake at
six o'clock — back
by four "

circle with the six o'clock hour marked with a twig showing he would be back about six o'clock. I made a good guess that he meant me to get a fire going in the cabin stove for supper. And sure enough he came back with a fine catch of trout.

It didn't take me long to find out what the Chief had in mind, for he loves the kind of trout chowder I make and he had even saved a few potatoes that he had brought in on his last trip to the settlement. I like my chowder without any bones, so I get rid of all skin and bones, and start by frying several thick slices of salt pork with chopped onions until they are well browned. This is put in the pot with the fish and raw potatoes cut in chunks with just enough water to cover. Then I add a generous amount of evaporated milk, which to my mind is even better than fresh milk for a chowder and many other kinds of cooking. When the chowder is done after cooking slowly for about an hour it is golden brown and Hank and the Chief love the flavor of the fried pork and browned onion.

AUGUST

Harvest of the Wilderness

Now COMES the most favorable time of the year for traveling in the north country. The mosquitoes, black flies, and midges are about gone and the weather tends to be clear and settled, with fine warm days and cooling nights. What is more, this is the harvest season.

The berries are ripe and ready to pick, but you have to know the right places. Besides the big frosty blueberries, there are the low-bush or ground cranberry which hides its small pink and white face deep in the moss, as well as the high-bush kind that grows in or near the swamps. In the sunny clearings and sometimes in shady places where you would never think to look, the juicy blackberries hang on their canes, and among the slash and blowdowns are rasp-berries bigger and sweeter than any ever grown by man. Until you have lived in the woods a while you have no idea how much fine food nature provides if you know where to find it. Take a ground cranberry, for example. It is as hard to spot as a woodcock in October, unless you learn where the moss grows in places the little fellow likes.

I have had to learn some of my woodcraft the hard way, but what you learn that way you seldom forget. One thing I had to find out from experience is that when you travel in the woods you have to plan ahead with care, taking every-

"High-Bush Cranberry" isn't really a cranberry at all. It's a Viburnum —much closer to the Elderberry.

thing you need in the way of equipment and food, for often there is no turning back, no one to borrow from.

I used to think that going light and roughing it was the thing to do. That is all right if conditions require it, but I find that the good woodsman is a man who takes what he needs to live comfortably, making use of what comes to hand wherever he is. Although I like a balsam bed in the woods, if a fellow wants to carry an air mattress that is all right with me. No need to be uncomfortable just because you are camping. And just in case you think air mattresses are new fangled contraptions, dig back into history and you will find more than 1600 years ago Roman soldiers slept on bags which were filled with air from a bellows. I believe the Emperor Heliogabalus worked out the idea.

As I said, I like a balsam bed in the woods, but in my bunk at the cabin I have the best mattress I could buy. Funny how it came to Cache Lake, too. When I decided to order it I wondered how I would pack it in from the settlement, for if there is a mean and ornery thing to carry, a mattress takes the grand prize. But I didn't have to tote the thing in after all, for my friend the pilot of the lumber company's patrol plane, said he would bring it in on one of his trips.

Sure enough, one day I heard him over the lake and by the way the plane was weaving about I knew something was wrong, so I got in the canoe and made ready to give a hand. When he finally came lurching down I couldn't make out what was going on, but when he landed I could see what the trouble was. It seems my friend rolled the mattress up as tight as he could and tied it with a cord so it would fit into the little cabin. Everything went well until about halfway in to the lake the cord broke and the mattress came to life with a wild bound and just about filled the cabin, with the pilot crouching under it. He was still there, peering out under one edge, when he landed and crawled out. He said he would as leave take ten wildcats for a sight-seeing trip as to keep company in the air with a spring mattress again.

A while back I was talking about my cooking outfit, which

has all anyone needs. Add to that a tent, a good oiled tarpaulin, which has many uses in addition to its main purpose as a ground cloth, an axe, which is more important than any other piece of equipment, two heavy all-wool blankets, fishing gear, a good pocketknife as well as a sheath knife, a small file, needles and linen thread for making repairs, a simple medical kit, a few candles, and plenty of matches in waterproof containers or set in paraffin as I described before. With this outfit packed in a large packsack and duffel bag, and a tump line for extra carrying, you can take care of yourself in any kind of summer or fall weather.

The amount of provisions you need in the woods depends on the time of the year and whether you are traveling steadily and working hard or spending part of the time in a permanent camp. Almost every woodsman knows the old general rule that calls for three pounds of food per day per man, one pound being meat and the rest all other foods. By and large that is a good foundation rule, but I have found that most men, especially those that are fresh to the woods and not in hardened condition, will eat more than they think they will.

Another mistake to watch out for is making up your provision list with the thought that you can get part of your food from the country. Right now, when berries are plentiful and the fishing is good you might figure that you could cut down on some of the staple rations, but I have been on a trip in August through country where there wasn't a blueberry for a hundred miles and the fishing for one reason or another was poor. Many a man has run out of rations because he figured he would get meat on the way.

Seeing that there is no provision store around the corner once you get into the woods, the wise thing is to plan on taking all the food you need for the full time of your trip. Better to end your journey with a few pounds of food than to work the last day on an empty stomach.

I am going to give you here the ration list that the Chief

There's always competition for
blueberries — bears love
them too!

and I worked out after many years of experience. The amounts given are for one man for one week.

RATION LIST

Flour	4	lbs.
Bacon	5	lbs.
Cheese	2	lbs.
Rice	1¼	lbs.
Lard	½	lb.
Oatmeal	1	lb.
Sugar	1½	lbs.
Tea	¼	lb.
Bar chocolate	½	lb.
Coffee	½	lb.
Beans (dried)	1½	lbs.
or small cans of baked beans	5	cans
Butter (in can)	½	lb.
Dried fruit (prunes, apricots, peaches, pears, or raisins)	1½	lbs.
Onions	1	lb.
Dried soups	3	oz.
Dried milk	12	oz.
or evaporated	2	cans
Potatoes (fresh)	5	lbs.
or dehydrated	4	oz.
Baking powder	4	oz.
Salt	3	oz.
Pepper	¼	oz.

A few words about these provisions. Part of the amount given for flour can be corn meal. If you are starting out from a place where there is a store that keeps bread, it is nice to take along several loaves to carry you two or three days, but bread doesn't keep well in woods traveling and don't cut down the flour ration because you carry a few loaves of bread.

As for bacon, make sure that you get a lean strip. By the time you fry up fat bacon there is not much left but grease. We include lard on our list because it is a fine fat, although the Chief and I usually leave it out and use bacon fat in its place. It is tastier, I think. If you are on a canoe trip where the portages are short and the weight of your outfit is not so important, you might want to cut down the amount of bacon by taking two cans of good corned beef, but always remember that canned goods have a surprising way of gaining weight on a two-mile portage. Some folks do not care about cheese in the woods and I will agree it does not keep too well in hot weather. But it is nourishing food for hard work though not so good for a loafing diet. Some old woodsmen might snort at including chocolate in a ration list, but all the experienced explorers know its great value as a food. It belongs in the meat part of your diet. Many a man has been saved from hunger by carrying a bar of sweet chocolate in his pack when he went out on what he thought was a short tramp.

I would give up a lot of things before I left my rice ration behind, for rice is a democratic sort of food that mixes just as well with sugar and dried fruits as it does in a stew. I like it best hot with milk and maple sugar.

Coffee is included on our list, although most men in the north find that tea makes a much better drink for woods living. Dried soups are wonderful things to have on the trail. They are light, very nourishing, and can be added to stews, mixed with rice, or taken just as warm drinks. You will have to decide for yourself whether you will take dried milk, which is the lightest, or cans of the evaporated kind, which means that you are toting quite a lot of water. Some like condensed milk, but as it is very sweet it does not fit into general cooking.

My weakness is butter and I will give up other luxuries to have it with me on a trip. The only practical kind comes in cans and it keeps well. Beans are a foundation ration and the quantity on our list represents a surprising amount of energy. If the traveling is easy and you do not mind carrying the extra weight, canned beans are convenient. There is not much manpower in an onion, but many a stew has been made the tastier for having an onion chopped up in it. It is my theory that food that pleases a man's appetite does him a lot more good than victuals that do not appeal to him.

The prepared mixes for hot biscuits and dumplings, corn muffins, griddle cakes, gingerbread, and other things are all fine to take along. Some woodsmen do not bother with potatoes, but if we can get them we always have them in our grub bag for part of the trip at least. Sugar is important because of its value in giving energy, and the craving for sweets in the woods, especially when you are living on the heavier foods, is surprising. Some travelers will tell you that part of your sweetening ration should be saccharin tablets because they are very light and have a powerful sweetening effect. However, a doctor friend of mine tells me that saccharin doesn't take the place of the sugar the body needs and that steady use of saccharin is bad.

In the woods
~ or even in the
city - there's no
flavoring more
useful than onion

Our provision list totals up to about thirty pounds of working rations. By that I mean rations chosen to keep us fit for steady paddling day in and day out, heavy packing on the portages or cross country tramping. You may have ideas of your own, and almost every woodsman I ever knew had some secret luxury that he liked to tuck in one corner of his food bag. As for me if I can get my hands on a chocolate cake I will lug it with the greatest care for about two days, counting on the time when I can get my teeth into it, and then when I can't resist any longer I have myself a feast.

Every woodsman has his own ideas about tents and all types have their good points. To my way of thinking it is pretty much a matter of what kind of country you are in, the season of the year, and how long you are going to be out. If it is a "short and light" trip, a small tent of "balloon silk," which is really Egyptian cotton duck, will serve you well. But for a permanent camp give me a good wall tent of eight or ten-ounce duck with a fly to carry off the rain or keep it cool, for the air moving between the roof of the tent and the fly has a lot to do with the temperature inside. In addition I favor a vent or window in a tent for circulation. It can be very uncomfortable on a warm night when a tent has to be closed up to keep out insects.

I rely on a wall tent for general year-round use, for it provides more headroom, has more usable space, and can be made comfortable in any weather. As a matter of fact, I spent most of a winter in a wall tent with a small stove to keep me warm and it was very snug, I can tell you, even when it was thirty-five below zero.

The only difference between my summer and winter tents was that for winter living I used a double wall, a tent within a tent, one separated from the other by an air space of two inches. The inner tent was held in place by canvas loops fastened to the outside tent at the various places where it would be supported in the ordinary way of setting it up. The air space between the two tents is of great importance in keeping out the cold, and I have since learned that when a dead air space is used for insulation two inches is just right. If it is any more or any less you begin to lose the insulating value of the air trapped between the two walls.

To gain more headroom for my winter tent I built a foundation of logs about three feet high, chinked it with moss, and laid a double floor of saplings with four inches of sphagnum moss between, keeping the double floors separated by three logs so that the moss would not pack down and lose its insulating value. Then I set the double tent on top and tacked the lower edges to the logs with light saplings to keep out the wind and banked it with pine needles and boughs. It

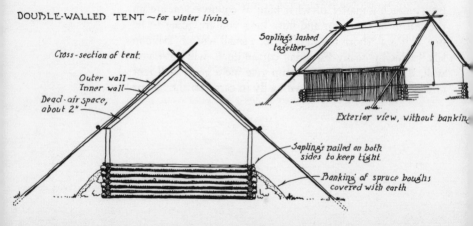

DOUBLE-WALLED TENT ~ for winter living

Cross-section of tent:

Outer wall
Inner wall
Dead-air space, about 2"

Saplings lashed together

Exterior view, without banking

Saplings nailed on both sides to keep tight.

Banking of spruce boughs covered with earth

was supported by a ridge pole set on shears which are easily adjusted and hold well in almost any weather. Frost that forms on the inside of a warm tent in winter sifts down on you and can be a miserable thing, but in a double-walled tent it falls down between the walls.

The double-walled shelter is not new in the north woods, for some of the Indians built their tepees of hides, covered the shelter with a thick layer of moss and then laid on a second covering of hides or bark. Hides were used not only because they made a strong, tough covering, but also because the hair that was left on gave extra insulation. The secret of this insulation was not only the thickness of the hair, but the fact that each individual hair of the deer is hollow, thus providing added insulation in the form of tiny dead air spaces. The hair of the caribou is said to be the warmest of all.

These tepees had floors laid deep with balsam boughs and hides laid around the outer edges to keep out drafts as much as possible. The door was covered with a tightly stretched skin held in place by pegs. Some Indians still use them although many tepees you see are made of canvas and some Indians have even turned to the white man's tent.

Another tent that I like very well is one shaped like a lean-to. This type is not so practical during the fly season, but fine in the fall. You can lift the front, support it on a couple of poles and have a roof while you are cooking in the open. On a cold evening you can get a lot of warmth by building your campfire in front of the lean-to, for the slanting roof reflects the heat down.

For a short trip where comfort is not the main thought the wedge or A-tent is a handy shelter, but it ought to be large enough so that if you get weather-bound and have to stay under cover you will have room enough to sit up. Never will I forget two cold, rainy days one fall that I spent on an island in what is called a pup tent. A good name, for it was a dog's life!

Some folks like a bottom sewed into a tent and to be sure

it helps to keep out insects, but walking on the canvas floor soon gets it dirty, and if the weather is wet and you come in dripping it holds the water. I would rather have a good tarpaulin ground cloth which I always have anyway to keep the dampness from striking through, and if the insects are bad I can tuck it in around the edges of the tent and hold it tight with small logs. Rubberized ground cloths are good, too, but heavier than oiled tarpaulins. If you are in country where the flies and mosquitoes are bad, which is almost everywhere in the north, a mosquito net across the front of the tent is worth its weight in gold. Instead of having it split down the front I like one made in one piece with plenty of room so that it can be hoisted up out of the way. The kind with an open front is hard to make tight against the pests.

For use in winter, you can get tents with stovepipe openings made of asbestos or metal. I like the kind that takes the pipe out through the back wall rather than through the roof, where there is apt to be leaks. The tent stove I like best is the plain box type which gives room for cooking as well as providing heat. I have noticed that some people build their balsam beds too close to their stoves which often get red hot. A balsam bed in a few weeks becomes so dry and inflammable that it takes only a spark to start it blazing, and once it is on fire there is not much you can do to stop it before your tent is gone. I always have a piece of wire netting to put over the top of my stove pipe to keep sparks from falling on the tent, for even if they do not set your shelter on fire they are apt to burn holes in it.

Getting burned out in the woods in cold weather is a serious business and if a tent catches on fire while you are asleep you may have a time escaping with your life. I make it a practice never to go to sleep with a fire in my tent stove. But I always have plenty of dry twigs, birch bark and small pieces of wood so that I can start the fire quickly. Another thing to remember is that if you move a tent in winter when the temperature is low and the duck is stiff or frozen it may crack when you try to fold it. The answer to that is to get it warm and as dry as possible before you begin to handle it.

A tent can be waterproofed with plain paraffin, which should be chipped into small pieces and spread evenly on the fabric with a moderately warm iron. This method is effective, but it also makes a tent very inflammable. A safer method is to make up a waterproofing solution of powdered alum and sugar of lead. Dissolve approximately one pound of alum in a water pail—about four gallons—of boiling water. The softer the water, the better, and rain water is ideal. Meantime dissolve one-half pound sugar of lead in about four gallons of water. When the ingredients are dissolved and the solution has cleared, pour the alum water into a large tub and then add the sugar of lead solution. Let this mixture stand four or five hours and then carefully pour off the water, being sure to keep all the sediment. It is in this soupy solution that you soak the tent thoroughly, working it around until every inch is saturated. Then wring it out very lightly and hang it up loosely to dry. If you do not want to take the trouble to make your own waterproofing solution you can buy several types ready for use.

In good weather when the flies are not a problem I don't bother with a tent. Sometimes I throw up a few poles in the form of a lean-to and tie my ground cloth over it and have made many a trip with no other shelter than my canoe turned on its side, which is a pretty good makeshift roof. If you know your country you will place the bottom of your canoe toward the direction from which the storms come and after making a balsam bed, pile up boughs around the ends of the canoe for a wind break.

When you spread your ground cloth on the bed, roll up the extra length at the back of your shelter where the side of the canoe touches the ground and then pull it through and turn back over the top and peg it down in front of your bed. If it rains in the night you will be well protected. To

EMERGENCY CANOE SHELTER

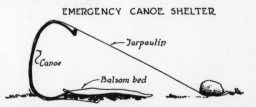

Tarpaulin

Canoe

Balsam bed

My canoe is a pretty good makeshift roof

be sure, it is not a shelter for a long spell of bad weather, but for a short trip where weight and time count, it is handy.

Maybe you think it queer that three men who make their home in the woods enjoy a camping trip every summer, but it is just as much a change and adventure for us to explore some new part of the north as it is for other people to visit a strange city in a different part of the land. To be sure we have seen a lot of the north country, but if we lived a hundred years longer we would not have time to visit the thousands of lakes, big and little, that have never known the ripple of a canoe. So when we travel we are adventurers exploring new territory, never being sure what we will find. The days, the weeks, and the months are ours and we live by the sun and pay no heed to clocks.

This year we traveled across country by way of a chain of lakes and streams to Lake Waweashkashing, which means "a grassy place in the water." And that's what it is, for the west shore of the lake is shallow and there the grass and wild rice grow thick. In the fall it is a regular stopover for geese and ducks. The Chief can remember when Indians came there to lay up a store of smoked waterfowl for the winter. From the head of the lake we portaged to a stream that brought us to a clear, deep lake up on the height of land. Two-Ways-Out Lake, they call it, and the Chief says that in the spring when the water is high it flows from two outlets, one stream heading north and the other south. Anyway the fish think it is a fine place to live and we had some rare good sport. Never saw such fighting squaretails as I hooked in that little lake, which is spring-fed and cold enough to suit any trout. We made our camp on a fine little spruce-covered island near the north end of the lake and, in addition to fishing, took some trips so the Chief could look over the country for possible trapping come winter. He found a deserted cabin where he can camp if he decides to trap in those parts.

I am just a plain fisherman, not very skillful at fly-casting, and only a little better with a bait rod, but I am expert at trolling! When I need fish somehow I catch them. There was a time when I believed in all the notions that many fishermen have about the weather, the kind of day, and exactly the right kind of fly, but after I had lived with Chief Tibeash a few years I got over most of that. The Chief doesn't pay much attention to the weather if he wants fish and he is not too particular about special flies or certain baits. One thing he is fussy about is going to places where he knows there are fish and why they ought to be there. He says that it is knowing the water and the feeding habits and what to expect during the various months of the summer that has a lot to do with getting what you are after.

I have seen him working up a strange brook on a hot July day when the trout lie deep in the dark cool water, dipping his hand in the stream every once in a while and moving on. That is his way of hunting a spring hole. I have seen him pass pools that made your mouth water to think of the trout that should be there, but he would shake his head and go on. Then, further along, dipping his hand into the stream again he would nod and I knew we were near a cold spring-fed pool. I do not believe I ever saw him fail to get fish once he has found the right water conditions.

It took me a long time to learn the Chief's trick of testing the temperature of the water, but once you get the hang of it you can detect a spring quite a distance off and it is downright surprising how you can follow a cold current to its source.

I have watched the Chief pick up a caterpillar along the bank, fix it on a hook and drop it into a pool to get a strike almost before it hit the water. Once I saw him pick up a bright feather dropped from the wing of a moosebird, quickly tie it on a bare hook and land a trout in no time.

The Chief does most of his fishing early in the morning or late in the day, although that is not always so. I have seen him catch trout in a heavy summer thundershower at midday, and he pays no attention to a little sunshine on a brook. Furthermore, if the Chief ever heard that "fish will not bite when the wind blows from the east," he never lets on, for I

have seen him take fish in an easterly wind many a time. I
suspect that a lot of those superstitions about fishing conditions came about because they describe the kind of weather
that fishermen, rather than fish, dislike.

The difference between the Chief and most fishermen is
that he fishes when he needs food, but that doesn't mean that
he does not enjoy it, and I might say that he is fond of fish
right often. An old prospector friend of mine says that fishing
is like panning for gold: you never know what is going to
come out of the stream on the next try, and it is the lure of the
unexpected that keeps you at it. It is a harmless form of
gambling that once you start is apt to keep you dreaming of
fast water and dark pools for the rest of your days.

The Chief and I have certain choice pools spotted all over
these parts and there is not a time during the season that we
cannot go out and get a mess of trout when we need it. Once
in a while we go after the big-lakers, which give quite a
tussle, especially in surface fishing in the spring with a good
lively spoon. As you know, the lake trout is a lover of deep
water and, although he comes into shallow places to feed,
you will not find him anywhere where there is not deep
water close at hand. Reefs or boulder-strewn shoal places
that run out toward deep water are likely spots.

We have done some deep-water trolling with a hundred
yards of copper wire and a pound sinker, but you have to
know where to fish if you don't want to waste a lot of time
and it is not as much sport as casting. It is what the Chief
calls "provision fishing." I am partial to bass, which give a
wonderful fight, but I don't care much for pike or pickerel
fishing, though I do not mind holding my end of a line with
a mad muskellunge on the other end.

When you are back in the woods you may not always have
all the special flies and lures that you read so much about.
The only thing to do then is to make the best of what is at
hand. As I said, the Chief can catch fish with almost anything, but there's a lot of woods knowledge behind what he
turns out, even though it may look crude. I have seen him

Lake Trout lie deep ~ and come big!

The Chief's
SPINNER

1.

2.

make a little spinner out of a piece of mussel shell, but it was not just any mussel shell. He would look over a lot before he got just the color he wanted. That is one way to make a spinner in an emergency, and it often brings surprising results. Once I saw the old man cut off a little forked twig with arms about an inch long, bore a hole through the main stem and whittle the arms into the form of propeller blades so that when he pulled it through the water it whirled. Then he spread it with spruce gum and glued on some tinfoil and went to work in bass water. We had fish for supper! He whittles out all sorts of wooden plugs, decorating some with paint, and others by tying on bits of feathers and dyed deer hair. I have also seen him cut up a tomato can and fashion whirling or wobbling lures that were sure-fire killers, although they didn't last long and weren't meant to.

Most of the time we eat our fish soon after they are caught, but if we want to keep them a day or maybe two while in the woods, the Chief places them in the sun for a very few minutes. When the skin has dried to a point where it feels stiff he removes the eyes and gills and wraps them in dry moss well separated from each other. If you need to keep them several days, clean the fish and rub salt along the backbone, wipe as dry as possible and wrap in paper or dry cloth. Cleaned fish also keep well if they are hung tails up in a cool place where the air circulates freely. They should be enclosed in a piece of mosquito netting, if possible, to keep the blowflies away. To let fish die slowly spoils the flesh, to my way of thinking, and so I kill them at once by tapping them over the head. Bending the head back quickly is another way of doing it.

Our tent on the little island in Two-Ways-Out Lake was pitched in the shelter of a big spruce and we lived in comfort and took life easy. Hank brought along his canvas bed. It is quite a contraption. Just a piece of canvas seven feet long with the sides stitched together to make it about three feet wide. It looks like a big bag with both ends open. At each end he sewed strips of canvas with open ends to the top to put small saplings through so the head and foot won't sag. If you don't want to use it on a sapling frame you can stuff it with grass or balsam tips. On the trail Hank folds his blankets and stuffs them inside the canvas and then rolls it up and carries the whole thing on a tump line. One sharp night last fall when we were on a two-day trip, Hank made a sleeping bag of his canvas bag by putting the blankets inside and laying it on top of a balsam bough bed. So, as you can see, it is a pretty useful rig.

Night in the forest is a time of mystery and adventure, for with darkness come sounds never heard at any other time. To be sure we all know the cheerful song of the tree frogs and the snowy crickets in the branches overhead. But to this day I am not certain what some of the others are. The crash of a falling tree in the night is pretty sure to mean beavers at work and once you hear it, you never mistake the sharp slap of a beaver's tail on the water when one gives an alarm. A moose can walk like a mouse and there are times when a mouse makes sounds like a moose. You never can be sure, and there are always new noises to make you wonder.

Lying on a deep bed of balsam boughs, I love to listen to the voices and the sounds of the night. Now and then you hear a squeak and the rustlings of a traveling white-foot. And once in a while something—maybe a bear—thrashes through the woods like a logging team breaking a new road. You never forget the scream of a bobcat.

Far back in the woods where they seldom see human beings, the northern rabbits often play around the camp all night. That's when you may hear a sudden swish of wings and a quick high-pitched scream when a great horned owl dives for a catch. If it misses and the ground is hard and dry you may catch the drumming of the rabbit's feet running in fear of winged death in the darkness. There is no other sound just like it.

Once in a while on a still night when the moon is full you

CANVAS BED
AND PACK SACK

You can notch the logs and drop the side saplings in there if you like, but these end-stakes spread it better.

Drive these end-stakes in well to spread the saplings and hold the canvas taut.

The cheerful song of the tree frogs overhead

may hear the call of a loon and more often at this time of year the soft quacking of black ducks resting on a lake. I like best to listen to a brook talking to itself. And if you are within ten miles of fast river water you will hear the thunder of the rapids, rising and falling, now far away, now very close and clear, as the night breeze stirs, drifts, and dies. Often in late August you will hear the faint chirping of roosting small birds telling each other that all's well. After a while the night sounds of the woods blend into a slow, soft song of sleep and the first thing you know the night is over. Another day is breaking!

I guess I made one mistake on our trip. I got to bragging about food, and Hank and the Chief let me talk until, before I realized it, I was elected cook. What could I say? But just between you and me and the frying pan I like to cook, and if I do say so we had good food—and they washed the dishes!

One dish Hank and the Chief always enjoy is a pot of baked beans. So after we had settled down I dug a bean-hole. In case you are interested this is how I make baked beans:

Two cups of beans (I like the white California kind,
     plain white or yellow-eyed)
Half a pound of bacon (salt pork will do if you boil it
     a while first)
Two teaspoons of salt
One small onion
Half a cup of brown sugar or light molasses.

For baking beans in a hole you need a pot with a fairly tight lid so dirt won't get in, but not so tight that it won't let the steam escape. To begin you soak the beans in the pot overnight. In the morning drain off the water and set them to boil slowly in fresh water. Let them simmer until they begin to break out of their hides. Then drain off the water again and put several pieces of bacon in the bottom of the pot. Add the salt, onion, and molasses, stir them in a little, and finally add part of the bacon cut up into cubes, poking it down in the middle of the beans, but keep several chunks to put on top. Now you are all ready for baking in the hole, after covering the beans with water and bringing them back to boiling.

The trick is to get the hole heated while the beans are boiling. The hole should be about a foot and a half deep and just about the same square. If you can find some rocks to put in the bottom and line the sides it makes a better hole, to my way of thinking. Some people don't bother with the stones. Anyway, you start a fire of dry twigs in the bottom and keep on firing with large dry pieces until the hole is filled with fire. Pile more on top so the burning embers fall into the hole and keep it up for an hour or so. By that time the earth and rocks should be good and hot.

Now step lively! Dig a place deep in the hot ashes for your pot, put it in very carefully and pile the ashes back around it. I usually put a chunk of sod on top of the pot and then pile on more hot earth and ashes until the hole is full. If it rains you will have to cover the hole with boards, a box, or pieces of bark to keep it dry. Let them cook overnight and if you don't think my baked beans are the best you ever tasted I will be disappointed. You can try it in your back yard.

One night Hank said: "How about trout baked in clay tomorrow?" Then the fun began, because you can't find clay everywhere. But Hank paddled over to the mainland and after a while came back with hunks of gray clay and put it to soak so I could work it down like dough. Cooking fish in clay is easy. One thing to remember is to clean the fish through a small cut. Don't slice him the whole length as you generally do. The next step is to build a fire of dry wood that leaves a bed of hot coals. While you are getting the fire just right cover the fish with clay to a thickness of about half an inch. If the clay is soft like putty it goes on easily.

BEAN-HOLE BEANS

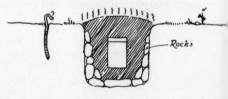

A lid that fits over the outside of the can is best to keep out dirt. A 5 pound baking-powder can or lard pail works well.

Rocks

When that is done and the fire is a glowing bed of coals, hollow out a place for the fish and cover it with hot ashes and coals. The fish will cook in thirty to forty minutes, according to size. When you lift the fish from the fire if you break the clay off carefully it will take the skin with it, leaving your fish white and clean, steaming hot and ready for salt and pepper. A few slices of bacon go well with baked fish.

Along with our fish we had a batch of nice brown biscuits baked in the reflector oven I made from a couple of gallon-size tin cans flattened out and a wire shelf from an old refrigerator. Makes the nicest biscuits you ever bit into. Of course you can also bake fish or chickens or partridges, not to mention rice pudding, in a reflector oven. Sometimes just for a change I made my biscuit dough extra stiff, pull it out into a sort of rope, wind it around a green stick and push it into the ground in front of the fire. Turn the stick every few minutes and you will have something worth eating or I don't know good food. Once in a while I wrap apricots and a little sugar in the dough, and there you have one of the best "long-tailed pies" you ever ate.

I always put up some blueberries for winter eating, for I like blueberries for pies and muffins when the snow flies. I follow the method used in olden times. Make sure that the berries are clean and free of any leaves or stems, then boil them up with just enough water to cover the bottom of the kettle until they are soft, and no longer. Then pour into jars that have been cleaned and boiled. Sprinkle a little bit of salt on them; you don't need any sugar. Of course when it comes time to make a pie or muffins you add what sugar you want.

The Chief has his own way of preserving berries. He lays them out on sheets of birch bark and lets the sun dry them, being careful to take them in at night or when it rains. In

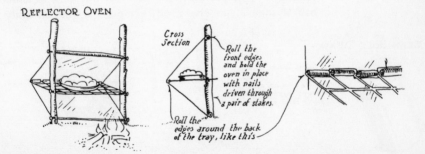

REFLECTOR OVEN

Cross Section

Roll the front edges and hold the oven in place with nails driven through a pair of stakes.

Roll the edges around the back of the tray, like this

about a week to ten days the berries are all shriveled up and to look at them you wouldn't think they were worth keeping. When it comes to cooking you soak them for a while just as you would prunes and use them like any other dried fruit. They are delicious. The Chief is apt to put a handful in his flapjack batter which is also a good idea.

LONG-
TAILED
PIE

— or
ROPE
BISCUIT

SEPTEMBER

The Moon When the Birds Fly Away

THE NIGHTS are getting cool now and the Northern Lights
are beginning to play in the sky, for summer is over and
fall is on the way. The Indians call September Benasee Jewan,
the Moon When the Birds Fly Away. For all of us here in
the north, man and beast, it is time to get ready for winter.
The driving snow and the bitter cold have no mercy on the
man who fails to prepare, but if you have plenty of wood
and food to carry you through there is no need for fear.

Most of my chores are done, for I have already banked the
cabin foundation with pine spills, moss and boughs, with
earth to hold it down, and I'll be as snug as a beaver when
the blizzards come. Banking is best done before any frost
gets into the ground. If I didn't leave the cabin again until
March, I would still have plenty of provisions to live on. The
wood I cut last February to season through the summer, all
twenty cords of it, is stacked handy to the cabin and covered
with bark, and there is more on the porch. I am ready, come
what may.

The days are clear and often warm, but as soon as the sun
goes down the air chills quickly, and in the morning likely
as not the lake is covered with a frosting of mist. Generally
we have quick flurries of snow before the month is over. For
the animals, especially those that sleep the winter away, this
is the fattening season and the bears are already gorging
themselves on berries, beechnuts and grubs against the time
of denning up. The seeds of plants and the wild grain are

191

dead ripe now and the mice, squirrels, and chipmunks are making the most of the harvest and filling their caches with food to keep them alive when the snow is deep and food is hard to come by. The squirrels are fond of mushrooms and the way they hold them in their paws and turn them round as they nibble makes me hungry.

The beavers are already beginning to cut the young, sweet, green wood—poplar, alder, and the like—which they store in the mud in the bottom of their ponds to feed on in the winter. They are also repairing the dams and making their lodges weather-tight. The muskrats are likewise busy on their houses which are something like the beavers' lodge, but smaller. They are usually made of bulrushes and the stalks of water plants with a few small twigs worked in and are entered through a tunnel. They store away pieces of root and other vegetable matter, but not wood as the beavers do. Musquash, as Chief Tibeash calls muskrats, move about under water in the winter and in a pinch they can exist on the material of which their houses are built. If by chance they live on a creek they burrow into the bank from below water level and work up to hollow out a dry, warm room. In the summer they live a good life, getting their food from water-lily roots and other water plants.

The does and their fawns, and even the yearlings, are moving about together, while the bucks keep out of sight in quiet, shadowy places until the points on their antlers finally harden. The deer, which spend a lot of time around the rivers and lakes feeding on water plants during the summer, are now beginning to move back into the woods where they find plenty to eat. One of their favorite foods is beech mast. Just in passing, venison that has fattened on mast is mighty special eating. About this time you notice that the deer are shedding their reddish summer hair and the darker "blue" coat that will carry them through winter begins to come in. Now the spots on the fawns disappear. Most of the fur-bearing animals look pretty ragged, what with losing their summer fur and getting ready to put on their winter overcoats. About this time too the bright colors on some of our fish begin to fade.

Most of the birds are through molting and the bright feathers of summer have been replaced by the darker traveling colors they wear on the journey to the south. The migration is already well started, for many birds began drifting away in August. If it were not for the arrival of birds that spent the summer still farther north of us, the woods would seem deserted.

The colors of birds and the reasons nature plans them that way is very interesting. Many of the males have bright summer coats, while the females wear dresses of dull hues so that they will not be easily seen by their enemies while they are on their nests. Take the scarlet tanager with his bright red feathers and black wings, you would spot him on a nest in a minute, but the olive green of his wife is so like the color of the leaves that you can hardly see her. However, not all the males have bright feathers. Both the male and female of some species, such as the various sparrows which spend most of their time on the ground, wear dull colors. On the other hand a few females of the kind that nest in holes or underground have as bright colors as their mates, for their nests are out of sight and color doesn't matter.

Just as the tide of feathered creatures flowed north in the spring, now it has turned and as the leaves begin to color the birds are flying toward the tropical forests of the south. If you keep your eyes open these days you will see them gathering in flocks, sometimes sitting in trees and chattering, and then flying off to whirl and turn as if they were drilling in formation for their long flight. The older males leave first, while the females and the youngsters that were hatched in the summer follow at a slower pace, for they are not as strong flyers. I've already heard many flocks of Canada geese flying through the night honking to each other. These mornings when I get up around five o'clock there are almost always black ducks feeding in the shallows across the lake. They'll be flying down from the Hudson Bay country for

quite a while yet, and to see one of those fellows come hurtling down with feet set for a landing always gives me a thrill.

The robins left last week, big flocks of them, and I have noticed the white-throated sparrows and the wood thrushes passing on their way. The vesper sparrows that nested nearby have gone, too. I haven't seen a bank swallow or purple martin for days, and the kingbird that used to sit on a dead limb of the pine out front hasn't been around for a week.

A fellow might feel a little lonely if he didn't stop to remember that they will be back in the spring. One thing I can be sure of, my friend Gabby, the moosebird, will be here with me all winter. He is tough and bold and I keep him well fed when the snow flies. He waits for me in the pine by the porch every morning for his breakfast and scolds if he doesn't get it on time. When the blizzards come he goes down in the black spruce swamp to roost in a shaggy tree where the snow can't touch him.

There is much we have to learn about the birds and their ways. Nobody has figured out how they know when to start their migrations, nor how they find their way thousands of miles over land and sea from the Arctic barrens to the jungles of the tropics. Who gives the signal to go? In August you see the robins and the swallows gathering in flocks, small at first, then by the hundreds. Suddenly one day they are gone, flying south through the night. They rest and feed during the day. Yet one pair of robins has come back to my cabin to build a nest for three years running. How do they find my little place deep in the woods year after year? It's a mystery that many people who study birds would like to solve. Some day they will.

Speaking of birds, they tell me that down in Mexico there is a woodpecker that caches his victuals in the hollow stems of certain plants. He bores a hole just below a joint and drops in nuts and acorns and when he needs food he bores another hole lower down the stalk and they drop out just like gum drops out of a slot machine. In the western part of the country there is a woodpecker that drills holes in the soft bark of trees and stores an acorn in each hole. As a matter of fact, blue jays like to store nuts in holes.

The coming of the first Canada geese reminds me to tell you of our wild rice, for this is the harvest time. Some call it Indian rice, or water oats, and for hundreds of years the Indians have gathered it in the northern part of the country. At one time it was found in almost every lake in the north, but now it is getting scarce. You have to know wild rice to be sure of getting it, for the grain ripens very quickly and unless you know just when to gather it, it will suddenly drop into the water. We watch it until it is just ripe and then I go with the Chief down on Snow Goose Lake and we gather it together. We paddle the canoe very gently through the rice, and with thin sticks strike the heads of the plants so that the grain falls into the canoe.

I flail my rice on my tarpaulin to get the grain from the husks and fan the chaff away, but the Indians in some places parch the grains over a low fire and then separate the grain from the husk by fanning it. You can buy wild rice in the city, but it costs plenty. It is wonderful with roast duck. The Indians used to pound it into a sort of flour to thicken their stews, and some made a kind of bread from it. Usually they boil it whole with meat.

Now that the waterfowl are on their way through, Hank is spending a lot of time on photography. He has studied nature photography for years and his pictures of animals and birds are the best I have ever seen. As Hank says, it takes the patience of Job and plenty of time to photograph the wild things. One thing we learned from the Chief a long time ago was that if you sit still in the woods the birds and animals that are frightened when they first see you soon forget all about you and go about their business as if you were not there. That is the way Hank gets some of his photographs; he will sit almost motionless for hours and finally the bird he is watching for comes within range of his camera. Just sitting and keeping quiet is the best way to learn about wild things and their habits.

Most people, Hank says, snap their pictures before they are close enough to get anything worth-while. Take a bird, for instance; a lot of folks click the shutter when they are ten feet away and think they have really got something. Of course that is closer than they usually get to a wild thing, but the bird is still a long way from the camera. When you try to find that bird on the print, it is like hunting for a gnat on an alder. Hank takes most of his photographs of small birds and such like at a distance of one and a half to three feet. If he is unable to get that close he doesn't waste his film. That kind of photography often calls for hours, sometimes days, of planning and waiting. If he wants to get a picture of a mother bird feeding her young in the nest, he sets up a little black box or something that looks like a camera right close to the nest. In a day or so the bird is so used to seeing that box that she doesn't pay any more attention to it. Then, when she is away looking for food, Hank puts his camera in place of the box and gets out of sight. When she comes back the camera is all focused on the nest just the way he wants it, and all he has to do to take the picture is pull a long cord, or better yet, use a super-long cable release which he has.

Hank is a great fellow for building himself blinds so he can get up close to the animals. If you were to be up here in the woods and saw a stump get up and walk away, you could be pretty sure it was Hank; or maybe a small spruce tree begins moving down toward the lake where he wants to get a close-up of a black duck and her family of downy little ones. I've know him to build a blind high up in a pine tree to get pictures of a horned owl feeding her young. He uses an old piece of canvas dyed about the color of the trees, and leaves it up there for several days until the birds get used to it. Then when they're away he climbs in and when they return takes the photographs without them ever knowing it. In that way he gets pictures of the owl in the air just about

PHOTOGRAPHIC BLINDS

You've all seen photographs like these. To get ones that are really worth taking requires not only time and patience, but also ingenuity, luck, — and often as not, a blind.

Don't fool around pulling long strings. You can get pictures that way, but it's no where near as satisfactory as using a blind, or—

Some people make wooden cutouts, size and shape of a man, and set it up in front of a nest for a few days until the birds get used to it. Then all you do is replace the dummy box with a camera, stand behind the figure, and shoot away. Works well

A simple blind is made of brush and branches on the spot, but of course it dries up fast. You can use a cover made of burlap bags and daubed with brown and green paint, with either a knockdown frame, or one made of saplings in each location. It's rough and not very pretty, but it will give a lot of good service.

Here's a very effective portable blind, one of the best types. Made of bamboo rods which fit into holes in a circular block at the top, and in a wooden ring at the bottom. The cover, thrown over this frame, is made of green cloth imitation grass. Easy and quick to put up.

ring folds up

to land with a rabbit in his talons and then others of the young ones feeding.

One thing about birds, except possibly crows, they cannot count above one. Often when Hank has to go to a blind while the birds are watching, he takes me in with him. The birds see us enter and stay away, but when I come out again and go off they think the blind is empty and come right back. I wouldn't mind obliging Hank this way if he only wouldn't put so many of his blinds in such hard places to get to, like tops of pine trees.

Pictures of jumping fish are about the hardest kind to get, but Hank has a special high-speed flash lamp and a supply of patience the like of which I never have seen. Of course patience is not the only thing in getting good wild life photographs, for you have to know a lot about the animals and their habits. Hank will watch a partridge for weeks to decide just where he can get the best chance of a close-up. I have known him to spend most of a day sitting in a blind with corn spread all around it to get a photograph of a crow, which, just in passing, is one of the wariest critters in all the woods.

When I went over to visit Hank not long ago I found nobody home, but it didn't take long to find out why, for there, out on the lake, was Hank in his canoe chasing a swimming moose. And it didn't take very much guessing to know why, for to Hank any wild animal means a photograph. Sure enough when he was close up on the moose I saw him drop his paddle and grab his camera. The way be paddled back made me pretty sure he was satisfied with what he got.

As long as there are blueberries we eat them almost everyday. They are mighty nice with evaporated milk and a little

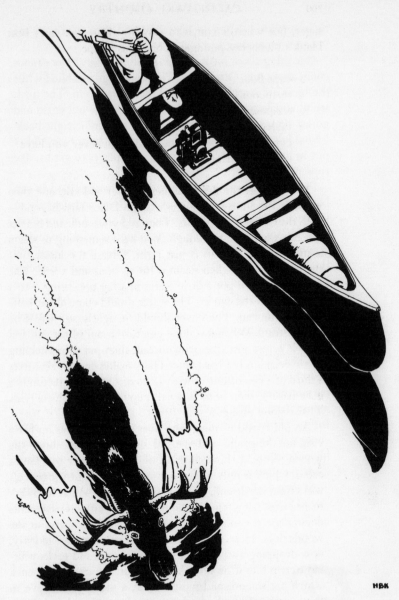

Hank was chasing a swimming moose

sugar, but when it comes to cooking them you can't beat Hank's blueberry pudding. This is his recipe:

   2 cups flour
   4 teaspoons baking powder
  ½ teaspoon salt
   2 tablespoons shortening
   1 cup milk, fresh or evaporated, whichever you have
   1 cup blueberries

Mix and sift the flour, baking powder and salt, and then work in the shortening—fresh bacon fat or lard is good—with the tips of your fingers. Then add your milk and berries and mix them into the dough. You need something to steam it in and a coffee can is just right. Grease the inside, put the cover on, and then steam it for an hour and a half. The easiest way is to put a little water in a big pot, bring it to a boil, then set the can in. The water should come about half-way up the can. The cover should fit tightly so there'll be lots of steam. When it is done you turn it out of the can and slice it across just like brownbread, then put a big helping of a special kind of hard sauce Hank makes on top. He mixes a third of a cup of butter with a cup of sugar (confectioner's if he has it), then beats in a half cup of mashed blueberries. That is good eating!

An old friend of mine who lives in the city was up for a visit not long ago and we did some tramping about the woods. Now, I think nothing of walking over to Hank's cabin, which is only about two miles away, but the trip always tired my friend, and that worried him. What he didn't realize was that a fellow who walks in the city on pavements doesn't use the same muscles that a man who walks in the woods does. Here the trails twist and turn, rising suddenly, now dropping away over a ridge, with ruts and rocks waiting to trip him if he doesn't watch out. On city pavements, which are smooth and mostly level, a man doesn't have to think very much about the ways of walking, but here in

GOOD!

the forest every step is a matter of balance, and you learn
to feel the ground as your foot touches it whether you are
walking in daylight or in the dark. The feet of a good woodsman tell him where the trail is, no matter how dark it is, for
even in heavy boots they become very sensitive to the lay of
the land. The constant change in the trail is what tires the
muscles of a city man. The woodsman develops an easy, ef-
fortless rolling gait that takes him over rocks and windfalls
without a lot of labor. He walks from the hips down, while
the city man, as the Chief says, walks from head to foot. The
feet of a woodsman move straight ahead and not at an angle
as many city folk walk, and the body above his waist leans
slightly forward.

Knowing how to take care of your feet has a lot to do
with comfortable traveling in the woods. I believe in bathing
as often as I can. Walking in wet footgear is hard on the
skin. If the going is damp it is my habit to take off my socks
which are always pure wool, and wring them out if I have no
dry ones with which to replace them. Another important
thing is to have shoes or moccasins that fit. After a day of hard
traveling, when your feet are apt to be pretty tired and sore,
it is very restful and beneficial to bathe them in warm water
and salt.

When a shoe begins to chafe, particularly on the heel or
the toes, you are almost certain to get a blister, and one way
of easily avoiding the trouble is to rub candle wax on the
toe and heel of your sock. That makes it slip easily and prevents friction on the skin. I know several woodsmen who do
that regularly whenever they take a long tramp because it
also keeps their socks from wearing out. Nothing will make
you more miserable than undersized socks, for a short sock
cramps your toes and tires your feet, which means being
tired all over. Socks should be a size longer than the foot,
for wool is bound to shrink a little. Just in passing, never
wash your woolen clothes in hot water. It should be not
more than lukewarm, for hot water shrinks and hardens
wool and robs it of that springy softness that traps air between the fibers of the yarn and acts as insulation.

TRACKS ~ of
a City Man....

....and a Woods
Indian

If you get a blister on your foot don't pull off the skin. Doing so may cause a serious infection. I have known woodsmen to take a clean needle and run a thread through a blister cutting off the thread after it is through, which helps the water to drain off. The Chief very seldom has any trouble with his feet, which are toughened by years of walking, but once when he got a blister he spread balsam pitch on it and wrapped a clean piece of cloth over it. Pitch is also good for corns.

Every year in September a friend of ours comes up for a little late trout fishing and as he always wants to take some home to his folks we smoke them for him. The squaretails are at their best now, hard and fat, and the sport is good. Smoking fish is a job that cannot be rushed and if you do it well the results are mighty satisfying. There is a flavor to smoked fish that leaves you craving more, especially if you freshen them for an hour or so in cool water and then cook them slowly in milk. Before starting to smoke fish split and clean them and then rub salt on the inside. If you are going to eat them right away very little salt is needed. For keeping any length of time soak them for a night and a day in brine, which is made by adding salt to water until it will float a small potato, before smoking begins. The old Chief loves to work the smokehouse. First he builds a good hot fire, then puts on a lot of damp or green wood. Birch punk is best to my way of thinking. In time the fire just smolders along giving off a thin smoke. The Chief digs himself a lot of fine spruce roots and ties the fish by their tails to short green saplings to hang in the smoke flue. Then he lets them stay in the smoke for two days. You can smoke fish and meat over a smoldering open fire, on mesh wire over a barrel, or even in the throat of a fireplace chimney, but I have a smokehouse which does a better job.

Fish is not the only thing you can smoke, for the Indians smoke geese and ducks, as well as deer and moose meat. You

plan view

...tied to green saplings with spruce roots

SMOKE HOUSE

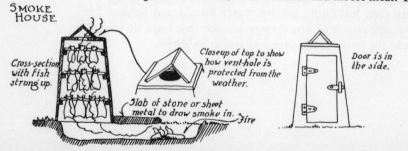

Cross-section with fish strung up.

Closeup of top to show how vent-hole is protected from the weather.

Slab of stone or sheet metal to draw smoke in. Fire

Door is in the side.

can also smoke partridge. As a matter of fact when I get a side of bacon that I have to keep for a while, particularly the mild-cured kind, I hang it in my smokehouse for a couple of days and make sure that the blowflies don't get at it. Before I put it in the smokehouse I rub on a syrup made by melting maple sugar in just a little water—honey would do just as well—and I daub it on because sugar makes meat tender while salt is apt to toughen it. One thing about smoking that you must remember is that you do not want too much smoke. It is not only smoke, but a little heat that does the job.

Every fall the Chief smokes quite a few geese. He plucks and cleans them, rubs a little salt on the inside, and hangs them up in a smokehouse made of birch bark laid over a sapling held up by short shears and blocked at each end with pieces of bark, leaving vents at both ends near the peak. Last year I saw him use an old hollow log buried in a trench to carry the smoke from the fire. In the old days the Indians built a little staging near the top of their tepees where they hung strips of meat and whole fish to cure slowly in the smoke that drifted up from the fire in the center of the shelter. In many ways that was a fine method, for slow smoking is good smoking.

When the Chief smokes venison or moose he cuts the lean part of the meat into strips about an inch thick and hangs them on a wire in his smokehouse. Usually in the early fall when there is not much rain he keeps a slow smudge going for about four days. The Indians do not use much salt, which, generally speaking, is right, and when their dried meat is done it is about as hard as rawhide; but if you cut it up in small pieces and boil it a while it's mighty tasty and nourishing. That is what they used to call "jerked meat."

As I said, rotting birch is a good wood for smoking. The main thing is to keep away from pine, balsam, and spruce, which give an unpleasant and bitter flavor. If you have any hickory handy that is fine, and I know that down in the farming country apple wood and pear are used, not to mention corncobs.

Smoked partridge to my way of thinking is wonderful eating. I like to skin the bird, rub a little salt and pepper inside after cleaning it, and hang it up by its feet in the smokehouse for twenty-four hours. It is the white meat of the partridge when smoked that tastes the best.

I have been smoking meats for years and I have discovered certain little tricks that are mighty handy in a pinch. Supposing you have a chicken and you are hankering for the smoked flavor. All you have to do is to boil it for the usual time until it is tender, set it aside to cool, and then hang it in the smokehouse for about an hour. When you bite into the meat it will have that wonderful smoky flavor that people will go a long way to find.

If you are fond of smoked cheese cut it up in small chunks and spear them on twigs to hang in your smokehouse for about an hour. Don't have much fire when you smoke cheese, for heat melts it. All you need is a whiff of good smoke from damp wood.

Salt is another thing I smoke because it gives a fine flavor to my foods. It is especially good in soups and stews. What I do is take a cup of salt in the bottom of the bag it comes in and hang it up in the smokehouse. I wet the bag, for the dampness seems to carry the smoke through the salt better than if it is smoked dry. By the time it is smoked through the salt is a hard lump but it breaks up again easily by running a rolling pin over it. I have no wooden rolling pin but a bottle does the job for me in all my cooking very nicely.

If you want to try smoking things you can easily do it in your own back yard; and a friend of mine who lives in an apartment in the city smoked his in the flue of his fireplace and got fine results once he located some hickory which he had to soak in his bathtub before it gave off enough of the right kind of smoke. If you want to build a temporary smokehouse all you need is a few flat stones and a little ground flue to carry the smoke to the bottom of a stack which can be made of a piece of stovepipe or even wood if you make your ground flue long enough so it won't catch fire. Then you can

Stick

Pipe

SALT
SMOKE
HOUSE

hang your salt and other things to smoke on a wire across the top of the stack.

The Indians who have spent the summer on Snow Goose Lake are heading north for their trapping grounds and most of them have already passed up Cache Lake with their canoes riding low with heavy loads of winter supplies which are chiefly flour and salt pork. Their traps, snowshoes, and hunting sleds have been cached all summer on stagings at last winter's camping places for they are not needed during the summer and to cache them saves a lot of heavy packing.

The Indian women generally take back with them quite a lot of cotton goods for making dresses, especially the brightly colored calicoes. One of the most important items of the trappers' supplies is ammunition for their guns, although any Indian worthy of the name could live on the land without ever firing a shot.

As they pass Cache Lake they nod to me, for Indians don't show their feelings very much, but the children wave and shout as all children do. No matter, I am proud to know that I would be welcomed as an old friend in the lodges or cabins of any of the Indians who pass my way.

I remember one Indian I called Joe who came to me last summer and told me without complaining that his wife was sick and he needed a few supplies until he could replenish them. What he wanted most was tea, which the Indians love, salt, sugar, and for himself, a little tobacco. I started to make up some packages for him, but he shook his head and spread out his red bandanna on the floor. Then he asked me to pour about a half pound of salt in one corner, some tea in the other, sugar in the third and tobacco in the fourth corner. He knotted each corner to make a little bag, rolled up the big kerchief into a ball and left without a word. Not that he wasn't thankful, but that was his way. On the trip north sometime later he paddled up to the shore, called me to come down, and handed me one of the finest pairs of snowshoes I have ever owned. His wife and little boy smiled at me and then he nodded and pushed off without further conversation.

The Indians are heading north

Sitting around the stove one night when it was chilly enough outside to make the fire feel good, we got to talking about our experiences in the woods. I recalled the time years ago when I capsized while running rapids in a strange stream when I was traveling alone. I had a ten-foot birch bark trapper's canoe, the kind the Indians use, broad and flat in the middle with the ends drawn in pretty fast. They are light and small, but carry a lot of freight. I was on my way south and in a hurry to get home so I decided I would rather take a chance on running the rapids than carry around them. I was almost through when the canoe swung sideways, hit a hidden rock and over I went.

I made shore all right, for my clothing was light and I had moccasins on. I never wear anything else in a canoe for if you go over with boots on your chances of landing are pretty slim. When I began to round up my belongings in the dead water below, all I had left was the canoe with a hole in the bottom, a little can of tea and about a pound of prunes that I had wedged up in the bow to keep them dry during a rainstorm. But the important thing was that I had a little watertight bottle full of matches in my pocket, so I knew I could get along.

After I had patched up the canoe with spruce pitch and bark and got under way, it took me five days to get back to civilization. On an island in one of the lakes I found gulls' nests and, not being a man to turn down anything edible in case of need, I took some of the eggs. Once I got myself a mess of trout by damming a little brook with close-set stakes and driving the fish down into a small pool. Another time I got a single fool hen, knocking it off a spruce by swinging my paddle edgewise so she couldn't see it coming. As luck would have it after I lost my outfit I never laid eyes on a porcupine, the starving man's meat, although usually there are plenty of them around. What I missed most was a little salt on my victuals. As all my pots and pans were gone I had to boil my tea in a little birch bark rogan. I roasted the gulls' eggs which, I can tell you, do not please a man's appetite, since they are so fishy in flavor.

I am not a superstitious person, but from that day on I have always kept some tea and prunes and a little salt wedged high up in the bow of my canoe, and I lash my packs to the thwarts before going into lively water. I also learned from that experience that a long portage is often the safest and shortest way home. When going into new country a man should make allowance for what people tell him about traveling conditions. A woodsman who knows his country may overlook the fact that a rapids he can shoot without any trouble may be dangerous for a stranger. A river can be safe during times of high water and just the opposite when the level drops.

I have started Tripper's training as a sled dog. He is not very big yet nor very strong, so I made him a little deer hide harness and I am teaching him to get used to the feel of it by pulling a little piece of dead spruce pointed at one end so it will not catch on roots and discourage him. As I have said before, he is a smart little fellow and already he is getting so used to the feel of the drag that he doesn't even turn around to see what he is pulling. It weighs only a few pounds and in a month I will have him ready to hitch to my hunting sled for the next step.

The Chief and I have been clearing out a few trees down in front of the cabin so I can get a better view of Faraway See Hill. To make sport of it we had a contest to see which one of us could drop a tree exactly where we wanted it. One thing is to size up a tree and if it is leaning more in one direction than another the wisest thing is to drop it on that side. The wind also has something to do with where you drop a

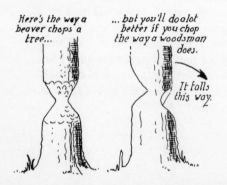

Here's the way a beaver chops a tree...

... but you'll do a lot better if you chop the way a woodsman does.

It falls this way.

tree. The notch or kerf on the side on which the tree will fall should be cut first and must be a little lower and deeper than the notch on the opposite side. The Chief taught me long ago to make sure before I started chopping that all nearby brush is cut away, for you can have a mighty dangerous accident if your axe catches on anything when you begin to swing it. The Chief won the contest by dropping a tree across a piece of birch bark which he had laid down as a target.

The WINTER WOOD PILE

A piece of bark keeps out a lot of weather.

When you're splitting, always put the piece on the far side of the block.

That way it won't fly up and hit you unexpectedly.

OCTOBER

Frost on Scarlet Leaves

U P I N the timber country they are putting the camps in shape for the winter cutting and I have to go there every so often to make plans with the bosses. Logging is not what it used to be forty years ago when big horses, the pride of the tote teamsters, did all the heavy hauling. Only a few horses are seen in the camps these days, for tractors have taken their place. They do a fine job, but I miss the horses, the shouts of the drivers and the sight of fine teams with vapor steaming up from their shining backs in zero weather. It was grand to see them snaking logs out to the skidways where the sleighs picked up their bunk loads and hauled them down to the banking ground by the river. Those were days when the push had to be a man who not only knew logging, but could knock down any lumberjack in the camp and keep order. They call him the foreman now.

There is no finer picture of teamwork than to see two good men making a sharp crosscut saw sing its way through a big stick. And for handling a double-bitted axe you can not beat those fellows in the logging camps. To watch one of them balanced on a downed tree, his axe flashing in the dazzling winter sunlight as he slashes off the limbs, is worth seeing. They used to spend a lot of time whetting the edges of their axes and I have seen a man prove an edge by shaving himself. When the trees fell the swampers got busy clearing away the limbs and brush so the teams could drag logs to the skidways.

Keeping the tote roads in good condition was important and all day long road monkeys were busy repairing places that broke down under the heavy loads. On cold, quiet nights when the frost cracked in the trees and the zero air burned in your nostrils with every breath, the sprinkler, a sleigh fitted with a big wooden tank, would go out over the roads, water trickling from two holes over the ruts to fill them in with new ice.

Teams often left the camp soon after three o'clock in the morning and in an hour there wouldn't be anybody left there but the cook and his crew, the wood butcher, who built and repaired the sleds, and who could shave out a toothpick with an axe, and the barn boss who had charge of feeding the horses.

Nowadays most of the heavy work is done by tractors and in the silence of the woods you hear the roar of their engines that leave a trail of smoke that taints the good north air. That's the way it has to be, for things have got to move ahead, and if there is a better and faster way of doing a job I am for it. Be that as it may, I will always be glad of my memories of men and horses working in the woods in winter and the great spring drives when the logs that were piled on the ice crashed through and started on their way down stream.

Tamarack, Hackmatack, Black Larch, they're all the same. Sheds its leaves every fall — "Deciduous Conifer," it's called.

Sometimes the Chief comes along on my trips to the timber limits and on the last one we went up by way of Faraway See Hill to look over the country. We do that almost every year about this time, for in the fall the view from the top just about takes your breath away. It is a mite over four miles as the herons fly, but seven by the trail from my cabin.

When we got to the top of the hill where the winds of winter blow too hard for trees to live, we looked down on a giant-colored map made up of the scarlet of the maples and the bright yellows of the birches and poplars laid out on the dark green background of spruce and pine, with patches of lighter green where the tamaracks stand in the swamps; and in between lay the rivers and the lakes, blue in the sunlight, silver when a cloud passed across the sun.

Just before sunset we made camp by a brook at the foot of the hill and I cooked some flapjacks, bacon, and tea while the Chief built a shelter. Bending down a slender birch sapling until the top was about his own height, he lashed it with our tump line to a stake, and against it on both sides at intervals of a few inches he slanted dead spruce saplings. These he tied at the top with spruce roots and then beginning at the bottom shingle-wise, he laid on pieces of birch bark stripped from a dead tree, spiking the strips over the stubs of the spruce branches to hold them in place until he could pile on a thatch of balsam boughs. A long strip of curving birch bark laid along the ridge finished the job. It was as snug a shelter as a man could want, tight and warm.

Close by our camp was an out-cropping of iron pyrite, Fool's Gold, and although I had not tried it for years, I made fire by striking two chunks of it together. When struck a sharp, glancing blow pyrite gives off sparks which can be used to kindle a fire. It is not as easy as it sounds, for there's a knack to it, and you have to have good dry tinder. The Chief shredded some birch bark, but I failed to light it, so he got a piece of fungus, the kind that grows on dead birch logs, and scraped it with his knife until he had a little pile of powder on a strip of birch bark. Then after several tries I got it glowing and by blowing on it gently, we got a fire going. To be sure, matches are handier, but as pyrite is pretty common in these parts it is a trick worth knowing. It is an easier way of starting a fire than striking sparks with flint and steel.

To an Indian the woods furnish nearly all he needs for living, be it shelter, fire, or food. It was not by chance that we came upon that camping site with plenty of dry birch bark and saplings ready at hand. The Chief's roving eyes had been watching for what he wanted. And it wasn't just luck that

Saplings lashed to birch tree

Balsam over bark

Bark over ridge

Young Birch

Line to hold birch down

Stake

THE LEAN-TO

Strips of bark pushed over limb stubs to hold in place

there was a brook to give us water and a stand of heavy timber to the northward to shelter us in case the cold wind came in the night. Yet we had not gone out of our way nor wasted time in coming to the place.

On the trail the Chief walks as quietly as a lynx and his eyes see everything. Not an animal track is missed and he can pick up scents like a wild creature. "Moose not far," he said soon after we had started on our way the next morning. Sure enough in a few minutes he pointed to fresh tracks crossing the trail, for this is Wisac, the Mating Moon, and the deer and moose are roving the forest. While stopping to study the tracks, the old man pointed out a stalk of grass slowly lifting from the soil into which it had been pressed by the hoof of the animal, and because the ground was dry little specks of soil crumbled from the edges of the hoofprint. Without saying a word, but by holding up his hands, touching his nose, and indicating direction he told me that the moose had passed not ten minutes before; that the animal had wind of us and was hurrying was shown by the distance between the hoofprints and their depth in the damp earth.

I have seen the Chief trailing a bear in light tracking snow and before he had gone very far he told me the bear was a large male and that he was in no great hurry or had no special place to go to because the tracks wandered hither and yon, which indicated that he was probably looking for food. That proved to be true for later on we came across several logs that he had clawed in search of grubs.

When an animal is running for its life its tracks are deep and clean cut, but when the beast is taking its time the prints are more likely to be blurred or shallow, and without sharp edges. Talking of bears, the Chief said you could tell a young one by sharp claw marks, while the claws of an old-timer, worn by much traveling, have rounded points.

Studying the tracks of a big dog wolf one day he explained that the animal was moving very slowly and had stopped once in a while to listen and pick up a scent, for the snow in some of the footprints was faintly glazed, showing that the animal had stood still long enough for the warmth of his foot to melt the snow which quickly froze when he moved on.

When as a youngster I began trailing game with the Chief he made sure that I understood that wild animals depend on scent, sound, and sight to protect themselves against their enemies. The hunter, therefore, tries to keep down wind from his game, moves very quietly and guards his movements. Ever watch a cat stalking a squirrel, creeping ahead when his quarry was not looking, freezing when it turned its head or showed signs of alarm? That's the way the Chief gets close to a moose or bear. If the hunter is standing as motionless as a rock when the animal looks his way it may not recognize him for what he is, especially if he is in timbered country. But let him so much as twist his head or move a hand and the wild creature will see it.

Chief Tibeash likes to show how good a woodsman he is and at times I have found it hard to pick him out in the forest. Once I discovered him not twenty yards away, chuckling to himself because he had been coming up on me for several minutes, freezing in his tracks when I looked his way, silently hurrying on when I turned my eyes in another direction. "Good thing," he said, "you are not a moose or you would be my meat."

I recall the days when the Chief taught me how to call moose. After I had practiced with him for a while I went out one fall evening alone without a gun for a little calling on my own hook. I wandered down to a point on the east shore of Snow Goose Lake and let loose with my birch bark horn, rolling it toward the ground and raising it high just the way the Chief does. It was a quiet evening and after listening for a while I gave some more calls, ending up with a few mooselike grunts. When moose answer a call they may come tearing through the bush without thought of caution, but once in a while they steal up as quietly as a cat. That is just what happened to me. Not fifty yards away a big bull suddenly

A big bull suddenly appeared on the shore

appeared on the shore. He saw me about the same instant that I caught sight of him, and I could see he was mad. It was my good luck to be standing near a big spruce with limbs that came down pretty low, and it didn't take more than a jump and ten gasps to get twenty feet up that tree. The moose hung around for a while, snorting and pawing the ground, and then he went away. Then I started home like a snowshoe rabbit with a fox on his trail. It took me a week to begin to feel proud that I could call a moose.

If you called the Chief superstitious he would be angry, yet he and many other hunters and trappers have certain beliefs about hunting and fishing that have been handed down from generation to generation. One afternoon early this fall when the old man and I were sitting talking I noticed that he was listening to something else, and then all of a sudden he got up and went out the door very quietly. I had some meat on the stove so I didn't follow him for a few minutes and when I went out he was standing under a tree looking up and talking his head off in Cree. It took me a minute to see that he was addressing several bluebirds which were then moving down on their way south. Every few seconds he would stop and listen, and finally I heard one of the birds chirp and then another. At that the Chief turned back to the cabin with an air of great satisfaction. The Indians in these parts believe that if you talk to the bluebirds before you start on a hunting trip and they answer, the hunting will be good, but if they make no reply then you can expect no game.

Aside from banking the cabin I have had a lot of other chores to keep me busy this fall. One of them was to build a new stage for my canoe at the back of the cabin where I store it under birch bark when the ice makes on the lake. I have also replaced the stay wires on my chimney pipe, for the fingers of the winter gales are strong and searching, and checked over the roof and tarred some of the seams. A good tar paper roof is hard to beat if you keep it tight.

CANOE STAGING

With no room in the cabin, and no storehouse, we have to store our canoes outdoors all winter. But with bark and boughs for cover, held off the ground on stakes, they come through in good shape.

Inside I have set up my old barrel stove which with the cookstove keeps me as warm as I please all winter. That kind of heater, which some call a drum stove, gives off a lot of heat and I get an extra supply by using a long pipe that runs down the middle of the cabin and then across to the chimney. You would be surprised the amount of heat a long pipe will throw off instead of pulling it all up the flue. When it comes to making a hot fire it is hard to beat tamarack, which is sometimes called larch or hackmatack. To my mind it is better than white birch and equal to yellow birch for a lasting fire, and a good deal hotter than either. The fact is that it is so hot it is apt to burn out the stove irons. You cannot find any better wood for foundation posts or fencing, since tamarack resists decay so well it lasts for years. A mighty useful tree in all ways.

During the summer the pipe lengths, greased with bacon fat to keep off rust, hang by wires from the roof, so the mice and squirrels can't get at them. Once the critters make the jump from a rafter and skid off the greasy pipe they decide there are easier ways of getting their victuals. While I was putting up the pipe I found some of the chinking was loose between the logs high up on the east wall, so I yanked off the saplings that hold it in place and tucked in plenty of clay and then dry sphagnum moss.

Now that the nights are getting colder I have packed in the storage bin I built under the cabin floor all the provisions that would be damaged by freezing. The first one I made was a failure because it was built of boards and the mice got in, so I got myself an old oil drum from the abandoned mine, burned it out to clear away all smell of oil, and then painted it with tar on the outside so it wouldn't rust. I set the drum in a box four feet square with a foot of sphagnum moss on the bottom and plenty of dry moss around the sides so that it is well insulated and if any mouse gets in there he will have to bring along a hacksaw. The lid is a piece of sheet iron and I reach into the box through a trap door in the

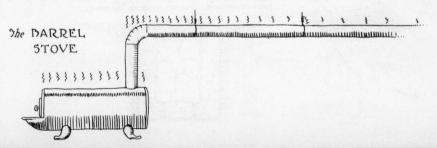

The BARREL
    STOVE

floor. Potatoes and any other vegetables that I happen to get, as well as canned goods, keep perfectly in this little store bin. If I leave the cabin for a trip I have a heavy pad of sphagnum moss in an old bag that I put on top for insulation. When I am home the little amount of heat that leaks through the floor keeps it at just about the right temperature.

Another little job was to paint my weather vane which is the shape of a big pike. I relined the hole which fits over the nail on top of the pole with a small piece of metal tubing so that it will turn easily in the slightest breeze. I always enjoy watching the weather vane to keep track of wind direction. You can make weather vanes in all sorts of shapes, such as flying geese, arrows, guns, or a canoe with a man in the stern. Once after I had visited an old sea captain down on the coast I copied one he had made in the shape of a whale. It is easy to whittle one out, and to make sure that the vane minds the wind, put a metal washer under it so that it won't rub on the top of the pole.

Mice have been troubling me lately. The critters got into my flour sack and I had to work fast, for once they break into your grub they send out word to all their friends and relatives to come on in and share alike. The way I stopped that was to make a water trap. All you need is a large can or pail and a sliver of wood which should be light and thin, about ten inches long and an inch wide. Find the place were it just balances on the rim of the pail and cut a small notch just back of that so the end outside the pail will be the heaviest. Then lean a piece of firewood against the pail so the critters can climb up. Balance the sliver of wood on the rim after tying a small piece of bacon on the end over the pail. It should then be set with the notch on the rim so that when your mouse walks out to get the bait the stick drops down and he slides into the pail. You can put water in it or leave it

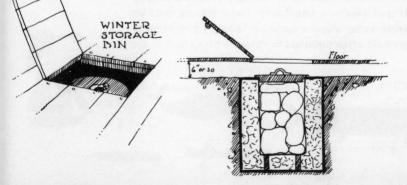

WINTER
STORAGE
BIN

Floor

6" or so

empty if you like, for most mice can't climb out of a pail. However, be sure your stick is short enough so he cannot use it for a ladder and climb out if it falls in too. If you have balanced your sliver of wood just right it will swing back into catching position after it dumps each mouse. And, by the way, rub a piece of bacon on the stove wood and out along the trigger strip so the mice will follow the trail to the bait.

I must tell you about something interesting I tried after reading a story about South American Indians and how they use blowguns for hunting. I didn't think much more about it until the Chief and I were poking around the old deserted mine when we went over after my oil drum. In what was left of the blacksmith shop I found a piece of quarter-inch brass pipe about four feet long. Well, that put an idea into my head so I took it home and started in making slender little arrows to see if I could make a blowpipe. For the arrows I used slivers of spruce with a small nail in the head to give them weight and a sharp point, and on the other end I wrapped a little strip of cloth until it was large enough to fit easily into the bore of the pipe. The idea of the cloth, which should be loosely wound, is that when you blow the air expands the end and makes a good seal to let your breath drive the arrow with force. I tried it out and the thing worked.

BLOW-PIPE ARROWS

The arrows of the South American Indians range from twelve to twenty inches long and the shafts are very slender, some being no thicker than a match. They feather them with some kind of vegetable wool or even soft bark wound in a cone form just as I wound the cloth. The blowguns are from seven to nearly twelve feet long and some of them are lined with a bore made of a smooth reed. I have even heard that some of the Indians wind the shafts of their arrows with bark in spiral form to start the arrow rotating just as the rifling in a gun makes a bullet turn. Don't think this is any toy, for those fellows down there can shoot accurately up to seventy yards. They even rig sights on their blowguns.

NEW WEATHERVANES

If you don't get a proper balance for free turning, put a plug of lead in the nose.

about ⅔ of the way back

What I want to do when I get around to it is to make one of wood like the native guns. My brass blowpipe throws an arrow fifty feet and drives the point into a pine like nobody's business. The way the Chief watched me made me pretty certain he will be doing the same. He always likes to try out something new.

We have had good hunting this fall and the Chief has a fine white-tailed buck hanging in the lean-to back of his cabin. Hank and I will also have venison before long to keep us going for some time. Once it gets cold and the meat freezes you can keep it all winter if you want to, and the longer it hangs the better venison tastes.

For waterfowl shooting we go down to Snow Goose Lake and I can tell you it is a beautiful sight to glide through the narrows and come out on the lake, blue against the gold and crimson forest, with an Indian summer haze to blend the colors. The air now is apt to be sharp even at midday, strong with the scent of dead leaves and swamp grass. Just as we came into open water we saw a bull moose standing on a little point that juts out from the tamarack swamp. He was one of the biggest we have seen for a long time and his antlers must have had a spread of at least sixty inches. I don't believe there is anything so downright impressive as a moose in the open where you get a better idea of the size of the animal than when you come on him in heavy woods. He watched us for a minute and with a snort that sent jets of vapor from his nostrils he went off with that peculiar trot which takes a moose over the ground much faster than you realize.

The Chief's favorite duck shooting ground is in the shallows where the wild rice and the water grass grow, and at one place where the water is only a few inches deep he will step out and twist a bunch of grass into the rough shape of a duck for a decoy. You wouldn't think those tufts of grass would bring in the ducks, but they do.

The geese have been coming over strong lately, great flocks of them flying in wedge formation, and the Chief has

spent a good deal of time down on Snow Goose laying in a supply of them as well as ducks which he smokes and puts away in a cool place for good eating later on.

This is the crazy season when some of the partridges seem to be out of their minds, flying wildly by day and even by night. Often they crash into trees or limbs, and even houses. What makes them lose all their cunning no one seems to know, but many a time I have seen them in spells of madness when they seemed to lose all fear of their natural enemies.

On one of our hunts we stopped on the way home and Hank brought in five partridges to make a fine Sunday meal for us. While he was working up the slope of a low ridge looking for birds he caught sight of a big black bear busy on a rotten log in search of grubs. The place was strewn with blowdowns and the trees, crossed this way and that at all angles, made some of the worst jackpots he had ever seen, so Hank couldn't get close enough for a shot. Fat and well-fed for his winter sleep, he was, Hank said, and his fur was thick and purple-black. You can tell a lot about the health of an animal by the condition of the fur and when it is rich in color and shining you can be pretty sure the critter is in good health.

The way we like our grouse is to skin, clean, and bake them. I put the whole bird in a pan and lay very thin strips of bacon across the breast. In that way you baste the meat while it is cooking and it comes out moist and sweet. All you need then is salt and pepper and some hot biscuits. With ducks it is little different and Hank is certain he can cook them better than anybody else. A duck, he will tell you, must be picked, singed and then drawn and washed. Then you wipe it dry and tie the legs together, turning in the neck close to the breast. After that you season with salt and roast for about twenty-five minutes. The next step—and it is important—is to put a tablespoonful of cold water inside the duck, which keeps the juices from hardening. Anyone will tell you that a little currant or beach plum jelly to eat with the duck makes it perfect. Of course, as Hank says, there are plenty of fancy stuffings and basting with wine and such like, but if what you want is the taste of duck, that is the way to get it.

On the way home the day we got the partridges we struck back into the woods to look over a little brook that we had not visited for two years. The place was so changed we hardly knew it, for the beavers had been busy and instead of a brook we found a good-sized pond held by as fine a dam as you could find. The beavers are busy now getting in their winter food supply and all about back from the pond on higher ground the young poplars have been neatly cut and dragged to the water. While we were watching, a beaver came out on the far end of the pond and started swimming down with a newly cut length of sapling. The instant he saw us there was a quick, hard splash and only the widening rings on the water showed where he had been. It is not often you see them by day, for they do most of their work after dark.

With young Tripper to take his place in harness this winter, I have made myself a new sled which is a little different from the kind we usually have up here. Instead of runners made of split ash, I used two old hickory skis that a fellow left here a year ago. My idea is that the extra width of the skis will keep the sled from sinking as deep into the snow as it does with the narrower runners. The skies are a shade heavier than the regular runners, but I allowed for that by lightening up on the rest of the sled so it weighs just about the same as the old one. The new sled is just six feet long, which is small, but plenty for two dogs. I never believe in overloading them.

Old Wolf loves a sled and all the time I was building the new one he was nosing around inspecting my work and trying to show me he liked it. When I got out the harness to make sure it was in good order he just about went wild. That's the kind of sled dog you like to have.

Tripper has been doing fine in his training. The harness I use has a round collar made of moose hide and filled tight with pieces of old blanket, wrapped around heavy wire to

The beaver are busy getting in their winter food supply

DOG
HARNESS

This is the
top view, and
below is the way
it looks on Old
Wolf,
the lead dog.

— and on
succeeding dogs

stiffen it. The collar has a strap on each side to snap onto the traces, and one on top fastened to the cinch strap. Now Tripper steps right along behind Wolf and pulls his share like a good one. He has learned to stop when I shout "Whoa," and puts his shoulder to the load when I give the command, "Mush!" One thing you have to remember is not to over-work a young dog. At first you carry no load on the sled and you have to be careful not to let it run up on the dog and hurt him. Patience and more patience and firm kindness is the secret of training a dog, or any animal for that matter. You want him to love his work and good sled dogs do.

After a training trip I always give the young dog a little piece of meat as a reward, but that is only during schooling. Experienced sled dogs work best when they are fed at the end of the day, but when a puppy is young he needs food three times a day. If you want a good sled dog don't make a pet of him. You can be good friends, but a dog that is a pet is almost sure to be spoiled and does not obey as he ought to. You must earn a dog's respect and he has to know who is master.

The Chief and I have been dressing the skin of his first buck which will make fine moccasins later on, although he wants to get a moose, too, for its hide will stand more wear. His method of making buckskin is the one the Indians have used for generations and it is fairly simple.

A lot of hard work goes into making a good skin, for the only skin worth having is one that is soft and will stay soft even after it has been soaked time after time. To begin with, the Chief mixes about two quarts of wood ashes in half a wash tub of warm water and puts the skin in to soak so that the hair can be scraped off easily. This can usually be done after the hide has soaked two or three days.

To scrape off the hair, hang the skin over a log set up at an angle to make it easy to work on, and scrape with an iron tool with the edge ground flat. The one the Chief uses is made of a piece of bucksaw blade set in a slotted handle, and it works fine. An old flat file makes a good tool.

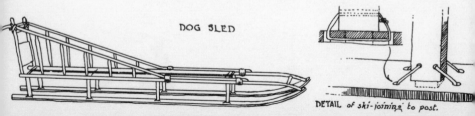

DOG SLED

DETAIL of ski-joining to post.

When all the hair has been removed and the top layer of skin cleaned off, turn the hide over and start what is called "fleshing" it, which is the job of scraping off every trace of flesh and fat that was left on the hide when it was pulled off the animal. This is hard work and you can save yourself many a backache if you have your fleshing log at the right height so that you can put your full weight on the scraping tool as you push it down and away from you.

When all the hair is off and the skin has been thoroughly fleshed it ought to be rinsed in clear warm water and then wrung out. It is a pretty awkward job to wring out a wet deerskin so the Chief and I rigged up a crude sort of wringer made of two short lengths of spruce logs with a handle on one, and set in a frame. It does a pretty good job too.

When you have all the water out of the hide the job of tanning begins. This is something that ought to be prepared for in advance. The Chief saves the brains of the deer, dries them very slowly in a pan at the back of his stove so they won't cook, and when they are dry he puts them in an old sugar bag and boils them slowly until they are soft. When the boiled brains have cooled off so that he can stand to put his hand in the mixture, he pours them in the wash tub and adds just enough water so that the hide can be thoroughly soaked in the mixture where it must stay until the skin is just as soft as an old glove. In place of brains you can use common brown kitchen soap which is melted up until you can make a rich solution. Homemade soap, the kind made with lye in it, is even better, but the Chief never uses anything but brains.

While the skin is soaking it should be thoroughly worked every once in a while to help soften it, and after it has been soaking for a few hours take it out and pull it in every direction with all your strength to make the fibers pliable. This process of pulling and working dries the hide, and if it is then still stiff put it back to soak and repeat the process.

When the skin is properly done you should be able to squeeze water through it. The real secret of making good

Fleshing Log

buckskin is to work it by kneading and stretching it until it is thoroughly softened. There is no easy way and it is safe to say that you can hardly work a skin too much.

The final drying should be done by squeezing all moisture out in the wringer and then working and pulling the hide until it is dry and smooth. The final step which keeps the skin soft even after it has been wet through use is smoking for several days in the same kind of smoke that you use for curing meat. It is important that as little heat as possible reaches the skin. To get an even smoke the skin should be turned over from time to time and the job is done when the hide has taken on a beautiful soft yellow tone. When the hide is used for moccasins some folks give one side a dressing of neat's-foot oil.

On my cabin floor is a fine bearskin rug which the Chief, Hank, and I tanned. Where you want to keep the fur you don't soak the skin in water and ashes, but after fleshing it stretch the hide by lacing it on a frame in a place where it will be sheltered from rain. Then you paint on a coat of the brains mixture made just as you do for buckskin. Several coats should be applied at intervals, between which the skin should be pulled and worked thoroughly to soften it. I remember we laid it out where the pine needles were thick, fur side down, and beat it with saplings to help soften the fibers. After it was thoroughly softened we gave the fur a good washing in the lake, stretched and worked it until it was dry, and then smoked it for several days. The hide is just as soft now as the day we finished the job, and mighty comforting to the feet on a cold morning, not to mention being downright good looking.

While we were working on the deerskin we got talking about the way we used pyrite to start our campfire and other methods, such as whirling a stick with a bow which is difficult, and using a magnifying glass, a fine method when the sun is out. But one of the best fire makers I have ever seen is the fire piston which they say was invented ages ago and is still used by primitive natives on small islands in the faraway

Pacific. They make their fire pistons of wood, but try as I could, I never made one of wood that would work, although I'm going to try it again one of these days. But I did make one of a short piece of quarter-inch brass pipe that does a good job.

The fire piston works on the principle that air gets very hot when compressed under high pressure. Anybody who has ever worked a bicycle pump will recall how hot it gets when you pump it for a while. Well, the fire piston works that way only you take just one stroke to compress the air which may reach a temperature of more than 800 degrees Fahrenheit.

The secret of making a piston is to have a small, smooth bore cylinder, one end of which is closed, and a plunger with packing on the end that allows no air to get by it when it is thrust quickly into the cylinder. The end of the plunger is hollowed out to a depth of not more than one-eighth of an inch and in this little hole, which should be wider at the bottom than at the top, put a little wad of tinder. I have used charred cotton rag and also finely shredded cedar bark, but it has to be thoroughly dry.

To start your tinder glowing you pull the piston almost out of the tube, put the end against something solid like a tree or a wall and give a quick thrust. The speed and force of the thrust has a lot to do with getting your tinder lighted, and in case you try it I want to tell you that it takes patience and practice, and don't be disappointed if the first piston doesn't work. I should also mention that the plunger must reach to within three-sixteenths of an inch of the bottom so that you get high compression.

FIRE PISTON

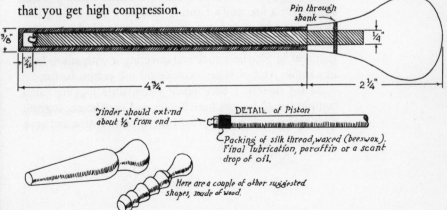

Pin through shank

³/₈"   ³/₁₆"   4³/₄"   2¼"   ¼"

Tinder should extend about ⅛" from end —

DETAIL of Piston

Packing of silk thread, waxed (beeswax). Final lubrication, paraffin or a scant drop of oil.

Here are a couple of other suggested shapes, made of wood.

I made my plunger out of a nail cut off square with a groove one-fourth of an inch wide filed as close to the bottom end as I could make it for winding on thread for packing. I also took care to sandpaper the nail very smooth so that it would travel freely and on top of that the packing should be greased. I found that a little candle wax mixed with bacon fat worked well. The natives of the Pacific have a belief that a fire piston will work only if it is greased with dog fat, but I love my dogs too well to go that far.

On the top end of the piston I fastened a wooden handle of a kind that you can grasp between your fingers and thrust hard with the palm of your hand. I have made several designs for wooden ones and sometime I am going to see what I can do. To my way of thinking the wood should be very hard so that after use you get a fine glassy finish in the bore.

In the long winter nights when we three get together we sometimes make miniature models of cabins and the like, using flat weathered rocks or a weathered slab of silvery dry-ki.

Hank made a model of his cabin and even put in little trees made of dry green moss, the kind you find growing in thick woods away from the water. This moss grows in the natural form of beautiful little trees and is just right for our purpose. The Chief whittles out beautiful models of canoes and also makes some of birch bark. One of his models showed an Indian tepee set up on thirteen poles as the Indians used to do, each pole representing one of the moons of the year. He set it on a flat rock that looked just like a little island. There was a canoe on the shore and a little fleshing beam, a place for a fire, and a hunting shed on a little staging just as it would be stored during the summer. He has an idea that he will make a winter scene sometime by putting a thin coat of glue on a rock and covering it with salt to look like snow. And of course you could use cotton batting.

As for myself, I once made a miniature logging camp complete with hovels, bunkhouses and cookhouse, logging sleds loaded with little logs held together by chains, and even tiny peaveys, as well as a bateau six inches long. But that wasn't all. I finished it up by carving two horses to go with one of the sleds and a teamster two inches high standing alongside. It was mighty good looking if I do say so.

NOVEMBER

Gray Skies and Cold Rains

THE THIN ice that makes in the coves now is waiting its chance to creep out some quiet cold night when the lake is asleep, for this is Kuskatinayoui, the Ice Moon. High winds will drive it back for a while, but after a few days of steady cold as we near December it will bind the lake from shore to shore and hold it fast until spring. This is a month of many gray days when heavy clouds hurry across the sky. The Chief says the color and rolling motion of them make him think of the great caribou herds he saw years ago on their winter migration.

If you have done what you ought to do to be ready for winter, this is a month of contentment. When the late rains come, rains that often freeze as they fall, you can stay indoors with the fire going strong and leave the woods to the storms. But it is not all wind and rain in November, for on many nights the woods are so quiet and cold you can hear the thunder of the Manitoupeepagee rapids as if they were close by. Chief Tibeash is fond of the river and tells stories of the men of the fur brigades sitting by their campfires many years ago listening to the "voices of the rapids." In the ever-changing sounds of falling water you can hear, if you want to, the pealing of church bells and deep-throated organ music, the songs of the north country, the voices of men and the laughter of children. You can hear the roar of the north winds and the whisper of a summer night breeze in the pine tops. Sometimes when the wind changes the sound fades and

the music of fiddles will come clear and sweet. And I have
heard the wild booming of Indian drums echoing in the hills.

It is on these still nights that you also hear the chorus of
the big timber wolves back on the ridges. They are beginning to run now that it is getting colder and their hunger
grows.

I can hardly describe the contentment that comes to me in
November. Maybe it is a feeling of security, which is what
every one of us is looking for. The way I look at it, security
and happiness are one and the same thing. On a stormy
night when the trees thrash in the high winds that claw at
the eaves, I sit listening to the murmuring of the fire in the
big stove, at peace with myself and the world. Give me food
to keep me strong, wood to keep me warm, good friends to
talk to me, fine books to read, and I have all I need. I know
men who think that's not enough.

Late fall brings ice storms that make the going slow and
dangerous and for a while after the ice forms and before the
heavy snows come you need something to help you on the
lake ice. We don't have creepers up here, but we made some
wooden soles the shape of our feet with lacing to hold them
on and a heel plate to keep them from shifting, and shod
them with spikes made of wood screws and even stove bolts.
One kind that Hank made had sharp iron cleats screwed to
the bottom and they worked well. For holding the lacing we
used staples at first and later cut slots which were more
secure. To be sure you don't use creepers very often, but
when you need them nothing else will do. I will have to get
some caulks next time I go to the logging camp.

Once the snows come and winter settles in we will need
our snowshoes so I have taken mine down from the wires

E CREEPERS

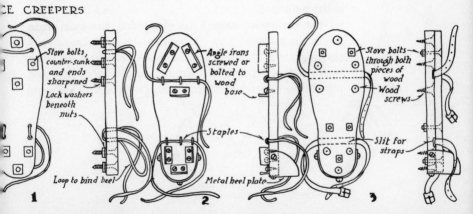

Stove bolts,
counter-sunk
and ends
sharpened
Lock washers
beneath
nuts

Angle irons
screwed or
bolted to
wood
base

Stove bolts
through both
pieces of
wood
Wood
screws

Staples

Slit for
straps

Loop to bind heel

Metal heel plate

1   2   3

hanging from the ridgepole. That is the only way to keep them away from the mice and the squirrels that love to chew the babiche. I have a pair of bear paws, a very handy type about three feet long and eighteen inches wide, which are fine for breaking trail for the dogs in old snow. For traveling in deep snow and heavy woods, especially if you are carrying a pack, the Indian hunting type, about a foot wide and from four to five feet long, is best. You cannot beat this kind of snowshoe if you can get a pair with the toes turned up, which saves a lot of tripping in heavy brush. For a fast trip in open country and on the frozen waterways give me a pair of runner's snowshoes about ten inches wide and from six to seven feet long.

Once in a while when we are working in hilly country we tie on the bottom of our snowshoes a piece of moose hide with the hair running back. This helps to keep us from slipping backwards. The idea is much the same as using sealskin on skis.

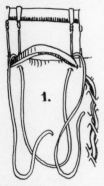

1.

I like a permanent toe strap on my snowshoes. It should be about three-quarters of an inch wide and should loop across the toe hole, the ends being woven into the mesh on either side. To my mind the toe strap gives you better control of the snowshoe and with a good hitch you can travel a long way without much adjusting. There are several good snowshoe hitches, but Hank's drawing shows the one that most of us up here use. Our hitch can be made permanent so that you can slip your foot in and out of it very quickly and not have to make a new tie every time you put your shoes on. Another good idea is a snowshoe harness made like the toe of a boot with the end cut off. It has a lacing on top to adjust it to the foot, and loops to fasten it to the snowshoe.

Once in a while you see a pair of wooden snowshoes made

2.

SNOWSHOE
HITCH

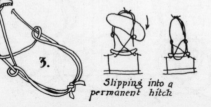

3.

Slipping into a
permanent hitch

when a fellow got caught out in the woods in a heavy storm
without his regular snowshoes. They can be made by splitting a dead cedar or pine log into thin boards and rounding
the ends to snowshoe form. Our snowshoes are woven with
moose hide babiche, the best of which is made from caribou
hide which stretches very little when it is wet, but the caribou are gone from here and moose hide serves very well.

Snowshoeing is strenuous work and unless there is a bitter
cold wind you don't need as much clothing as you might
think. Many a time I have tied my mackinaw on my pack,
leaving me free to swing along in my shirt, but when you
stop you have to put on your coat at once, for you will be
sweating, and a sudden chill is the half brother of pneumonia.
That is one of the most important things to remember in
the woods, summer or winter.

The Chief loves a little fun and one snowy night last
winter when he started home he reversed his snowshoes un-
beknownst to me and went on his way. When I looked out
later on to size up the weather there were snowshoe tracks
coming to my cabin but none leaving and that had me
puzzled for a minute. To this day the Chief still laughs over
his trick. They tell me that in the old days outlaws used
it to throw followers off their trail.

One evening when sleet was picking at the windows the
Chief, puffing thoughtfully at the black pipe he loves so
much, began talking about old-time Indian games. The
grownups had a lot of gambling games, he said, and the
youngsters, as well as the older ones, also liked to play games
of skill. He told me about the tops that he and his brothers
used to spin on the ice. They were whittled out of pieces
of pine or tamarack, about four inches long and two and a
half inches wide and tapered to a point at one end. Sometimes a little bone point or nail was put in the end to make

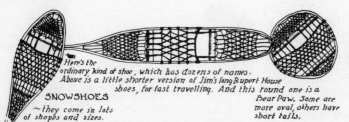

Here's the
ordinary kind of shoe, which has dozens of names.
Above is a little shorter version of Jim's long Rupert House
shoes, for fast travelling. And this round one is a
SNOWSHOES   Bear Paw. Some are
~ they come in lots   more oval, others have
of shapes and sizes.   short tails.

This is really an
emergency shoe, which
can be cut out in the
woods with an
axe from cedar
or anything handy.
Good for slush.

them spin longer. This kind of top was kept spinning by a whip made of a little stick with a piece of rawhide on the end. They would start the top spinning by twirling it with the fingers and then keep it going by whipping it as fast as they could. They also made tops out of acorns and nuts as well as bone, and sometimes stones, when they could find the right shape.

Other tribes had different kinds of tops. Some were made with a thin, pointed stick driven through the centers of a wooden disk about four inches wide and slightly less than an inch thick. The spindle running through the top was about seven inches long. Once his father came back from a hunting trip up north and brought an Eskimo top shaped something like an arrowhead. Some of the Indians made tops that looked pretty much like the ones I used to spin when I was a boy by winding the cord around the top and throwing it. I guess all boys are the same, be they white or red, for the Chief got to chuckling over the top games he used to play when he tried to split the other fellow's top. I have played that game many a time myself.

The old shell game played at carnivals is nothing new, for the Indians had their own games of that kind, using little pieces of wood, pebbles or bone, which they changed from one hand to another and let the others guess which hand held the right piece.

The Indians even had their own form of football, which was played with little chunks of wood two or three inches thick and maybe six inches long. There were many rules for playing the game, but one of the favorites was to choose up sides and then the piece of wood was buried a few inches in the soil on a playing ground with two stakes at each end

INDIAN
STILTS
or
"WALKING
WOODS

INDIAN TOPS

Here are a few Indian tops and whips. Most of them are very simple, but the kind that intrigues me most is the one that is started by pulling a cord through a hole in a holding stick

... and of course there are the little "finger tops" like this acorn top ~ used in a number of games.

(the stick is held with the left hand and a foot)

just about like the goal posts on a football field. The players
had to dig the piece of wood out of the earth with their toes,
for they were not allowed to touch it with their hands,
and they would then kick it along the ground, dodging the
opposing players until they got it through the goal posts.

The Chief tells about Indians in other parts of the country
who used a kind of football made of rawhide stuffed with
hair and grass. There was also another game in which the
Indians used a soft ball of hide or fabric with a short cord
attached to it. To play this game a player would lie on his
back and sling the ball backward over his head. The man who
could throw it the farthest was the winner.

They also had a lot of fun with stilts made of the limbs
of trees on which a short stub of a branch would be left for
the footpiece. Sometimes they would wrap the stubs with
fur and thongs to make them more comfortable for the feet.

Another great Indian game was played with darts, some
of which were made from corncobs with sharp bones set
in one end and feathers in the other. The target was often a
ring of grass or branches bound together with thongs. The
target was laid on the ground and the players tried to get
the darts inside the ring. Other tribes made darts by binding
a single feather to a sharp sliver of bone or horn.

Although the Indians do not play it very much now, the
Chief, Hank, and I have a lot of fun in the winter playing
with snow-snakes, which are pieces of birch or ash about
five feet long and an inch thick, with one end shaped up
like a snake's head. You can play it on snow or ice and the
idea is to throw it so that it will slide a long distance. Sometimes you build up a little hump of ice or snow so that when
the stick is thrown horizontally it shoots out in the air just
above the ice and gets a good start before the slide begins.

Now that the cool weather is here my pet deer mouse
visits me almost every evening and the dogs know him so
well they don't even look up when he scampers across the
floor. Tripper used to chase him, but now that mouse is so
spunky he will wait until the dogs are through eating and

SNOW-
SNAKES

*Here's the way a snow-snake
is held for throwing*

then go over and pick up what scraps they leave. He is the fussiest mouse about his looks and is always sitting up and washing his face with his paws.

Hank had a tame skunk for a while and he was as nice a pet as a man could have. Used to follow him around in the woods and made friends with the dogs which had a right healthy respect for the little black and white fellow. Hank never removed his scent sac and his skunk never misbehaved. But just the same that is taking a chance because no matter how tame a skunk is a sudden fright may make him forget his manners.

It takes time and a lot of patience to tame a wild animal. The easiest and best way is to get them young and bring them up. I had a bear cub once and he was about the most comical rascal you ever saw, but when he got big his playing got pretty rough, so I took him back in the woods and turned him loose to make his own way in the world. Another time I brought home a fawn that was lost and reared him on canned milk until he could take care of himself. He was as tame as a lamb and followed me through the woods everywhere I went. When he was about six months old he went back to his own kind, which is the way it ought to be.

The way to attract wild animals is to feed them the things they like. Put the food in the same place at the same time every day so they will learn to expect it. That's how Gabby, my moosebird, was tamed. I used to sprinkle crumbs on the edge of the porch every morning after breakfast and he soon learned to be there when I came out. At first he would sit in a tree and fly down when I went away. After a while he came closer and finally he would light on my shoulder the minute I came out of the door. One thing to remember in working with animals is not to make any quick movements. Don't try to rush the taming. The birds and animals have so many enemies they are afraid to take any chances. Once they know they can trust you they are your friends.

All this talk about animals reminds me of the time I went on a trip with a young fellow from the city. This friend,

Pete, was new to the woods and he couldn't get over the way the rabbits are attracted by a campfire and come around at night out of pure curiosity. One night about two o'clock he poked me awake and whispered:

"One of those rabbits is nosing around the tent close to my feet. Here is where I get a chance to tell the boys back home I kicked a rabbit in the face."

With that he pulled back his leg and let fly. His foot landed with a thud and I knew then it was no rabbit. So, Pete jumped up and stuck his head out of the tent. It was bright moonlight and what he saw was a big black bear high-tailing it for the tall timber. I don't know which was scared the most, but I know Pete lay awake the rest of the night. It so happened that our bacon was stored close to the foot of his bunk, which was what the bear was after. I still laugh about that night and I heard that when Pete got home he made a pretty good story of how he kicked a "giant" black bear in the face, leaving out the part about the rabbit.

There is always something interesting going on at Cache Lake and one of the reasons is that you never know what Hank will do next. Not long ago he got an idea to dye an old piece of canvas the color of the marsh grass like the camouflaged jungle suits used by the marines, so he could make himself a blind to help in photographing the snow geese. Neither of us knows very much about dyes, so we called in the Chief and sure enough he could tell us. The color Hank needed was a soft yellow which is close to the color of the grass in the shallows of Snow Goose Lake, so the Chief boiled down some bark from an ash tree and got just about the right color. He said he was not sure how much weather it would stand, for one must have alum to set the color. The young leaves of the birch in early spring also make a fine yellow, he told us.

The boiled-down juice of many of the berries gives bright dyes. One of the fine reds comes from the ground cran-

The Bear
That Walked
Like a Rabbit.

berry. For coloring moose hair and porcupine quills for decorating their moccasins the Indians make other kinds of red from elderberries and bearberries. A dark red dye can be made from the pinkish inner bark of hemlock, and dark brown from pine bark. Boiled blueberries give a purplish-red dye.

Rotting wood is used to make blue dyes and a grayish-blue color is made by boiling down shredded alder bark. A black dye comes from boiling the shredded bark, roots, and berries of the sumac, and the Indians also used soot from their fires mixed with fish oil to make a black paint. Green comes from boiling the leaves and bark of cedar. The Chief says to try a lot of different kinds of leaves and barks to discover new dyes, so we are going to try it. If you find any colored earth you can dry it on the stove and then sift it through coarse cotton cloth and mix the powder with oils to make a fairly good paint for indoor decorations.

The Chief, Hank, and I have been having a wonderful time building a crystal detector radio receiver. It all began when a friend of ours, Mr. Beedee, a radio engineer, came up for a week's rest last fall and got an idea it would be a real achievement to build a radio from the odds and ends of material you could find lying around a camp in the north woods. Of course, we couldn't expect to find materials to make earphones, but he thought if we worked hard enough we could dig up the rest. Before he left he made a diagram for a set and said he would send the earphones. So we started a search for parts.

It was like one of those scavenger hunts you hear about. When the three of us put all our findings together we had some pieces of well-seasoned pine board, various bits of metal, two or three dozen brass-headed tacks, an empty spool, a handful of assorted screws, and an old cardboard salt box.

The two main problems were the tuning coil and a variable condenser. Following Mr. Beedee's diagram we found we would need about 150 feet of insulated copper wire. Any

Porcupine quills come in a variety of lengths — but they all have the same sharp points!

—and those barbed points under a microscope are wicked.

size between number 22 to 28, or even finer, would do. For a while it looked as if we were not going to have any radio, but Hank got an idea and we snowshoed over to the old abandoned mine to see what we could find there. As luck would have it, in one corner of the blacksmith shop where it had lain for nigh on to twenty years was an old ignition coil once used for firing a gas engine. I certainly was excited when I pulled that thing apart and saw what was inside. Sure enough, there was a winding of fine wire, just the kind we wanted.

The salt box turned out to be just the thing for winding our coil on, so we cut off one end four inches long and soaked it in melted candle wax so it wouldn't take up moisture. Then we began winding, beginning one-quarter of an inch from one end of the box and put on a total of 166 turns. At the start of the winding we anchored the wire by passing it back and forth through three pinholes punctured in the cardboard tube so the wire wouldn't slip. Every seven turns we twisted a little loop to make a tap until we had eight of them. Then we wound on 40 turns without any taps. From then on to the end we made a tap every ten turns, scraping off the insulation on each tap to make a good connection. Those taps, connected by short wires to the switch points, make it easy to use any desired number of turns on the coil to tune in a station.

When all the turns were wound, the end of the wire was again fastened by passing it back and forth through pinholes in the tube. Then we painted the coil with candle wax to keep the wire in place. While we were doing that the Chief made a little wooden disk to go on top of the coil to hold the crystal detector.

Making the movable condenser had us puzzled for a while, but we looked on the diagram and it said tinfoil would do, so we started to hunt and it wasn't long before the Chief thought of the tinfoil lining of the packages our tea comes in. We got enough to make two sheets four by six inches and the Chief smoothed it out very evenly with the edge of

a knife. We also needed some waxed paper and found what we wanted on a package of dry cereal. Meantime Hank cut out a pine baseboard for our set 14 inches long and 12 inches wide.

The first thing we did then was to start on the condenser and you will get an idea from our friend's diagram how we made it. Out of an old piece of tongued and grooved siding I cut two narrow guides and from another piece of the board we made a slider five and one-quarter inches wide and six inches long. Fitted between the two guides, this piece slides back and forth very nicely after being shellacked and waxed, making it easy to adjust the condenser.

The next step was to use shellac to fasten one of the sheets of tinfoil onto the baseboard at a 45-degree angle, leaving one corner free to connect a wire, and then covering it with waxed paper extending the full width and length of the guides which are twelve inches long. Then we screwed the guides in place on top of the waxed paper, making sure that the slider board moved back and forth freely with just enough clearance so it didn't touch the baseboard.

On the bottom of the slider at a 45-degree angle we fastened the other sheet of tinfoil, which was also glued down with shellac, leaving one end turned up over the edge of the slide for connecting a wire. The slider ought to be shellacked, too, for you want to keep all wood parts as dry as possible. Then the Chief screwed the spool on top for a handle, fitted wood strips at each end as stops for the slide, and our condenser was done.

I used two narrow strips of brass cut from the name plate of an old canoe for the two switch blades and then copper wires from the various taps on the coil were brought down and fastened under brass-headed tacks. The connections for the earphones, antenna and ground were made of little bits of copper wire, but we hope to have something better, such as a binding post, or spring clips, some day.

For a cup to hold our detector crystal we used one of the Chief's .38-55 caliber rifle shells cutting it off about one-

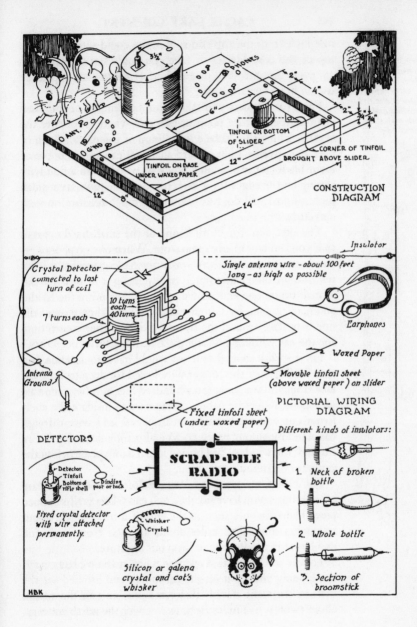

PHONES

3½"

4"

6"

2"

4"

2"

¾"
¾"

TINFOIL ON BOTTOM
OF SLIDER

O ANT.

O G'ND.

TINFOIL ON BASE
UNDER WAXED PAPER

CORNER OF TINFOIL
BROUGHT ABOVE SLIDER

12"

12"

8"

14"

CONSTRUCTION
DIAGRAM

Insulator

Crystal Detector
connected to last
turn of coil

Single antenna wire - about 100 feet
long - as high as possible

10 turns
each
40 turns

7 turns each

Earphones

Waxed Paper

Antenna
Ground

Movable tinfoil sheet
(above waxed paper) on slider

Fixed tinfoil sheet
(under waxed paper)

PICTORIAL WIRING
DIAGRAM

Different kinds of insulators:

DETECTORS

Detector
Tinfoil
Bottom of
rifle shell

Binding
post or tack

SCRAP·PILE
RADIO

1. Neck of broken
bottle

Fixed crystal detector
with wire attached
permanently.

Whisker
Crystal

2. Whole bottle

Silicon or galena
crystal and cat's
whisker

3. Section of
broomstick

HBK

half inch from the cap end so that we could screw it to the top of the coil. Matter of fact you could use the end of a 28 gauge shotgun shell or even one of those little cups they use on brass curtain rods.

To keep antenna from snapping if attached to swaying trees, carry supporting wire at one end over pulley and weight with stone or sand bag.

For a cat whisker you take about two inches of fine steel wire sharpened to a point at one end where it touches the crystal, which should be a little lump of galena or silicon or even iron pyrite. I have heard that you can use a couple of razor blades set in slots in a block of wood, with a fine wire resting on the edges for a detector. Some fellows say a small piece of coal will do, but I don't put much reliance on such detectors.

The best detector of all is one of the small fixed crystals that you can buy in any radio store. When our earphones arrived, tucked in with them was a fine fixed crystal and I can tell you we didn't lose much time putting it in place. It has a small tip on one end, so we set the large end in the holder and made it snug by tamping in tinfoil and then wound the fine bare wire around the tip to make the other connection, for the cat whisker is inside these manufactured detectors.

For a spell it looked as if we would have no antenna, but then I thought of the copper wire I used for deep trolling for lake trout and we stretched a hundred feet of it between two jack pines above the cabin, taking care to insulate the ends. From one end we brought an insulated lead wire through the window to our receiver. We also took some bare wire through the window and buried it in a damp place below the eaves for a ground connection.

For insulators on our aerial we used pieces of broken syrup bottles, but if you have no glass you can take a well-seasoned piece of hardwood, such as the end of a broomstick, about six inches long, drill holes about an inch from each end and boil it in candle wax to keep out moisture.

I never will forget that evening when at last we had everything ready and I put on the earphones and listened for the new government station that has been built in the woods about twenty-five miles from us to cover the north country.

At first I didn't hear anything so I changed the little switch blades and moved the condenser slider and all of a sudden I heard a girl singing Annie Laurie, clear and sweet!

But the radio hasn't taken up all of our time, for a while ago when Chief Tibeash was up near the carry at the head of the lake, three wolves drove a deer out of the woods. It was a long chance, but he let go with his .38-55 carbine, and brought down one of the gray killers. The others ran and the deer escaped. Having nothing but a small shoulder pack, the old man made a travois of two twelve-foot birch saplings lashed together with crosspieces and skidded the wolf down to my place. In addition to having a fine pelt, he will get bounty to boot. Not often do you get close enough for a shot at a wolf. What really took the Chief up the lake were signs of an otter slide at an open place in a creek. He has an idea he will have a fine skin one of these days.

From the window of my cabin I can see a porcupine sitting in a big pine at the edge of the clearing. He has been there nearly a month feeding on the sweet inner bark and paying no attention to cold and snow squalls. Their habit of girdling trees causes some damage, but porky is about the only animal a man can get without a gun when he is badly in need of food. By the way, don't pay any heed to that old tale about them throwing their quills. It isn't so. Porcupine liver is not bad when it is fried with bacon and the meat can be stewed or roasted after parboiling, but I cannot say I like it.

The snowshoe rabbits are turning white and on quiet, moonlit nights they play up on my ridge as I can see by their tracks, but they are always on the alert for weasels, owls, and foxes, their mortal enemies, and once in a while a scream that sounds like a hurt child marks the end of a rabbit. You have often heard it said "only the strong survive," and that is certainly true up here, for most of the wild things have their enemies and they all have to fight the cold and hunt food to keep alive. The weak ones die and the strong live on. That is nature's way of improving all living things.

In the woods where your life is controlled by the weather

TRAVOIS

Undersides of the butts were bevelled to slide easier.

The snowshoe rabbits are up on my ridge

there is naturally a lot of talk about weather signs. I suppose
you have heard the old one about the breastbone of a goose
in November. Some folks believe that if the bone is thick
the winter will be cold and snowy, but if it is thin you can
expect a mild season. And there are some that believe that a
heavy storm this month means snow right through to spring.
Others tell you that as the wind blows this month so it will
blow in December. I know a man who is dead sure that the
kind of weather you have on November twenty-first will
tell the kind of winter to look for. But, as I have said before,
it is not one sign but many that give you some idea of what
to expect. Even then things can change fast and a snow squall
can turn into a blizzard.

The company's patrol plane has gone over for its last trip
before the freeze-up, for there is always a waiting period
when the plane can't land on wheels or pontoons and must
wait for snow to land with skis. But as soon as the ice is
solid and cushioned with snow he will be back. Circling over
the cabin to say good-by he dropped a bundle of magazines
that were mighty welcome, for Hank and I are great readers.

I had quite an experience lately and I might have known
something strange was afoot when Hank came over with a
mysterious air and asked me to visit him next day, providing
there was a breeze blowing. That is what puzzled me. I was
just that curious that I hiked over the next morning, since
it was a fine clear day with a light breeze. When I came in
sight of Hank's cabin the dogs ran ahead as they always do,
but this time they set up such a commotion I knew something
special was happening. There was no sign of Hank at the
cabin, but it didn't take me long to locate him, for the dogs
led the way out onto the lake, which was a sheet of glare
ice, it being almost December.

Never before in the north woods or anywhere else have
I seen such a sight, for there was Hank tearing over the ice
in a contraption which you might call an ice boat made from
the natural crotch of a tree, with a smaller crotch reversed
to make a bowsprit. On it he had rigged a mast and hoisted

his canoe sail. Rough and ready as it was, that ice boat certainly did cut capers on the ice and you could see that Hank was more than pleased at my surprise.

When he had shown off for a while and had the dogs almost tired out chasing him, he swung up in front of me with a fine flourish and gave me a chance to look over the craft. It didn't take me more than a glance to account for Hank's mysterious trips to the abandoned mine and all the hammering and banging that had been coming from that direction for several days. He had explained that he was just picking up scraps of iron that might come in handy, and on the ice boat they certainly did. The runners, which were about twenty inches long, were made of three-eighths inch angle iron, four inches wide on each side, and judging from the work on them I suspect Hank wore out several hacksaw blades. With an odd assortment of bolts he had fastened the runners to blocks which were then bolted to the end of the tree forks, two in front and one on a pivot on the stern for steering. He had dragged over some boards to make a platform, or, as you might call it, a cockpit, and with a spruce sapling for a mast held in place by three wire stays, and another sapling for a boom, the strange craft was ready for sailing.

I knew that the hardest part of that job had been to find a tree fork with evenly balanced arms and Hank agreed that he had got himself a crick in the neck walking in the woods to find just the right kind.

I tried out his boat and it handled well. Flying over the ice at fifty miles an hour is next to riding in an airplane for speed, but it seems faster because you are so close to the surface. The next thing was to get the Chief over and give him a ride. The wind being just right Hank gave the signal on his horn and in a couple of hours the Chief hove in sight. The old Indian is a fine sport and when Hank suggested that he come for a ride he didn't hesitate a second. When they came back the Chief crawled off and walked around the ice boat thoughtfully two or three times. If you expect him to show

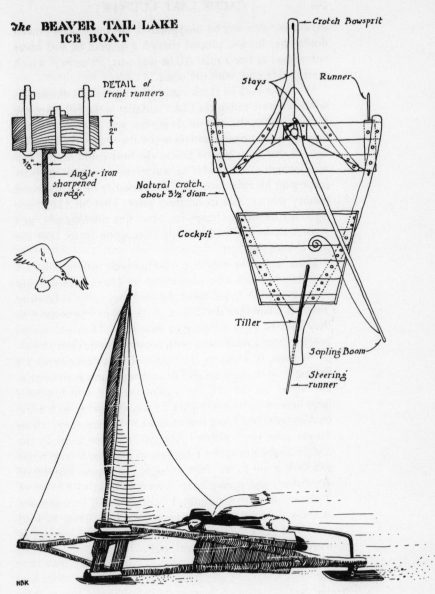

The **BEAVER TAIL LAKE ICE BOAT**

DETAIL of front runners

2"

3/8"

Angle-iron sharpened on edge.

Crotch Bowsprit

Stays

Runner

Natural crotch, about 3½" diam.

Cockpit

Tiller

Sapling Boom

Steering runner

HBK

excitement you will be disappointed, but there wasn't much doubt that he was pleased though I suspect he had never before had as fast a ride. All he said was "Pimasiw," which means, "He goes with the wind."

We went back to Hank's cabin for a good hot dinner and while we were eating the Chief said that in the fall when the first ice makes, the ice boat, being fast and quiet, would be a fine thing for chasing wolves when they cross the lake. He figured that with a good breeze the boat could outrun any wolf, which is true, and if he was stretched out on the platform with his rifle, he'd run a good chance of getting some bounty money, not to mention pelts. That hit Hank just right for he sees a chance for some fine photographs, so I suspect those two will be wolf hunting on an ice boat the first chance they get.

Hank is not the only one who has been making things. I worked out a new kind of cooking pot I have been wanting to try ever since I read about the kind they make in faraway Tibet. It seems they don't have much fuel in that country so they have to make a little go a long way. Their pot is supposed to heat a whole stew with not much more than a handful of grass. It is like an old-fashioned tin coffee pot with a flue right up through the middle so that the heat works on the bottom of the pot and the wall of the flue, which gives a large heating surface. We have no way of making such a fine cooking pot, but I had one of those cake pans they call an "angel cake tin," which has a tapered open cone in the middle. Same idea as the Tibet pot, so we filled it with water and took it out to try. Sure enough, just a good handful of dry balsam and spruce twigs boiled nigh on to a quart of water in about five minutes. I figure we will be using one of those pans on future camping trips. I am going to send away and get a bigger one with the center flue crimped in without solder so it won't melt out.

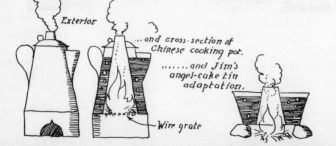

Exterior

...and cross-section of Chinese cooking pot.

........and Jim's angel-cake tin adaptation.

Wire grate

Blizzards and Wailing Winds

Snow lies deep on the land and the lakes, and the branches of the hardwood trees are gray skeletons swaying in the wind. In these parts a blizzard comes like a stalking lynx, quietly at first, then striking with whirling fury, screaming in the hills, clawing at the tree tops. At last it moves on with a wailing sound, leaving the land white and hushed, with sharp-edged drifts and deep wind rings around the trees.

There is no sign of any living thing on the white blanket that stretches away across the lake, up and over the Cache Lake hills, on and on through the dark woods into strange valleys and over other hills that few men know. I wouldn't enjoy flat country where one always knows what lies ahead as far as the eye can see. I want hills that lead you up to look beyond.

When I get up in the morning now the windows are covered with frosty crystals that sparkle blue and white if the moonlight strikes them. Some of the designs on the glass are like little curving plumes, wonderful miniature fern fronds, and leaves. Others are small balsam twigs on the end of a branch and many are miniature spruce trees of shimmering ice. I have seen some that looked like the spreading tail of a peacock and many that made me think of the geometry problems I had in school many years ago.

You need a microscope to see the real beauty of frost crystals, for some of the lines are too small for the eyes. Last night I picked out oak and maple leaves, the blossoms of tiny

Cree
Jack Frost

flowers, and even a spider web with what looked like a spider near the center. And there were grass blades and moss and many other designs.

If you want to see how frost pictures grow, go into a cold room on a midwinter's night when the window is coated with frost and hold a candle near enough to the glass to melt the frosty coating. You can do the same thing by blowing your breath on the glass for a few seconds. The warmth will cause the melting frost to form a thin watery film. As soon as that happens step back and almost at once the frost begins to draw new designs. You will notice them beginning to form around the edge of the melted spot. Often they take the form of slender lances or glistening stars, working out toward the center of the clear spot as if some invisible hand were drawing them with white fire.

These designs will form only where the glass is wet and stop at the edge of any dry place. If you observe closely you will find that between the larger designs very fine pictures gradually begin to appear. Some of them look like pieces of coral and others may look like finely cut gems. In time the frost begins to cover the dry places with an even white coating that shows no design and looks at first like sanded glass. This is a granular form of frost and it always keeps away from the beautiful designs as if it didn't want to spoil them.

Various combinations of temperature and moisture affect the formation of frost crystals and for that reason the designs are never exactly alike. The thickness of a pane of glass or its finish, and whether it is clean or dusty, have something to do with the kind of frost crystals that form on it.

Looking at the wonderful designs on a window pane, it is hard to realize what a powerful thing frost is, for it is frost freezing the moisture in the trunks of great trees that splits them in zero weather with explosions like shots out of a cannon.

We are so used to frost that we don't often stop to think that it is constantly changing the shape of the land, breaking up the rocky formations, loosening the earth in valleys and on the hillsides so that very gradually through the years the face of the earth changes in localities where the winters are severe. One good example is the long frost crystals that raise the soil several inches in sandy or gravelly places. And you find another kind of frost, fine-grained and very white on the undersides of rocks and logs and often under leaves on the ground. The Indians call December Yeyekoopewe, the Month of the Frozen Mist.

Once in a while I hear the lynx that lives in the tamarack swamp on the other side of the lake and if you look you are pretty sure to see its tracks although you seldom catch sight of the animal. Do you know the difference between a lynx and a wildcat? Well, the lynx has little tufts on the tips of its ears, and a black-tipped tail, whereas the wildcat has no ear tufts and its tail is black-tipped only on top and is white underneath. Furthermore, its legs are shorter and its feet smaller than those of the lynx which has large, furry foot pads that act like snowshoes.

Lynx

Wildcat

Weasel tracks are plentiful and often mixed in with them you will find the tiny foot pads of a white-footed mouse which is one of the weasel's favorite foods. The weasels which turn white with the first snow are known as ermine in winter when the pelts are very valuable. They are brown in summer but are known to turn white within a few hours after the first snowfall. It is pretty much the same story with the snowshoe rabbit.

Lynx and Wildcat tails — in a heavy snowstorm!

Did you ever stop to think why they change color? Well, of course the white is a protection so their enemies can't see them so easily against the snow, but the white is also warmer than darker colors, for it lets less heat escape than brown or black. An engineer who came up here to fish once told me if city folk painted their steam radiators black instead of white they would get a whole lot more heat out of them. But womenfolk don't like black, so you cannot get them to change.

The Lynx's big pads make fine snowshoes.

Getting back from women to weasels, maybe you have noticed that though the body of the animal turns a cream

The tiny footpads of a white-footed mouse

color or almost pure white, the tip of the tail is black. The
same is true of the snow buntings and ptarmigan, which have
dark tail feathers. Now at first you would think those dark
spots would show just where they are, but as a matter of
fact they keep the enemy's attention away from the animal.
I have proved it by covering the tail of a weasel (he was
dead) with snow and just as soon as you do that you begin
to make out the outline of the rest of the animal. It is the
black spot that catches the eye and fools their enemies. The
way nature takes care of its own is something to think about.

Grouse ~ Spike
Snow shoes

This is the time when the fur of the animals is at its best
and the northern trappers are out on their lines. The fur is
now dense and rich in color. You don't live in the old north
long before you discover that under the regular outer fur
the animals grow a sort of underwear of soft dense hair that
helps to keep them warm. I have read about mountain goats
in India that grow a soft fur called pashm, used to make the
wonderful soft Kashmir shawls and other fabrics.

The birds that winter up here also have an extra winter
covering. The outer feathers lie closer, overlap more, and
underneath these feathers they grow a wonderful coat of
down—little soft feathers that prevent water from reaching
the skin and keep out the cold winds. You see it best in some
of the ducks and geese. When winter is over and they shed
their underwear the waterfowl pick the soft down from their
breasts to line their nests. That is where eiderdown comes
from. The eider duck not only lines her nest with the down,
but covers up her young ones with it on cold spring nights.

Ptarmigan ~
Feather Snowshoes

And it is interesting to see how little extra spikes grow on
the toes of the grouse to help them walk over the snow and
dig deep for berries in the winter. Some birds, like the
ptarmigan, have an extra covering of feathers on their feet
in the cold months. Almost any day up here you can see
grouse running over the snow hunting for berries, cones, cat-
kins, and the like. And they will dig deep through the snow
to find such choice food as wintergreen, partridge, and snow-

Weasel chasing a Ptarmigan — and a Snow
Bunting!

berries, as well as the various cranberries you find in certain places. They know just where to dig, too.

Another thing you will notice, when the leaves are off the trees, is that the buds of those that break out their leaves early in the spring are covered with a protective sheath of scales which fall off and release the buds when the first warm days come in April or May.

This is the time of year I think about helping some of my bird-friends, especially the little chicadees. They can take care of themselves in almost any weather, but when an ice storm coats the trees and bushes they can't get at the bark where they find dormant insects and the like. That is where I come in and they know me for miles around. During the summer I raise lots of sunflowers and dry the seeds and later on I gather the ripe seeds of the wild plants. Then when winter sets in I put up bird-feeders, logs with holes bored in them, covered boxes and brush shelters. I even have a little box with a glass top outside my window. A friend of mine always sends up a bag of wild-bird food, including split pumpkin and squash seeds, which the chicadees love. I also feed them nut meats and the like. For meat I hang an old bone or a piece of bacon rind on a limb and stuff venison suet in the cracks in the bark of pine trees. Smart and cheerful fellows the chicadees are, and full of courage.

One thing I am really proud of is my squirrel-proof feeder. It is a piece of cedar log about three inches in diameter with a pointed top and holes bored here and there to hold the food. It hangs from a piece of wire which is attached to a screw eye in its tip. So far nothing unusual, but here is the squirrel-proofer. Punch a quarter-inch hole in the exact center of an old pie plate and run the wire through it so that the plate, upside down, balances on the point. The minute a squirrel slides down the wire and touches the plate it tips on its side. There's nothing for him to hold on to and try as he will there is no way to get around that teetering pie plate.

Hemlock

Ground Pine or Princess Pine

The only thing left is to make a jump for the ground or climb back up the wire and if there is one thing that is funny it is a squirrel going up a slippery wire hand over hand and slipping back every few inches. So far not one has passed the plate—for himself.

On Christmas Hank, the Chief, and I always decorate a big spruce with bits of the favorite foods of all the birds that stay with us, and sprinkle seeds beneath the boughs for the ground feeders.

One of the little problems of living in the woods in winter is coming home and having to get a fire going and wait for a meal to cook when you are hungry enough to chew rawhide. Well, I've got that one beaten, for I made myself a fireless cooker and now when I am away for a day I come back to a hot meal ready for me the minute I step in the door.

I don't know who invented fireless cookers, but they have been used for a long, long time, especially in the Scandinavian countries, where they were usually insulated with hay or straw and called "hay boxes." A fireless cooker is simple and inexpensive to make, for any kind of box that is tight or even a keg or a barrel will do. The important thing is plenty of good insulation to hold the heat in, and you can find the right kind wherever you are. I used well-dried sphagnum moss, but sawdust would have been all right. In addition to straw or hay, crushed paper, wool, ground cork, excelsior, or cotton batting are all good for insulation. Many of the materials made to keep houses warm, especially mineral wool and fluffy asbestos, would also do well as insulation for a fireless cooker.

The first step in building a cooker is to decide on the pot or pail you plan to use regularly, for on its size depends the kind of box you will need. Make certain the pot has straight sides so it will slip in and out of its compartment easily, and it must have a tight-fitting cover. Enamelware, aluminum, or stainless steel utensils are all fine for the purpose. The best type of pot is one which is about as wide as it is tall, for you

The BIRD'S CHRISTMAS TREE

Bone with scraps of meat on it.

Doughnut on a string

We bored holes in a log and stuffed them full of peanut butter and fat mixed with seeds.

Bacon rind.

Suet wound 'round and 'round with string

.....with seeds spread underneath.

don't want any more surface to radiate heat than you can help.

A fireless cooker does a much better job if you use a pre-heated round, flat stone, the diameter of the pot and about an inch thick, at the bottom of the cooking hole. Sometimes you can find a soft stone that can be chipped to size, but I cast one an inch and a half thick by mixing a little cement with sand and pouring it into a circular cardboard mold. I made a little hollow in the middle and set in a loop of wire so it could be lowered into place with a hook.

Once you have your pot you will know how big a box is needed, for the cooking well that holds the pot must be sur-rounded by at least four inches of insulating material, top, sides, and bottom. Before doing anything else, line the bot-tom and sides of the box with heavy paper, and then fill the bottom with four or five inches of insulating material. Next place the pot on top of the heating stone on the insulation in the center of the box and pack insulation evenly and not too tightly around the pot until it comes up to the rim and no more. Then work the pot around carefully until the hole is slightly larger, so it will slide out easily. Now slip in a cylindrical liner of cardboard to form a smooth wall for the cooking compartment.

When the insulating material has been packed to the top of the pot, cover it with heavy building paper or cardboard with the edges turned down and pasted to the sides of the box, the edge around the cooking hole turned down and glued to the cardboard liner. Then you make a cloth cushion four inches deep to fit the top of the box and stuff it with four inches of insulating material, for this top pad is very important. The last step is to make a hinged lid for the box that presses down snugly on the top insulating pad. Make a hook to hold it down, for the tighter the cooker the better it will work. If you want to make two cooking compartments make a partition in the middle and have a separate top in-sulating cushion for each side.

Once you have a fireless cooker you must know how to

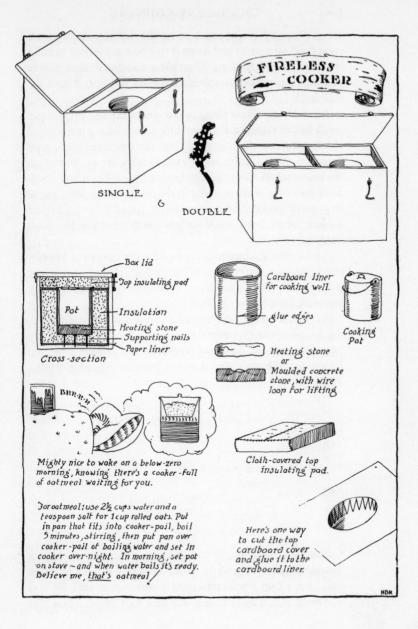

FIRELESS COOKER

SINGLE & DOUBLE

Cross-section
- Box lid
- Top insulating pad
- Insulation
- Pot
- Heating stone
- Supporting nails
- Paper liner

Cardboard liner for cooking well.

glue edges

Cooking Pot

Heating stone or Moulded concrete stone, with wire loop for lifting

BRR-R-R

Mighty nice to wake on a below-zero morning, knowing there's a cooker-full of oatmeal waiting for you.

For oatmeal: use 2½ cups water and a teaspoon salt for 1 cup rolled oats. Put in pan that fits into cooker-pail, boil 5 minutes, stirring, then put pan over cooker-pail of boiling water and set in cooker over-night. In morning, set pot on stove ~ and when water boils it's ready. Believe me, _that's_ oatmeal!

Cloth-covered top insulating pad.

Here's one way to cut the top cardboard cover and glue it to the cardboard liner.

HBK

use it properly to get the best results. Of course you start your food on a stove and bring it to a boil, meantime heating the stone for the bottom. Then get it into the fireless cooker as quickly as you can—instantly is none too fast. That's the real secret!

Another important thing to remember is that you will get much better results if the food fills your cooking pot instead of being half or three-quarters full, for wherever there is an air space, heat will be lost. Beans, cereals, stews, and soups are best cooked from eight to twelve hours, but many foods need only two or three hours in the cooker. You don't know how good food can be until you have tasted it from a fireless cooker, which keeps in all the fine flavors that usually steam away on a stove.

And if you are interested in fine flavors you would surely enjoy my overnight buckwheat griddlecakes. I would not want you to think I am taking credit for them because they are made by a recipe my aunt gave me.

But I don't want you to take my word for it, so I am going to give you my aunt's rule to try for yourself. Every year she sends me up a few pounds of buckwheat flour and I have griddlecakes almost every Sunday morning. Here's her rule:

> 2 rounded cups buckwheat flour
> 1 rounded cup white corn meal
> 1 cup boiling water
> ¾ cup milk
> 1 teaspoonful salt
> ½ yeast cake
> ¼ cup milk slightly warmed
> ½ teaspoon soda
> 1 teaspoon molasses

The first thing to do is to dissolve the yeast in about a quarter cup of lukewarm milk. It really should be fresh milk, but I find evaporated milk works pretty well. Be sure it is only warm and not hot, for heat kills yeast. Then take

Balsam

three-quarters of a cup of milk and mix it with a cup of boiling water. The next step is to mix the buckwheat and corn meal, which should be white if possible, and after adding salt, stir into the hot water and milk mixture. Now add the dissolved yeast and beat the mixture for about ten minutes.

All this is done the night before and when you have the batter mixed you put it in a warm place where it won't be chilled and let it stand overnight. Just before you cook the cakes add the baking soda and molasses and give the batter a good beating. The only thing you need is a good hot frying pan, but I want to warn you not to over-grease it. That is what spoils most griddlecakes. If you have butter it is extra nice. Put a little on a wad of cloth and rub it on the frying pan after each batch is cooked, but if you have no butter, bacon fat or lard will do a good job.

My aunt cooks her cakes on a wonderful oval soapstone griddle which just covers two holes of the old wood stove. It is bound around the edge with an iron strap and has a bail for lifting it. To be sure it takes a while to heat through an inch of soapstone, but once it is hot it makes the best cakes you ever tasted. A soapstone griddle needs no grease whatever and the batter never sticks, so you get the full flavor of the buckwheat.

As soon as the griddlecakes puff up and show little bubbles all over the top, flip them over and bake them on the other side until brown. Only a rank greenhorn ever turns a griddlecake twice. I guess I don't have to tell you what to do after that, but it is all the better if you have plenty of butter and real maple syrup.

We have already had the first sharp cold spell of the winter and the thermometer outside my door showed a steady thirty below zero for five days. When it gets that cold you need the right clothing, to be sure, but not as much as some folks think you do, for ideas on what to wear to keep warm in the winter have changed a lot in recent years. There was a time when a man piled on everything he could find or borrow, and he still couldn't get warm. The secret of keeping the body warm in cold weather is pretty much the same as insulating a house by having dead air spaces which stop the escape of heat.

Many a man who has been comfortable in a suit of heavy lumberman's woolen underwear has wondered why he felt the cold after it had been washed several times. The reason is that when he first put it on the chances are that it fitted him loosely thus keeping a wall of air about his body, but the way most men wash woolens by putting them into hot water, caused the garments to shrink, and all he can do now is to skin himself into it. Without that blanket of warm air the heat leaves his body quickly and he feels the cold. It is the same with animals. If you brought a short-haired dog here from a warm part of the country he would probably die of the cold, for he has grown no undercoat of soft hair to serve him as underwear and hold the heat to keep him warm. My dogs can curl up in the snow in a blizzard until they are nothing but white mounds, but if you run your fingers down through their heavy fur their bodies will be comfortably warm.

Another thing that makes a fellow cold is to sweat in the winter, for if his underclothes get damp from sweat the moisture carries off the heat of his body.

What I like for winter wear is a good all-wool, one-piece union suit that is fairly wooly so that it holds the air, and on top of that a good woolen shirt that doesn't fit tight, and maybe on top of that a light-weight loose woolen sweater. A tight-fitting sweater is a snare and a delusion on a bitter cold day. Furthermore if you use a sweater be sure it buttons up the front so that you can get it off easily if you are working hard. Then, with a pair of heavy woolen trousers, such as they make for icemen and lumbermen, and a mackinaw caught with a belt, you are pretty well fitted out for anything that comes. I have one coat that I had made up from a four point Hudson Bay blanket which is lined with closely woven cotton drill, which keeps out the wind in fine style. I had the armholes made extra deep so that if my hands get very cold I can pull my arms in and hold them against my body, poking the empty sleeves in under the belt to keep the wind out. This is a method that the Eskimos use and it is a fine idea.

One of the little miseries of traveling in bitter cold weather is that the stiff edges of your sleeves are apt to chafe your wrists and make them very sore. My grandmother used to knit me warm wristlets about six inches long which I slipped over my wrists before putting on my mittens, and somehow or other in addition to stopping the chafing I felt much warmer. The old lady had a theory that if your wrists get cold it chills the body. Be that as it may, I still wear wristlets and even the Chief has taken to them. They protect a spot where the arteries are nearest the surface and the cold can chill the blood.

There is such a thing as piling on so many pairs of socks in winter that your feet get damp from sweating and you defeat the whole purpose of the extra covering. The Indians have several good ways of keeping their feet warm. Some make little soft doeskin moccasins that come up just like a slipper, and then they wrap their feet in pieces of blanket about fourteen by eighteen inches in size. I have tried that and it works fine. But what I generally wear is a pair of light all-wool socks next to the feet and two heavy pairs on top. I would rather have home-knit socks than the manufactured ones, for they have a looser weave and hold the warmth better. Most important of all, you want the outer pair of socks long so that you can tuck your trousers into them. You pull the tops up just under the knee and tie them with a little thong to keep the snow out. I think I have said before that tight footwear whether it be a shoe or a moccasin is an abomination for it not only cramps the foot but gives you no air to insulate you from the cold.

You may laugh, but for sleeping up here I have a special set of one-piece woolen underwear, and when I go to bed I pull on this underwear and a pair of woolen socks, and I am as snug as a bug in a rug. A fellow wouldn't be very comfortable up here in pajamas.

Once in a while a fellow gets caught in a cold spell without enough clothing. In a case like that if you can get hold of some paper to put inside your coat it makes a good windbreak. The Chief says that you could probably use strips of birch bark for the same purpose although we have never needed to try it. But the thought of birch bark reminds me of the day the Chief came over to visit me and got caught in a freezing rain. When he got to my cabin he was wearing over his shoulders a large piece of birch bark with a slit and a small hole in it to put his head through, and it kept the rain off his shoulders in good style. As I have said before, the Chief knows what to look for in the woods, and how to use it, so that he can meet almost any situation.

Every once in a while you hear about somebody being found frozen to death on the trail in the north woods. When that happens it usually means that the man was either sick or didn't know how to take care of himself in the winter woods. If an Indian gets caught out on his trap line in a blizzard he knows better than to try to get back to camp unless he is in country where he recognizes all the signs and knows where he is every step of the way. If he is on a lake, where anyone quickly loses all notion of direction, he digs a trough in the snow and turns his hunting sled on its side as a windbreak and sits it out. That may sound crazy, but the secret of keeping on living in the bitter cold of a northern winter is to save your energy. You freeze to death when you drop from exhaustion and have no more energy to keep your blood circulating. If a man keeps his head, saves his strength, and stops when a storm closes in he won't freeze to death if he is dressed for winter weather. If you are in the woods you can always make a shelter of boughs and bark, and build a fire if possible, but the important thing is not to go on when there is any danger of getting lost. If you do you surely will be in trouble.

In the old fur trading days some travelers would dig themselves a shallow trough and lay snowshoes over the top and spread a blanket or tarpaulin on top of that and hold it down with a sled or toboggan. That was all right as long as a man didn't get drifted in and have his air supply cut off.

Everyone who goes into the woods should carry a first-aid kit. I am not one who believes in taking medicines every time you have a pain, but it is only good sense to be prepared for emergencies. In the old days I always carried iodine, which is effective, but can cause serious burns in open wounds. Now I take sulfadiazine or sulfathiasole in either the powdered form or in salve. It is wonderful stuff to prevent or halt an infection. My kit also contains laxatives, aspirin, vaseline, bicarbonate of soda, several rolls of bandages, and some surgical tape. The small prepared bandages for covering minor cuts are also mighty handy. If the Chief gets a small cut he just washes it and then covers the spot with balsam gum, which is a fine emergency treatment.

One year when I was home I took a first-aid course which included elementary surgery, and what I learned has come in handy many a time. My family doctor helped me choose a small surgical kit which included two scalpels, some surgeons silk, gut sutures, and a dozen surgeons needles, as well as a small pair of surgical pliers to hold the needles.

In an emergency requiring stitches ordinary household needles and cotton thread can be used, but only after the needle and thread has been thoroughly sterilized by boiling for at least ten minutes. Once you get the hang of it putting in stitches is fairly simple. You don't stitch a wound as you would a seam, for each stitch is put in separately and then tied. Once when I was alone in the winter my hunting knife slipped and I cut the end of the little finger on my left hand, but not through the bone. That was a test for my surgery skill as well as my courage. I didn't have anything to kill the pain but I hit on one idea. Why I don't know, but I figured if I got that hand numb enough I wouldn't feel it, so I went out and, plunging my hand into the soft snow, I held it there until it was numb. Maybe a medical man would say that was a dangerous thing to do, but up here where there is nothing to pollute the snow I figured it was a chance worth taking.

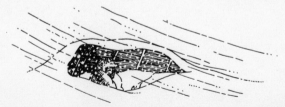

Hunting sled used as
a wind-break

Anyway I put four stitches in that finger and, so far as pain was concerned, I hardly felt it. It healed without any trouble and doctors who have seen the faint scar that remains tell me that I did a good job.

Once when I was on a railroad construction job the doctor in the emergency hospital we had beside the skeleton track (just a tar paper shack with oil lamps to work by) corralled me to give the anesthetic while he took off the arm of a man who had been smashed up in a dynamite blast. Once he got on to the fact that I had had a mite of training, he called me in for operations all the time I was there and I got so I could handle ether pretty well. Later on I kept a can of ether at the cabin, but it is dangerous stuff unless you know how to handle it and I don't advise fooling with it.

Walking around in the north somewhere is a fellow that I brought into the world in a little railroad shack with the assistance of a young engineer who gave me more trouble than the mother. One is enough for me!

I also learned to use a hypodermic syringe, but there again unless you are very sure of what you are doing and have a good knowledge of what is wrong with the man you are working on, it is wise not to use a hypodermic.

To go into the woods far away from medical men is taking a risk unless you know at least the simple rules of first aid, including the methods of stopping bleeding and how to take care of broken bones.

If you think time hangs heavy on our hands in winter up here in the north I want to tell you the days are not long enough for the things we want to do. A while back I read about a heliograph, an instrument used for signaling by picking up the sun's rays and flashing them long distances. It is much the same idea as flashing a mirror in peoples' eyes. The book had a diagram of a heliograph, so we planned one that could be built of things we had at hand. In place of mirrors you could use tinfoil smoothed out and pasted on circles of wood, or pieces of shiny tin, but it so happened we had two round shaving mirrors, the kind you can buy almost anywhere. They must be flat, not curved. We mounted the various parts on a board about two feet long and eight inches wide, but the supports or yokes for the mirrors were made of strips of white pine half an inch square and five inches high.

One mirror is used to pick up the rays of the sun from any position and reflect them down to the signal mirror, which then shoots a bright beam at the point where you want your signals to be seen. In the exact center of the signal mirror you scratch away the silver coating in a tiny circle about one-eighth of an inch in diameter. When you are ready to use the heliograph you stand behind this mirror and by sighting through the hole aim at your "target" which is located by bringing the two cross wire sights into line in just about the way you aim a gun. Of course the signal mirror must also be adjusted to pick up the most light from the sun mirror so that the beam you send out will be bright and sharp. If the sun is in front of the signal mirror you don't have to use the sun mirror. I might say that aiming a heliograph accurately is mighty important for the beam it sends out is quite nar-

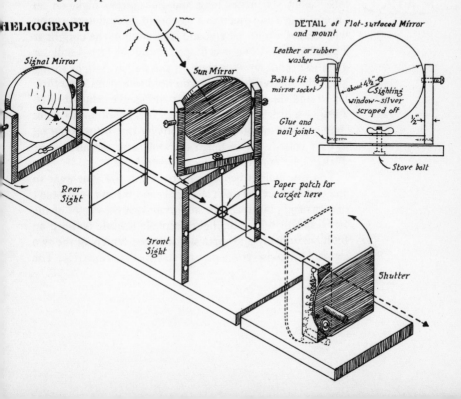

row and unless it is aimed right at the person watching for it, he may not see it.

If you signal for any length of time you may have to adjust your mirrors once in a while, for as you know the sun is always on the move. To help keep the mirrors in good adjustment after the heliograph has been sighted on the receiving station, you put a small round white paper patch, perhaps a quarter to half an inch in diameter, on the center of the cross wires of the sight that is shown below the sun mirror. When both mirrors are properly adjusted light passing through the small hole in the center of the signal mirror will not be reflected. Thus a small dark spot will appear on the little white patch, and as long as this little shadow spot shows in the center of the patch the heliograph beam is in good adjustment.

The shutter for making signals by shutting the beam on and off should be on a separate base so that when you work it you will not throw the mirrors out of adjustment. The shutter which you move up and down to make dots and dashes is very simple. We just mounted a very thin piece of pine, about six inches long and four inches high, on an upright nailed and glued to a baseboard. The shutter, as you will see, has a rounded end and is screwed to the upright at a point so that, when it is flipped up by the little handle, it gives the beam an open path to the target. A light spring keeps the shutter down and you need to experiment a little bit to find the right position for the handle which can be a nail or a little piece of dowelling. It is important that this shutter work smoothly and quickly so that by pressing on it with your finger in much the same way as you operate a telegraph key it moves up and down rapidly.

You can build a heliograph about any size you want to and the distance between the sights and the mirrors doesn't matter much, but it is very important that the center of the signal mirror where the light peephole is made be lined up both horizontally and vertically with the centers of the two sights. Otherwise you won't be able to aim accurately. The sights can be made with pieces of fine wire stretched up and down and across between supports. The sight next the signal mirror we made by bending a stiff piece of wire in the shape of a U, and then lined up our cross wires and twisted them on, and added a drop of waterproof glue to hold them in place.

Our heliograph works perfectly. The Chief was so interested in helping us that when the time came to test it he put on his snowshoes and hiked all the way up to Faraway See Hill to see if he could get our signal. Of course he had no way of flashing back to us for we had only one, but we agreed that if he saw our flashes he would light a smoke signal to let us know. I don't know any feeling that is akin to the thrill that comes when you make something and have it work just as you planned it, so we were mighty pleased with ourselves when we saw smoke curling up from the top of that hill miles away. And hours later when the Chief got back he was as excited as you ever expect an Indian to be. He is already planning to buy himself a couple of mirrors the next time he goes out to the settlement so that we can signal back and forth from the hilltops. Hank is studying the Morse telegraph code so we can send messages to each other.

Every year about this time the three of us make a trip out to the settlement to pick up some special luxuries for our Christmas dinner and get the parcels from the folks. But we have had a long spell of bad weather with heavy storms and we decided that we would have to wait for a better time. Maybe that sounds like a disappointment, but after you have lived in the woods for a while you don't think about such things as disappointments. You come to know there is something bigger going on than just your plans and if what you want to do doesn't turn out the way you hoped, you take it as it comes.

I've got plenty to do getting ready for Christmas and one of the little jobs I always enjoy is fixing up the candles. To be on the safe side I stick nails in the ends of short candles and then float them in glasses of water. The nail holds the candle with the top just about level with the water and because the wax is kept cool the flame burns in a little pool and lasts a long time. When the candle burns down to a stub the nail pulls it under and the light goes out. I will have candles burning in the windows when the Chief and Hank come down the trail on Christmas Eve. They say it wouldn't be Christmas if they didn't see those little beams across the snow.

We'll have Christmas candles in all our windows — safe candles.

Even though we didn't get to go out to the settlement, I had the new sled with the ski runners all ready for the trip, and the Chief had made new moose hide boots for my dogs in case we got into crusted snow, which cuts their feet. Dog boots are like little tobacco pouches which you tie around the top above the dogs' paws. Old Wolf is that fussy that he won't start on a trip when the footing is bad until he has his boots on, and he sits down and holds up his front paws to tell me what he wants.

One morning when the air was full of ice crystals and had that quiet silvery look that may mean anything, including a blizzard, the Chief, Hank, and I were out by the cabin putting up food for the birds when the old Indian, who can hear like a deer, stopped to listen. Pretty soon I heard it too; it sounded like a plane and yet I couldn't be sure that it wasn't the rapids. Then it came louder and clearer, and suddenly out of the gray we saw the lumber company's plane.

Our dog boot

He came diving down and roared over the cabin so low that the tops of the trees were bent down by the air from his propeller. Up he went again, circled over the lake, and came gliding down on the snow like a big black duck, for this was the first time he had been in since he changed from pontoons to skis. It wasn't good flying weather, but if anybody can take a plane into the north woods and get it through, it is my friend, Jack, the company's pilot. I knew why he had come, and I got a lump in my throat, for he had plenty of other things to do and a family of his own to think of.

He brought the little plane right up to the shore and when he jumped out he was lugging a pack-sack full of bundles. One of the things that tickled me the most was that my sister

The night before Christmas there will be a candle in every window

had sent the Chief a new pipe, which he needs badly, and a pound of the kind of plug tobacco he likes best. I don't believe I ever saw him so close to showing his real feelings as when he opened that package, for he didn't think to wait for Christmas. The company sent in a turkey, which the Chief has tasted only once before, and Jack brought as his own present to us a plum pudding and some brandy to burn on it. I don't believe any Christmas we have ever had will come up to this one.

While we were unloading the pack of Christmas parcels fine snow began whispering in the still air and in a few minutes the outlines of the trees across the lake had disappeared in a white smother. Jack was moving fast now for he knew the signs. The engine roared and he swung the plane into the wind to take off to the north. We couldn't hear his words, but we knew he was shouting "Merry Christmas" as the plane picked up speed and the propeller sent clouds of dry snow whirling back. In a few seconds he was lost to sight, but we heard the beat of his engine to the westward on its course for home.

On Christmas Day when we sit down to our dinner here faraway in the north woods we will be thinking of all our friends. And just before we begin Chief Tibeash will motion Hank and me to come to the door, as he has every year for a long time, and when he opens it he will lift his arms with his wrinkled brown fingers spread wide and say as near as I can write it: "Aslam nene-ti-une-non e-stays a-nouch-ke-se-cow!"—which in his language means "Come near our own brother today." And so he speaks to all our friends, near and faraway, on Christmas Day.

Woodcraft Index

Animal tracks
  carving, 65
  casting, 91
  identifying, 201, 245, 251, 253
Arrows, blow-pipe, 219
Axe sheath, 117

Bathing, steam, 82
Beaver
  dams, 113
  house, 35
Bellows, 100-3
Bird
  feeding, 37, 194, 255
  houses, 70-71
  migration, 110-12, 193-94
  tracks, 65

Camp equipment
  bedding, 184-85
  clothing, 259-61
  cooking, 117, 134, 137-39, 171-72, 248
  provisions, list of, 172-75
Camping in winter, 55-59
Candle
  holders, 99-100
  making, 267-68
Canoe
  hauling, 152
  paddles, 121-23
  portaging, 132-33, 158-59
  sails, 156-58
  storing, 216

Carving, *see* Animal tracks, Models
Chair, barrel, 65-66
Clothing, 259-61
Compass
  how to make, 141-42
  how to use, 43-44
  needles used for, 139-40
  watch used for, 47

Dewdrop
  formation, 145-47
  microscope, 120-21
Direction, how to determine, 46, 61
Distance, how to measure, 45
  barrel-hoop wheel, 46
Drum, 76-77
Dyes, 237-38

Feet, care of, 200-2
Fireless cooker, 255-58
Fires
  building, 212, 217, 226-28
  danger from, 178
  forest, 163-65
First-aid equipment, 263
Fish
  preservation, 184
  storage in ice, 60
Fishing
  flies, 72
  rod, 64-65

Fishing (*continued*)
  through ice, 73
  tricks, 182-84
Food
  on the trail, 59-60
  preservation, 184
  smoked meat, 202-4
  storage, 60, 160-62, 217-18
Frostbite, 61
Frost crystals, 249-50

Games, 233-35
Grass cutter, 153

Hammocks, barrel-stave, 153-54
Heliograph, 264-67
Hides, tanning, 224-26
Horn, 136

Ice boat, 245-47
Ice flow, 88-89
Ice creepers, 231-32
Insects, 148-51

Knife
  bread, 73
  hunting, 73
  sharpening, 115
  wood carving, 115

Level, carpenter's, 162-63
Lights
  candles, 99-100
  fireflies, 132
Logging, 93-94

Magnet, 140
Maple sugar, 68-69
Moccasins, 33-34
Models
  animal, 115-16, 135
  camps, 228-29
  tools for, 74, 115
Mouse trap, 218-19

Oven
  French Canadian, 124-26
  Reflector, 189

Pets, wild animal, 235-36
Photographic blinds, 196-99, 237

Rabbitskin robe, 55-56
Radio, 238-43
Raindrops, size of, 86-87
Recipes
  baked beans, 187-88
  baked fish, 188-89
  blueberry pudding, 200
  griddlecakes, 258-59
  Indian pudding, 75-76
  waterfowl, 221

Saws, 73-74
Sled
  dog, 222
  hunting, 52-53
  repairs to, 74
Sled dogs, 103
  harness for, 224
Sling stick, 119-20
Smoked meat *see* Food
Snow goggles, 37-38
Snowshoes, 232-33
  hitch, 232
  Mal de raquette, 32
Snow storms, danger from, 262
Stars, as guides, 61
Sundial, 167-68

Table, split-log, 99
Tanning *see* Hides
Tents, 175-78
Timber felling, 208, 210
Trail signs, 44-45

Vegetable garden, 104-6

Water, purifying of, 153
Waterproofing
  flour and sugar bags, 139
  matches, 124
  tents, 179
Weather signs, 142-47, 244
Weather vane, 218-19
Whittling *see* Animal tracks,
  Models
Wind gage, 31-32

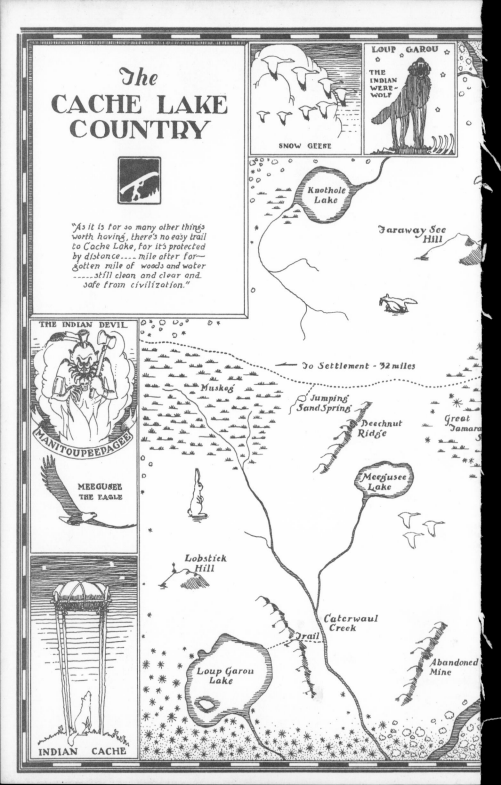

The
CACHE LAKE
COUNTRY

"As it is for so many other things
worth having, there's no easy trail
to Cache Lake, for it's protected
by distance..... mile after for—
gotten mile of woods and water
.....still clean and clear and
safe from civilization."

SNOW GEESE

LOUP GAROU

THE
INDIAN
WERE-
WOLF

Knothole
Lake

Faraway See
Hill

THE INDIAN DEVIL

MANITOUPEEPAGEE

MEEGUSEE
THE EAGLE

To Settlement - 32 miles

Muskog

Jumping
Sand Spring

Beechnut
Ridge

Great
Tamarac
S

Meegusee
Lake

Lobstick
Hill

Caterwaul
Creek

Trail

Loup Garou
Lake

Abandoned
Mine

INDIAN CACHE